D1545574

COUNSELING IN THE COMMUNITY COLLEGE

COUNSELING IN THE COMMUNITY COLLEGE

Models and Approaches

Louis V. Paradise, Ph.D.
Thomas J. Long, Ed.D.

PRAEGER

PRAEGER SPECIAL STUDIES • PRAEGER SCIENTIFIC

70886.

Library of Congress Cataloging in Publication Data

Paradise, Louis V., 1946-
    Counseling in the community college.

    Includes index.
    1. Personnel service in education. 2. Community
colleges. 3. Junior colleges. I. Long, Thomas J.,
1938-   . II. Title.
LB1027.5.P317   378'.194   81-5139
ISBN 0-03-058418-3   AACR2

Published in 1981 by Praeger Publishers
CBS Educational and Professional Publishing
A Division of CBS, Inc.
521 Fifth Avenue, New York, New York 10175 U.S.A.

© 1981 by Praeger Publishers

123456789 145 987654321

United States of America

Dr. Long would like to thank his wife, Lynette, and two children, Seth and Sarah, for letting him work on this book any time he wanted after 11 P. M. and then putting up with the mood that resulted the next day. Actually, Lynette has provided, through her own energetic writing, the motivation for doing this book, and Seth and Sarah the love that made it worthwhile.

Dr. Paradise is grateful for the continued patience, warmth, and understanding he received from those closest to him, Christopher and Gabrielle Paradise and Punko.

PREFACE

Community college counseling is rather unique, by virtue of its role and functions, in the field of guidance and counseling, just as the community college itself is a rather unique institution in American education. As a result, the community college counselor faces many problems and challenges quite removed from other counseling specialties. It is our hope to shed light on this unique and diverse area of counseling.

This book is intended to be a comprehensive introduction to the role and function of the community college counselor. We have written it to fill the need for a book that can be of value and assistance to all those interested in student personnel work at the two-year college level: counselors, students, student personnel workers, and administrators. Our purpose is to present useful and effective programs and approaches that are currently in use, with the intent of conveying the needed resources for the practitioner and student alike.

With over 4 million students in two-year colleges across the nation, the counselor has a unique and critical role. The material contained in this book should provide a thorough understanding of this multifaceted and challenging work. While this is a composite view of the field, the contents offer a practical and applied approach to helping students develop academically, emotionally, and socially.

Chapter 1 presents a historical perspective on the development of the community college and its relationship to the later development of counseling services. Discussed are the major educational and philosophical considerations that have contributed to the present community college system and its rapidly expanding counseling efforts.

Chapter 2 describes the need and rationale for counseling in the community college. The major work of the counselor is presented to demonstrate the varied nature of the counselor's role.

Chapter 3 provides a much-needed description of the diverse student subpopulations attending community colleges. Special emphasis is given the "new students" of the community college system— the older student, the woman student, and the foreign student.

Chapter 4 focuses on the organization and administration of counseling services. Organizational models and approaches, management strategies, and budgetary concerns, together with new and innovative trends in counseling service organization, provide new insights into this area of effective and responsible counseling management.

Chapters 5 through 8 deal with counseling programs and techniques. Various individual and group approaches are presented, including skill-building exercises. Of special interest is a comprehensive presentation on outreach programs and their effective use to further the goals and objectives of the institution.

The future of the community college counseling is the topic of Chapter 9. New programs, new students, and new commitments are all seen as part of the counselor's planning for the future.

We have not attempted to limit the scope and relevance of this book to only the two-year community college, since the material presented here will be equally valuable to all college student personnel workers and post-secondary-school counselors associated with community colleges, junior colleges, vocational/technical schools, two-year branches of state university systems, or, for that matter, four-year colleges and universities.

It is our hope that this effort will advance the goals and objectives of the community college counselor by developing new insights, provoking thought, suggesting new research and program development, and providing ideas useful in coping with the rapidly expanding role of the community college counselor in America.

ACKNOWLEDGMENTS

Several people have greatly assisted us throughout the development of this book. The single most important contribution has been made by Edwin J. Nolan, Director of the Counseling Center at the University of Tampa. Many of his ideas and suggestions have been incorporated in the writing of this book, and it is hard for us to overestimate the value of his contribution.

We would also like to acknowledge the technical and editorial assistance of Margaret Brooks, Barbara Howard, Susan Konzelman, and Barbara Siegelwaks. We would especially like to indicate our gratitude to Adele Chwalek, the world's most dedicated and capable librarian.

CONTENTS

COUNSELING IN THE COMMUNITY COLLEGE

1

HISTORICAL PERSPECTIVES:
EDUCATION IN TRANSITION

> Effective counseling is the keystone of the arch of a
> widespread education system dedicated to the prin-
> ciple of equality of opportunity.
>
> Conant, 1948

The counselor in the community college setting occupies a
central role in the educational, social, and emotional development
of the student. Because his is a multidimensional role, serving a
wide variety of students from all levels of academic ability, cultural background, socioeconomic status, and motivational interest,
the efforts of the counselor are crucial to the overall objectives of
the community college system of higher education.

The community college is a unique educational institution
peculiar to the United States. It has many commonalities with both
the public school system and the traditional university system of
education. Yet it is quite distinct and separate from both, exerting
tremendous educational and social impact on the communities and
individuals it serves. With four million students enrolled in two-
year colleges across the country and an additional three and a half
million participating in community education programs, the increasing recognition of community colleges as a major educational phenomenon cannot be overemphasized. Similarly, the community college counselor's increasing importance as a unique and dominant
force in the community college system must not be underestimated.

For counselors in this setting, an understanding of this uniqueness—in terms of the students, organization, function, and purpose—
is essential in order to be successful and effective. Therefore, the
overall role of counseling cannot be fully appreciated without some
inquiry into the historical evolution of the community college and
the development of counseling services within that institution. This
chapter will briefly outline this development along with a discussion

of the acceptance and expansion of the role and function of community college counseling. The aim is to provide the reader with a historical framework in which to critically view the practice of community college counseling.

THE COMMUNITY COLLEGE: WHAT IS IT?

Any definition of the community college concept would have to include a thorough explanation of its role and function, which would inevitably meet with some disagreement among leaders in the field. Nonetheless, the function and purpose of community colleges are essential to an understanding of their importance to the educational process. So, too, is this understanding important to the counselor's role within that setting.

In 1930 Ricciardi captured the essence of the community college in his early, insightful definition:

> A fully organized junior college meets the needs of the community in which it is located, including preparation for institutions of higher learning, liberal arts education for those not going beyond graduation . . . vocational training for particular occupations . . . and short courses for adults with special interests. (p. 549)

Monroe (1972) provides a more concise definition of the community college that reflects the purpose of this book.

> It may be said that a community college is the fulfillment of the American promise to its citizens for universal education; it offers two years of education beyond high school at a comparative low cost to the student, but not necessarily low to the public. (p. 25)

To this definition should be added the consideration that the relative educational position of the community college is unique: it is not a super high school, nor a mini four-year college, and not necessarily something in between, but an educational institution with its own philosophy, goals, objectives, and functions. In later chapters these distinctions will be further explored as they relate to the counselor's role, which is neither high school nor university counseling, but a separate and distinct counseling area with an identity all its own. For now, this definition is adequate for an examination of the evolution of counseling in the community college.

THE COMMUNITY COLLEGE:
WHERE DID IT COME FROM?

The origins of the community college can be traced to the principle of universal educational opportunity in early America. Acceptance and promotion of this ideal in the form of public schools provided the impetus for free public education as we know it today.
They also provided a philosophical framework, in later years, for
the establishment of the community college system.

The educational pioneers of the nineteenth century such as
Horace Mann, Henry Barnard, and Thaddeus Stevens led the campaign for the concept of free public education. It was not until after
the Civil War, however, that the public school movement became a
reality.

Monroe (1972) cites an 1872 landmark court decision that provided the first important confirmation of the idea that high-school-
age individuals should be educated at public expense. In this legal
case it was ruled that high schools in Michigan were to be supported
by public taxation. Similar court decisions in other states followed,
and by 1900 the principle of tax-supported public education was in
operation across America. Monroe concludes that the consequences
of these legal actions were a vital step in the evolution of the community college: historically, a direct extension of the public high
school. At the same time, state- and public-supported colleges and
universities were also becoming a reality.

The greatest advance in this area came from the federal government in the form of the Morrill Act of 1862. Under this law,
states received public land to establish colleges for training students
in mechanical and agricultural skills. The impact of this law on the
basic principles of education was summarized by Monroe (1972) as
providing low-cost education for the "common people," establishing
the concept of federal support for higher education, and presenting a
college curriculum that was nonsectarian and nontraditional in the
sense that it focused on practical and applied areas of study. All
three of the issues would later have direct influence on the educational philosophy underlying the community college and, therefore,
direct impact for the community college counselor. In that sense,
the ramifications of the Morrill Act can be considered the legal precursor to the educational philosophy underlying the creation and development of the community college in America.

Thornton (1972) delineates the basic philosophy that has led to
the rapid growth and expansion of community colleges as arising
from three main factors, which he identifies as the idea of widespread education for all people; the idea that increasing economic
wealth will increase the taxation base of the governing juristications—

the long-prevailing view that education will provide social and economic opportunity; and the continuing realization of the "American dream" that education is a social and individual good that society is obliged to provide its people. These three humanitarian and economic factors, outlined by Thornton, continue to play a prominent role in furthering the development of community colleges. Implicitly, they also provide much of the argument for counseling as a major resource for the educational objectives of the community college student.

As the effects of the Morrill Act were being felt, another trend was occurring in education that was destined to have an immeasurable impact on the evolution of the community college. Several midwestern university leaders, the most notable among them being Henry P. Tappan, president of the University of Michigan, advocated restricting the university to the intellectual elite, thereby relieving it of the burden of the first two years of college. Tappan felt that students who wanted to attend college for a general education or preparation for less than professional careers should not attend the regular university. His idea was of critical importance to the community college concept of today, for he suggested that the first two years of education be transferred to the secondary schools. His ideas, apparently, were greatly influenced by his experience with the German model of higher education (Brick, 1964).

Later, other notable university presidents made similar suggestions—Jesse at the University of Missouri, Folwell at the University of Minnesota, James at the University of Illinois, and Harper at the University of Chicago. It was only this last educator, William Rainey Harper, who achieved any degree of success with his ideas. "The work of the freshman and sophomore years is only a continuation of the academy or high school work. It is a continuation not only of subject matter studies but of the methods employed. It is not until the sophomore year that the university methods of instruction may be employed to advantage" (cited in Williams, 1969). With this aristocratic view of education, Harper saw in the junior college the opportunity for students who could not otherwise do so to obtain two years of college.

The concept of the two-year college was further promoted in the early 1900s by two educational leaders from California, Alexis Lange and David Jordan, who also sought to protect the academic standards of the university system from encroachment by less academically able students. Bogue (1950), in his account of the community college, cites Lange as the single most important person in the junior college movement before 1910. Lange felt that the junior college could promote the goal of universal education by offering both general education and vocational training. Certain historical ties to the current community college system can be seen in his 1917 address, delivered at the University of Chicago before a conference on secondary schools. In this speech, Lange is quoted as declaring:

> The state university, embodying in a higher indissoluble
> union of German and English university aims, rests on
> a foundation of fourteen grades of elementary and sec-
> ondary education, its first two years corresponding to
> the last two years of the four-year college. It retains
> the last two years of secondary education for a gradual-
> ly diminishing number of students . . . according to
> the junior college, in order to promote the general wel-
> fare, which is the sole reason for its existence, can not
> make preparation for the university its excuse for being.
> Its courses of instruction are to be culminal rather than
> basal. (Bogue, 1950, p. 356)

Beneath this rhetoric of the early 1900s, the remarks are clearly suggestive of present-day goals for the community college. It is paradoxical to note that certain historical roots for the community college, a truly egalitarian educational philosophy by present standards, rest with these early university leaders who were essentially elitist and aristocratic in their ideas about who should go to college.

Monroe (1972), in his comprehensive review of the history of the community college, discounts any impact on the development of the public community college of these leaders' ideas to adopt the German model of higher education. He concludes that if any historical influence was present, it was the upward extension of the public high school to include college courses. This occurrence, he contends, was a direct result of local school administrators responding to local community pressure for college work for the less academically able and less affluent high school graduates.

The impact of these university leaders, however, should not be underestimated, for they have exerted notable influence on the development of the two-year college. It was their early voices that conceived the two-year college as a continuation of high school, long before any community pressure or local school boards of education espoused the concept. In fact, Thornton (1972) credits Harper as strongly influencing the foundation of several of the public and private two-year colleges and obtaining the addition of two years to the Joliet, Illinois, high school program in 1901. Similarly, McDowell (1919), in an early publication on the development of the junior college, summarized the influences tending to further the development of two-year colleges. Prominent on his list was the university, with its rapid growth and tendency toward large classes, which felt the need to divide secondary work from that of the university. Thus the historical and philosophical roots of the community college are many and can be traced over the entire scope of public and higher education.

While the vocal support of educational leaders provided philosophical support, the legal machinery of the day provided more practical inducements to the community college movement. In 1907, under the leadership of Lange, Jordan, and others, California became the first state to pass legislation authorizing the establishment of local junior/community colleges. Specifically, the 1907 California law authorized high school boards of education to provide the first two years of college work by offering postgraduate courses in high schools (Morgan, 1930). Therefore, California assumed the leadership in the community college movement, a position that some would argue is still unchallenged.

The California legislation did much to facilitate the public community college, but the single most influential legal action to promote public community colleges came from the state of North Carolina. It had many similarities in principle to the court decision that legalized the use of taxes to support free public secondary education in Michigan in 1872. The North Carolina Supreme Court in 1930 upheld the legality of using public funds to support public two-year colleges. The implications of that decision had far-reaching impact on the entire concept of public-supported post-high-school education—the basic tenet of the community college concept of education. This was truly a landmark decision for the community college movement. The legality of financing an institution of higher education from public school funds was in doubt in the minds of many local officials and untested in the courts (Ogilvie, 1971).

By 1930 the community college movement had become an educational reality in America. Community colleges were successfully operating in more than ten states with many more being planned. Reynolds (1965) in describing this rapid expansion provides some impressive growth figures. In 1915, of 74 two-year colleges, 55 were private and 19 were public. By 1922, of the 207 two-year colleges, 137 were private and 70 were public, with the enrollment of the public colleges narrowly exceeding that of the private junior colleges. By 1960 there were 390 public and 273 private community/junior colleges, with the public colleges accounting for over 87 percent of the two-year college enrollment. Latest figures on two-year colleges report almost 4 million students enrolled as of 1976 (Chronicle of Higher Education, February 22, 1977), with over 3.8 million in public community colleges and slightly more than 150,000 in private junior colleges—a tremendous growth in the number of community college students over the last six decades.

Many reasons can be advanced to explain the rapid growth of community colleges since their inception in California in the early 1900s. The most obvious among these is the drastic increase in the total number of high school graduates desiring a college education— paralleling the increasing population of the nation during the first decades of the twentieth century. This, coupled with the rising expectations of an increasingly affluent society, provided an overabundance of students. Also paralleling this growth was the dramatic surge in the level of science and technology over this same period, bringing the demands of business and industry for trained personnel in wide varieties of mechanical and technical fields.

Others (Gleazer, 1971; Fields, 1962) have added to the list such considerations as the public concern among parents and local leaders who wanted their children to experience the fulfillment of a dream for a college education at an institution that was not beyond their financial or cultural reach. It was this concerned citizenry who facilitated legislation to support the concept of local higher education.

As more community colleges were established, their success encouraged the establishment of others. Additional federal government support, which had considerable influence on the growth and development of community colleges, came from two presidential commissions on higher education: the Truman Commission (1946-47) and the Eisenhower Commission (1955-56). Both of these commissions strongly recommended that the impending shortage of higher education facilities be resolved by considering the establishment of new two-year community colleges. Even more forcefully, the Truman Commission under the leadership of George Zook, a long-time spokesman for the community college concept of higher education, asserted that equal educational opportunity for all individuals to the maximum of their ability without regard to economic status, race, sex, color, creed, national origin, or ancestry was a major goal of democracy. "The democratic community cannot tolerate a society based upon education for the well-to-do alone" (Higher Education for American Democracy, 1947, p. 23). Considering the recommendations of both presidential commissions, together with a similar report issued by the Educational Policies Committee of the National Educational Association in 1964, the goals of universal educational opportunity appeared best achieved for the common individual by the establishment of community colleges.

Almost 25 years after the Truman Commission issued its appraisal and recommendations for higher education, the Carnegie Commission on Higher Education (1970) reported on a rather large segment of the population who were denied their rightful opportunity to attend college—those in the lower income brackets. They recommended that an additional 230 to 280 community colleges be in operation by 1980. The commission further recommended that community colleges charging no or very low tuition be located within commuting distance for all youth throughout the nation.

Thus government legislation, court rulings, learned educational committees, social and economic factors, and humanitarian ideals have all played a role in the emergence and rapid development of the community college system. Of even greater consequence, however, is the fact that these issues were to change the entire character and meaning of college education in America. By opening previously closed doors to new college students, the system greatly influenced the evolution of the community college counselor.

Cross (1972) in her analysis of the "new" college students of the 1970s comments further on this changing character and meaning in discussing the three major philosophies that have existed in this country concerning who should go to college. As was discussed in beginning this historical inquiry, an elitist or aristocratic attitude prevailed when the country was young. Students who attended college possessed financial and social status. The thinking of the time was that the only people who should attend college were those who needed it for their position in life; therefore the poor, the underprivileged, and woman as well could be excluded from college consideration, although Cross makes the point that the finishing colleges for women had the same elitist purpose as the private colleges of the day.

The second major philosophy, born out of a reaction against the elitist thinking, was that of meritocracy, arising primarily from the same spirit as the young American country founded on the high ideals of freedom and opportunity for all. The educational landmarks such as the Morrill Act provided a new impetus for a college education: entrance based upon merit. This growing philosophy, which was to become the dominant theme in U.S. education, gradually found unanimous acceptance, as it was in the best traditions and ideals of the founding fathers. Philosophically, educational meritocracy reached its peak in the 1950s, according to Cross (1972). To support her contention she quotes from a well-known study of the day sponsored by the Committee of Human Resources and Advanced Training:

> The democratic ideal is one of equal opportunity;
> within that ideal it is both individually advantageous
> and socially desirable for each person to make the
> best possible use of his talents. . . . The nation
> needs to make effective use of its intellectual re-
> sources. To do so means to use well its brightest
> people whether they come from farm or city, from

the slum section or the country club area, regardless
of color or religion or economic differences, but not
regardless of ability. (Wolfle, 1954, p. 6)

On one hand, the ideal of meritocracy served the development
of the community college, while on the other, it was later to become
its most vocal critic. Critics of universal higher education such as
Keats (1965), Lynes (1966), and Jennings (1970) have used the ideal
of meritocracy to challenge the philosophical foundations of the community college. The early educational pioneers who championed the
establishment of two-year colleges, it will be remembered, held the
elitist attitude that the two-year college would be a screening area
for the four-year university—to allow those who could benefit from
rigorous study to continue and those who could not to receive some
college training without placing any undue burden on the university.

The third and youngest philosophy of higher education has
been termed egalitarianism, the mainstay of the community college.
It evolved partly as an answer for all those individuals wanting an
education but unable to afford it, and partly as a response to barriers
that the meritocratic system had erected—the academic ability tests
(Cross, 1972). This criterion for admission to college under meritocracy systematically excluded large segments of the population.

Under the egalitarian system of open admissions and remedial
programs, a new sector of the population was being represented in
college, which Cross (1972) calls the new students of higher education. The community college has evolved as the institution of higher
education for these new students and for all students.

> We have devised all kinds of ways to make New Stu-
> dents eligible to participate in traditional higher edu-
> cation. Remedial courses are designed to remove
> academic deficiencies; counseling to remove financial
> deficiencies. However, if the answer to the question,
> Who should go to college? is to be an egalitarian re-
> sponse of "everyone," the educational systems will
> have to be designed to fit the learning needs of the
> New Students. (Cross, 1972, p. 5)

Cross (1973) summarizes this shift in philosophy as a complete turnaround from selecting students to fit the colleges (aristocratic philosophy) to creating colleges that fit the needs of its students (egalitarian philosophy). The focus was not only on those who
were academically proficient, as with meritocracy, but on all those
who had a desire to further their education and training: the under-
educated, the underprivileged, the minorities, and the poor. This

philosophy was truly the one suggested by the Truman Commission (Higher Education for American Democracy, 1947), as a result of its finding that only 16 percent of the college-age persons in America were in college and that half the college-age population could successfully complete two years of college. Thus the egalitarian approach embodied the American dream of low cost or free education for all those who desire it.

Today the aristocratic philosophy is no longer in existence, at least as a practical philosophy, for determining who should attend college. The meritocratic and egalitarian philosophies coexist, with the result that individuals from all segments of the population, young and old, bright and not so bright, rich and poor, have access to the American dream—a college education.

THE DEVELOPMENT OF COMMUNITY COLLEGE COUNSELING

Feder (1958) and others (Ogilvie & Raines, 1971; Williamson, 1961) have defined the role of counseling as consisting of those activities that supplement classroom programs and offer students the opportunity to develop personally and socially as a function of their education. Counseling, therefore, becomes central to the goals and objectives of both the student and the institution.

The emergence of this role, however, when compared to the emergence of public higher education, is relatively new, tracing its origin to the early 1900s under the pioneering leadership of Jesse B. Davis, a high school principal in Michigan, and Frank Parsons, a vocational leader and teacher in Boston. It was not until the 1930s that counseling as a separate and distinct profession entered the area of higher education.

Prior to this time the prevalent thought of college officials was that the students would be, or at least should be, self-reliant, mature individuals who could deal with the difficulties of academia and solve their own problems. The feeling was that the wise and scholarly academic faculty would counsel students when and if the need arose. The result of this was that counseling was left to deans of men and women and to academic faculty, serving essentially a disciplinary function with little effort going to any vocational or personal problem solving.

Monroe (1972) paints a vivid picture of those times with respect to the academic development of the student:

> If the function of a college is to provide an intellectual
> elite who, in theory, are wise and unselfish in their

leadership, then what personnel services programs
would best accommodate the needs of this type of college education? . . . To select and train a corps of
elite leaders . . . the educational process must continue the sifting process, even ruthlessly, so that only
a few of the best students survive the competitive
struggle for academic survival. (p. 151)

The academic leaders of the day believed in the principles of hard
work and rugged competition: an academic Protestant ethic. Any
consideration of help or remediation by counseling was unheard of
prior to the 1930s.

Not long after World War II the community college leaders
realized that if college were going to be offered to all those who
wished it, then the emotional as well as academic growth of the student would need to be considered. This concept of education, derived mainly from John Dewey's progressive philosophy of education for the "whole person," was reaffirmed in a 1949 report by the
American Council of Education. The report stated that the concept
of education is broadened to include attention to the student's well-
rounded development—physically, socially, emotionally, and spiri-
tually, as well as intellectually (Moser & Moser, 1963). In later
years many prominent educators and counselors were to underscore
the whole-person concept of education as the cornerstone upon which
the philosophy of guidance is based (Dolan, 1969; Koos, 1970;
O'Banion, Thurston, & Gulden, 1970; Rogers, 1969; Wrenn, 1959).
Counseling was beginning to make serious inroads into an area where
it was most needed.

The most significant federal action directed toward the realization of community college counseling was the passage of Public Law
85-864 in 1958, which stipulated that guidance was essential for the
best development of education programs. Even more significantly,
the law provided for funds to train professional counselors and to
give financial support to the states for improving the quality of
guidance services. This law was a crucial turning point in the development of community college counseling. Up to this point counseling programs were either nonexistent or terribly inadequate.
Several research studies on the utilization of counseling by the community college confirmed this fact (Anderson, 1961; McConnell,
1965; Medsker, 1960). Another disconcerting finding of these reports was that many colleges were using faculty members, sometimes unsuccessfully, on a released-time basis, to alleviate their
counseling deficiencies. The most conspicuous conclusion of these
reports, however, stated that professionally trained counselors
were a vital component of the community college system.

The concept of the community college as a viable and necessary educational institution quickly unfolded and blossomed during the 1960s and 1970s; and so too did the counseling programs under the direction and support of professionally trained counselors and college administrators, sensitive to the growing needs of students.

It should not be assumed that this development was, or currently is, without difficulties and problems. Indeed, it is probable that the development of community college counseling as an integral part of the educational system was more difficult than the development of the community college itself. It suffered setbacks and endured inadequacies as a function of individuals both within the system and outside it. The specific factors that have contributed to this difficulty will be discussed in later chapters, where their impact on the development of counseling will be more readily apparent.

One of the assumptions explicit throughout this book is the increasing need for better counseling programs and trained staff, greater administrative support, and a fuller realization of the interdependence between the academic and personal components of higher education at the community college level. Today few would argue with the scope and function of community college counseling. Its role has been expanded and its purpose has become more clear: that is, to facilitate the total educational development of the student in complete congruence with the needs of the student and the overall objectives of the institution. In this effort community college counseling has demonstrated that it can make a significant contribution to the ultimate goal of the educational system in helping to realize the American dream—higher education for all those who wish it.

REFERENCES

Anderson, L. A. Junior college counseling needs. Junior College Journal, 1961, 32, 100-103.

Bogue, J. P. The community college. New York: McGraw-Hill, 1950.

Brick, M. Form and focus on the junior college movement. New York: Columbia University Press, 1964.

Carnegie Commission on Higher Education. The open-door colleges: Policies for community colleges. New York: McGraw-Hill, 1970.

Chronicle of Higher Education, February 22, 1977.

Conant, J. B. Education in a divided world. Cambridge, Mass.: Harvard University Press, 1948.

Cross, K. P. Beyond the open door. San Francisco: Jossey-Bass, 1972.

Cross, K. P. Serving the new clientele for post-secondary education. Princeton: Educational Testing Service, 1973.

Dolan, R. E. Strategies for facilitating the development of student personnel programs at Chicago City College. Unpublished paper, 1969.

Feder, D. D. The administration of student personnel programs in American colleges and universities. Report of the American Council on Education's Committee on Student Personnel Work Study, Vol. 22. Washington, D.C.: American Council on Education, 1958.

Fields, R. R. The community college movement. New York: McGraw-Hill, 1962.

Gleazer, E. J. The rise of the junior college. In W. K. Ogilvie & M. R. Raines (Eds.), Perspectives on the community-junior college. New York: Appleton-Century-Crofts, 1971.

Higher Education for American Democracy. Washington, D.C.: Government Printing Office, 1947.

Jennings, F. G. The two-year stretch: Junior colleges in America. Change in Higher Education, 1970, 2, 15-25.

Keats, J. The sheepskin psychosis. Philadelphia: Lippincott, 1965.

Koos, L. V. The community college student. Gainesville: University of Florida Press, 1970.

Lynes, R. How good are the junior colleges? Harper's, November 1966, p. 59.

McConnell, T. R. A report to the Carnegie Corporation from National Committee for the appraisal and development of junior college student personnel programs. Washington, D.C.: American Association of Junior Colleges, 1965.

McDowell, F. M. The junior college. Bureau of Education Bulletin 32. Washington, D.C.: Government Printing Office, 1919.

Medsker, L. L. The junior college: Progress and prospect. New York: McGraw-Hill, 1960.

Monroe, C. R. Profile of the community college. San Francisco: Jossey-Bass, 1972.

Morgan, W. E. Junior college developments in California. Junior College Journal, 1930, 1, 64-73.

Moser, L., & Moser, R. S. Counseling and guidance: An exploration. Englewood Cliffs, N.J.: Prentice-Hall, 1963.

O'Banion, T., Thurston, A., & Gulden, J. Student personnel work: An emerging model. Junior College Journal, 1970, 41(3), 6-13.

Ogilvie, W. K. The Asheville case. In W. K. Ogilvie & M. R. Raines (Eds.), Perspectives on the community-junior college. New York: Appleton-Century-Crofts, 1971.

Ogilvie, W. K., & Raines, M. R. (Eds.). Perspectives on the junior-community college. New York: Appleton-Century-Crofts, 1971.

Reynolds, J. W. The junior college. New York: Center for Applied Research in Education, 1965.

Ricciardi, N. A radio broadcast. Junior College Journal, 1930, 1, 547.

Rogers, C. R. Freedom to learn. Columbus, Ohio: Merrill, 1969.

Thornton, J. W. The community junior college. (2nd ed.). New York: Wiley, 1972.

Williams, G. D. William Rainey Harper in Illinois. Illinois Education, 1969, 39, 212-214.

Williamson, E. G. Student personnel services in colleges and universities. New York: McGraw-Hill, 1961.

Wolfle, D. America's resources of specialized talent. Commission of Human Resources and Advanced Training. New York: Harper & Row, 1954.

Wrenn, C. G. Philosophical and psychological bases of personnel services in education. In N. V. Henry (Ed.), Personnel services in education. Fifty-eighth yearbook of the National Society for the Study of Education. Chicago: University of Chicago Press, 1959.

2

COUNSELING IN
THE COMMUNITY COLLEGE

> The guidance worker is the hub of the
> entire educational system.
>
> Thornton, 1972

The public community college can be viewed as providing two basic components of education to students. The first is systematically planned courses of instruction: the curriculum. The second is services that relate to activities outside the traditional classroom, provided to facilitate the overall development of the "whole" student: help in personal needs and problems. It is this latter component of the educational process for which the counselor is responsible.

This chapter will discuss the role of the counselor and provide a rationale for its need and importance in the educational process of the community college. The focus will be upon those elements that make the counselor unique, not only to the community college system, but unique in relation to other educational settings. It is the contention here that community college counseling is quite different from counseling in other settings and that a thorough understanding of this uniqueness is necessary in order fully to appreciate its need and importance.

THE NEED FOR COUNSELING

Patterson (1959) provides a general definition of counseling that is quite appropriate for the community college. He states that counseling concentrates on helping the individual remove obstacles to his optimum development. This definition is essentially similar to the broader definition of the Commission on Student Personnel Work of the American Council on Education, which has proposed that counseling is concerned with assisting the student in understanding and evaluating his potentialities and limitations, and in discovering and developing ways and means of working out problems so as to take full advantage of opportunities (Feder et al. , 1958, p. 7). These broad but accurate assessments are viewed as the essence of counseling in the community college. Such definitions could be applicable to counseling in any setting, since they convey the message that counselors help people to help themselves. If this is so, then how and why does counseling in the community college differ from counseling anywhere else? Foremost among the reasons is the fact that no other educational system in the United States opens its doors to such a diverse population—diverse in almost every measure of student attributes. Further, the role and mission of the university is distinctly different from that of the community college, and therefore the students and their needs are bound to be different. If counseling exists to facilitate the optimum development of the student, as the authors believe, then a good deal of how counselors go about this will be determined by the characteristics of those students with whom they deal.

Counseling has long been described according to the peculiar needs of its service population, and counselors often have added a modifying adjective to their titles to reflect their specialty. For instance, there are elementary school counselors, secondary school counselors, rehabilitation counselors, college counselors, community and agency counselors, employment counselors, Veteran's Administration counselors, and the list goes on. That the counseling profession has clearly recognized this need for counseling specialties is indicated by the number and diversity of divisions within the American Personnel and Guidance Association. Similarly, the American Psychological Association has an even greater list of subdivisions as specialties within the helping professions.

Therefore, counseling in the community college is unique to the extent that its students and their concerns are unique. And it is because of this major difference that the traditional ways and means of college counseling are not altogether appropriate. Given this perspective, the remainder of this book will present models and approaches for community college counseling.

To develop a more specific perspective of community college counseling and the need for its services, it is necessary to examine briefly the primary objectives of the community college itself. Monroe (1972) lists three main objectives held by the community college: the comprehensive curricula, the open-door policy, and a community orientation.

The comprehensive curricula are designed to meet the educational needs of a diverse student body. They include the first two years of the four-year college curriculum, as well as a variety of occupationally and vocationally oriented programs. Satisfying this wide-ranging objective is a challenge in which the counselor can play a prominent role. Admissions, recruitment, placement, and career and vocational counseling are just a few of the areas in which counselor efforts can facilitate the successful attainment of this objective.

The open-door policy, typical and almost peculiar to the community college, attracts students with varying needs, abilities, interests, aptitudes, past successes and failures, motivations, aspirations, expectations, and purposes. While it is true that many four-year colleges have amended their admissions policies to meet the ever-increasing competition for students, few have correspondingly amended the curriculum to meet the varying needs of these students to the same extent as have community colleges. For instance, in 1970 the City University of New York established an open-door policy providing for all New York City high school graduates to be admitted to one of the colleges in the CUNY system (Rosen, 1970). The CUNY system was soon overwhelmed with underprepared students and after a while it became clear that this policy was not viable. Severe financial limitations and faculty protests soon reversed the short-lived open-door policy.

The open-door policies characteristic of the community college are literally just that—open to the public almost without exception. In most cases those eligible to enroll in the community college are high school graduates, GED recipients, or anyone over the age of 18. Such a liberal admissions policy is effective only because the philosophy and practice of the community college movement takes into account and provides for the diverse needs of these students. As Hertz et al. (1977) state, open-door admissions and remedial programs go hand in hand. Many of the state land grant colleges are required by law to admit all in-state high school graduates; however, their goal for these students is to have them become more and more like university students in every way. In fact, many former land-grant colleges are now universities or attempting to gain university status. According to one Carnegie Commission on the Future of Higher Education (1970), the community college is now accepting, reshaping, and extending the service philosophy inherent in the land-grant movement.

Any policy that allows students to attend college without regard to intelligence, grades, and cultural or financial considerations poses a real challenge to the counselor, whose underlying purpose is to help those students develop socially, emotionally, and academically. Providing quality programs to help remedy deficiencies in all three areas falls within the scope of the community college counseling services. If an open-door policy is to be truly effective, the supporting programs that help the student cope academically, personally, and socially are crucial. Jencks and Riesman (1968) echo this sentiment in emphasizing that the community college student needs more counseling and direction than his more able and better-motivated counterpart at the four-year college.

The last objective, a community orientation, suggests that the community college must be responsive to the needs of the community. Within this goal the apparent tasks include the communication and exchange of ideas between the community and the college personnel; outreach activities in which the college makes itself and its programs available to all individuals in the community; and service as a consultant to the community in various civic and research programs useful to the improvement of community conditions. The implication is that the community college cannot be an isolated ivory tower of higher education, removed from the people and community it serves. It must open its doors not only to its students but to the community as a whole. The counselor can play a prominent role in facilitating this policy of involvement. The outreach programs under the direction of both the administration and the counseling service can be extended to all sectors of the community, providing needed services and enhancing a true community orientation.

Counseling can, and must, play a vital role in the achievement of the college's objectives. With the overall purpose of the community college being more than providing courses of instruction, the role of counseling is multipurposed, and the need for competent, well-trained counselors becomes of foremost importance.

Today, few would argue with the need for counseling in the community college. As discussed in the previous chapter, however, historically this has not been the case. It was not until the 1960s that the need for professionally trained counselors was finally accepted by community college leaders. During this time, several influential reports (Anderson, 1961; Humphreys, 1952; McDaniel, 1962; Medsker, 1960; Raines, 1966) took strong issue with the considerable inadequacy of counseling service programs in community colleges. The chief criticism found in these reports was that the college leaders failed to recognize the need and importance of quality counseling services. Reynolds (1961) summarized the lack of understanding of the need for quality programs in a statement delivered before the American Association of Higher Education. He concluded that it was unlikely any progress would be made toward remedying the situation until the value system of the community college leaders was expanded to include recognition of the significance of the counselor's role. Not until it was realized that counseling was able to serve effectively both the needs of the institution and the needs of the student was its acceptance as a vital and integral component of the educational system assured.

Dolan (1969) presents the clearest and most cogent rationale for community college counseling, underscoring the ideas presented thus far:

> 1) A college exists . . . for students to mature and effect in themselves beneficial changes, intellectual and other. The primary focus . . . should be on meeting the real needs of the students. 2) The student is a person and a citizen. Every student has inherent dignity. . . . Each student is unique. 3) As a person, a student functions as a whole being. The intellectual changes cannot be isolated from other changes and states. . . . 4) It is the chief responsibility of the student personnel services . . . to help the student develop an understanding of himself and to help the college share this understanding. (p. 156; emphasis added)

Today, as research on the community college suggests, counseling has found its place as an indispensable resource in achieving the goal of the American dream: an education for all (Medsker & Tillery, 1971). It must be cautioned, however, that while the counselor has defined his role and secured his identity, greater support and more effective programs will be needed if counseling is to keep pace with progress.

THE ROLE OF THE COUNSELOR

So varied and multifaceted is the counselor's role that McConnell and Raines (1965), in an appraisal of junior college student personnel programs, listed 21 separate functions ranging from student counseling to in-service education for the personnel staff. The functions were incorporated under the broad headings of orientation, appraisal, consultation, regulation, participation with student activities, service, and organization. The report, supported by the Carnegie Corporation, is a comprehensive and thorough treatise on the development and appraisal of personnel services in the two-year college. Currently, the development of new and creative programs together with the arrival of even newer student populations is rapidly expanding this list of counselor duties. Later chapters of this book are specifically devoted to these issues and their impact on community college counseling.

Functional Bases: Sources of the Counselor's Role

A clear awareness of the role and function of the community college counselor can be obtained by examining the functional basis of this role. Its sources constitute, in broad terms, counseling's overall responsibilities and include information, development and prevention, and crisis intervention and remediation. They are presented here as discrete categories only for the purpose of explication, keeping in mind the considerable overlap and interdependence among them.

Information

This category includes all those activities that have as their primary purpose the intent to convey information to the student that will help in making sound decisions concerning life goals. These may range from such areas as instructing students how to use the library to interpreting interest, aptitude, or personality inventories in helping students select their life work. The importance of information dissemination is evidenced by the accelerated pace at which knowledge is created and technology is advanced. Witness these projections by Abbott (1977):

> At the rate at which knowledge is growing, by the time
> the child born today graduates from college, the amount
> of knowledge in the world will be four times as great.
> By the time the same child is 50 years old, it will be 32
> times as great, and 97% of everything known in the world
> will have been learned since the child was born. (p. 28)

Freedom of choice is one of the basic rights in a democratic society, one that requires accurate and available sources of information if that choice is to be a responsible one. The task of the community college counselor is to insure that students have the opportunity to exercise this right. This is accomplished through an ongoing process of updating vocational, occupational, and educational information resources. Counselors cannot be expected to have all the information students require, but they should know where to find it.

Most community colleges conduct some type of orientation program specifically designed to provide students with considerable information during the first days on campus. Such programs are necessary, but are rarely sufficient to acquaint students with everything they will need to know about the community college. Needs change as students progress through their programs, and counselors must not only be available to handle these needs as they arise but must be able to anticipate them. This requires considerable forethought based upon a knowledge of those needs common to the individual subpopulations of the community college.

Many times a student will not be aware of needing certain information, and therefore it is incumbent upon the counselor to initiate the contact. Periodic surveys of student needs, coupled with a systematic outreach program, will ensure that the student is exposed to and has access to sufficient information to make wise choices.

Development and Prevention

The purpose of education, in its broadest sense, is to nurture and develop intellectual growth in a systematic fashion. Important as this is, it is not sufficient to guarantee that students will develop the necessary interpersonal skills vital to a healthy social and emotional life.

Developmental counseling (Blocker, 1965) is designed to teach life-coping skills for those inevitable life crises that cannot be averted and prevention techniques for those that can. Prince, Miller, and Winston (1976) have identified a series of behaviors they believe students need to master while in college. They have labeled these developmental tasks of young adults, which fall into three broad categories, as developing autonomy, developing mature interpersonal relationships, and developing purpose. Each of these categories is further divided into three specific tasks for a total of nine developmental tasks toward which college students strive. Monroe (1972) addresses the same issue, stating that all adolescents are expected to resolve four basic social and personal problems. He lists them as choosing a mate, making a career choice, deciding whether to become a mature, independent adult or to remain a dependent adolescent, and finally, choosing one's value system and beliefs. While various authors may differ on the number and categories of these developmental tasks, the fact remains that students are confronted with a number of inevitable and universal tasks that must be mastered. The way students go about accomplishing these tasks will, therefore, greatly influence the course of their lives.

On every campus there are students who will master these tasks with great poise and ease. There are other students who are successful only to some degree on each of these tasks, and there are still others who find little success with any of their efforts. The counselor's role is to help students to identify their own developmental tasks and other predictable life crises, and to help them plan the necessary steps to accomplish their tasks effectively and efficiently.

Crisis Intervention and Remediation

In the course of the student's life it is very likely that any number of frustrations that block immediate or long-term goals will be encountered. Many times the student is able to cope alone or with the help of a relative or friend. Other times this type of help is insufficient or unavailable, so the student looks for professional help in the form of counseling. It is important to keep in mind that a crisis exists to the extent that the person perceives it to be so. What may seem very commonplace to the counselor may be a traumatic crisis to the student.

The term "crisis intervention" brings to mind such areas as abortion counseling, drug-abuse counseling, 24-hour hot lines, and the like. These are important, to be sure, but represent only a small portion of community college crisis counseling. The community college draws many students who are not at all comfortable in their academic setting and who may overreact to situations that the academically sophisticated take in stride. In addition, many students attend the community college on a part-time basis in order to maintain their jobs, raise a family, and engage in other community affairs. As a result, students can and do bring problems originating elsewhere to school with them. The counselor must be aware of and sensitive to the needs of students, providing help and assistance and making referrals to appropriate resource individuals when it becomes necessary. Some cities now have consolidated referral services that act as intermediaries between the public and helping professions. It is necessary to keep abreast of these resource agencies in order to establish and maintain a professional working relationship to better serve the needs of the students.

Students do experience crises in their lives and the extent to which they seek counseling services will be determined by their knowledge of the existence and purpose of such services, their belief in the competence of such services, and their assurance of mutual confidentiality. Such efforts are possible only through extensive outreach and public relations activities and programs, and through counselors' reputation of being concerned, effective professionals.

The role of remediation needs to concern not only the personal and emotional crises of students; the counselor can also play an active part in academic remediation. Efforts to improve academic deficiencies, such as poor reading and study skills and low academic motivation, through special tutoring programs, are all part of the remediation effort. These functional bases are crucial for students who enter the community college. If the educational philosophy of the whole person, as discussed in Chapter 1, is at all valid, then the relationships among the academic, social, and emotion variables become essential to the student's successful development and overall educational experience.

The Work of Community College Counseling: Responsibilities and Rationale

The various areas of counselor responsibility within the community college are a direct result of the functional bases discussed in the previous section. A discussion of specific counselor tasks can help demonstrate the need for and the work of the community college counselor. The tasks covered below are far from exhaustive and are meant only to illustrate the far-reaching impact this work has on the needs of the student, the institution, and the community.

Choice Awareness

The open-door admissions policy, typical of the community college, attracts students with widely varying backgrounds and abilities. To assume that these students will have accurate assessments of themselves and will place themselves accordingly in the various curricular offerings is an overexpectation. It is this richness and variety of curricular offerings, implied by the multiple purposes of the community college, that causes Thornton (1972) to conclude that unaided selection by the student is almost impossible. Wrenn (1951) goes one step further in asserting, "The admission of students without regard to their chances of success is actually unethical. If students are to be so admitted, then it is incumbent upon the college to provide a reasonable opportunity for those students to find some success; anything less is clearly fraud" (p. 420).

It is the responsibility of the administration to ensure that curriculum offerings and staff support are available to meet students where they are academically and emotionally, and not where the college would like them to be. The dilemma, as Moore (1970) sees it, is to provide quality education equally to the academically able student and the high-risk student. The community college must be molded to the student and not the reverse, as is the case in many selective colleges and universities.

An essential facet of the community college support staff is a comprehensive counseling program designed to facilitate meaningful choices by the student. This is, perhaps, the most essential task of the counseling function, and one that must be an ongoing effort as the student proceeds through the educational process. For this experience to be effective and meaningful to the student, it must begin before enrollment.

Inherent in the notion of choice awareness is having access to an adequate and accurate source of information on which to base meaningful decisions. The counselor must be a director to, if not always the source of, that information. Students will require knowledge about themselves, the college and its offerings, the world of work, and possibly information on colleges to which they may transfer.

Self-knowledge

Meaningful decisions can best be made on the results of making an accurate self-appraisal of all pertinent factors. The student, with the assistance of the counselor, must take inventory of personal interests, aptitudes, abilities, study skills and habits, preferences, motivation, time commitments, and financial situation. There are probably many more factors that have an influence on a student's decision-making process; this listing covers only the major factors that each student must assess before launching an academic career. As situations change, which often happens, reassessments will be necessary for valid and meaningful self-knowledge.

The College and Its Offerings

After students have completed some form of self-assessment, they are ready to determine whether the community college can satisfy those needs. It is essential that new students be aware of all the options that are open to them. Since many students bring unrealistic expectations with them, they are bound to change their plans as a result of this new knowledge. Other students who arrive with certain academic deficiencies must be shown how to correct them, what their options are once deficiencies are corrected, and what the alternatives are for students who cannot or will not make the corrections.

Even with a considerable amount of information, many community college students will select what is perhaps the most popular community college major—undecided. Collins (1965) believes that up to 50 percent of all community college freshmen fall into this category and have no clear vocational choice. Helping this group of students can be the most rewarding—as well as the most frustrating— experience the community college counselor will face.

A considerable amount of information about the college can be provided during orientation, but counselors must be prepared to repeat and reinforce this information to the same students in the weeks and months that follow. Students are usually overwhelmed with more information than they can assimilate during a brief orientation session. The novel surroundings, new faces and old, anxieties about the unknown, and other distractions necessitate on the part of the counselor an ongoing contact with new students either through formal orientation classes or on some informal counseling basis.

McDaniel (1962) stresses the importance of providing sufficient and timely information to students and the possible consequences of failing to do so.

> Frustration, failure, and dropping out often result from lack of choice or wrong choice. Good choice is made difficult by inadequate information, faulty self-appraisal, peer influences, status values, family pressures, and conflict with immediate needs. (p. 20)

Time spent in trying to decide, or in failing to do so, can result in a waste of time, energy, and financial resources, items few students can afford to spend capriciously. Counseling, as a profession, has an ethical commitment to conserve human resources and this commitment is not fulfilled by allowing large numbers of undecided students to pass aimlessly through college.

Transfer to Other Colleges

One of the three major curricular missions of the community college is to provide, for those students who wish to transfer, an educational program parallel to that of four-year colleges and universities. Transfer students account for a significant portion of the student body and that number is increasing as more and more students begin their college careers at local community colleges. Gleazer (1968) reports that in 1968 one out of three students began at a community college, on a national basis, while in Florida 65 percent of the students did so. Further, he states that in California 75 percent of all full-time, lower-division students in public schools were in community colleges. Knoell and Medsker (1965) found that approximately 25 percent of the transfer students selected the community college because they were uncertain of their future plans. Similarly, Cross (1968) has reported that 27 percent of those who transferred had no college major, and of those who had, 36 percent changed their minds.

In a comprehensive review of community college transfer students, Nolan and Hall (1978) concluded that the academic and related counseling functions at the community college are the efforts most likely to ensure against transfer shock. Such a procedure can provide a smooth transition from the two-year college to the four-year college.

The counselor has a clear responsibility for successful ancillary programs directed toward the transfer student. It is important that students who show an interest in transferring be made aware of the differences in curriculum requirements between the transfer programs and the occupational/technical programs. Often the coursework in the latter programs will not be accepted by the four-year colleges and universities. Too often students are tempted to select courses on the basis of their availability rather than on the basis of curriculum requirements. While part-time students are the most likely to fall into this trap, they are not alone.

The counselor's professional library can be an excellent resource for the transfer student. Essential to this library are the college catalogs and transfer articulation agreements of equivalent coursework from each of the colleges to which students are likely to transfer. This source of information is vital in helping students to plot their academic future.

Decision-making Techniques

People are continually faced with situations requiring some sort of decision. The ability to act decisively in such problem situations will have great bearing on the course of one's life. Carkhuff (1973) points out the importance of this ability in his book The Art of Problem-Solving. In the preface to this book (p. i) he states: "Problem-solving is one of the skills essential to effective human functioning. The ability to resolve problems insures survival. The ability to resolve problems increases the probability of growth."

All situations requiring a decision are not necessarily problem situations, just as all community college students are not deficient in decision-making skills. It will be relatively easy, during initial contacts, for the counselor to identify those students who are deficient. Many community college students are quite willing to relinquish the responsibility for making decisions to the counselor, and the counselor must be cautious not to fall into that trap. There is a great temptation to appear the omniscient and benevolent helper, when in fact this attitude merely prolongs decision-making inability.

The truly helpful counselor adopts a systematic approach to teaching the student not only the how but also the why of making one's own decisions. Students who do not begin to make decisions and engage in systematic problem-solving activities are unlikely to develop to their full potential.

Conflict Resolution

It is sometimes difficult to accept—but it is nonetheless true—that the world has not been designed to meet one's every whim and want; thus, students are likely to encounter frustration and conflict in the course of daily living. The counselor may be called upon, from time to time, to help students resolve personal problems that are interfering with their learning experience or their emotional well-being. Moore (1970) contends that high-risk students are especially prone to spending a disproportionate amount of time just coping and worrying about basic needs. Conflicts will arise and the counselor must be prepared and available to handle this sort of emergency.

Sometimes, however, it is not enough to be ready, able, and willing. If students never seek counseling services, the best counselor can be totally ineffective. The challenge is to demonstrate to students that the counselor is a person who can help. Unfortunately, this task is complicated by the fact that community college students, in general, tend to maintain a comparatively strict set of values and beliefs, among which is the notion that to have personal problems is a sign of weakness, and that asking for help is a greater weakness yet.

Chapter 3 will explore the characteristics, traits, and special needs of the various student subpopulations of the community college. This should provide additional awareness of the complex role and responsibility facing the counselor in the community college.

Developing Potential

Herbert Otto (1967) has stated that few people use more than 10 percent of their full potential. It may be argued that such an estimation may be quite speculative, but the point Otto is making is clear: there are vast, untapped resources within each individual. Some are unaware of their potential and therefore cannot take advantage of it. Others may be aware of certain strengths, but are afraid to take the chance of trying for fear of failure, embarrassment, the appearance of being something they are not, or offending someone. Although these fears are based on what has been termed irrational assumptions (Ellis, 1962), they are very real to the student and therefore inhibit much potentially satisfying activity.

According to Moore (1970), the counselor must be a mediator, social worker, matchmaker, protector, confidant, and educator. This is no easy task, but it is required in many situations to convince students to use their resources in the most constructive, effective manner.

Summary

Certain broad areas of counselor responsibility have been identified in an attempt to demonstrate a need for counselors in the community college. With tight budgets, fiscal responsibility, and management-by-objectives, it becomes essential for counseling programs to continue to demonstrate and justify their existence.

This task is facilitated by each member of the counseling staff helping students to resolve problem situations, facilitating the development of their potential, and providing students with the information and skills needed to make wise choices and decisions.

It is not enough to convince students of the counselor's role—the faculty and administration must also be aware of the work of the counselor lest the attitude that Monroe (1972) notes become the dominant one:

> Today few, if any, faculty members would vote to discontinue the counseling and guidance functions; but, in my experience, most teachers would like to have the role of college counselors restricted to the task of assisting students to resolve their academic problems without becoming a crutch on which weak and irresponsible students rely for escaping their academic, classroom responsibilities. (p. 145)

Monroe's observation may not be totally accurate, yet it does suggest that the counselor's responsibility is to the needs of the student, without neglecting the parallel needs of the institution.

REFERENCES

Abbott, W. Work in the year 2000. The Futurist, 1977, 25-31.

Anderson, L. Junior college counseling needs. Junior College Journal, 1961, 32, 100-103.

Blocker, D. Issues in counseling: Elusive and illusional. Personnel and Guidance Journal, 1965, 43, 796-800.

Carkhuff, R. The art of problem-solving. Amherst, Mass.: Carkhuff Associates, Inc., 1973.

Carnegie Commission on the Future of Higher Education. The open-door colleges: Policies for community colleges. New York: McGraw-Hill, 1970.

Collins, C. Junior college counseling: A critical review. Personnel and Guidance Journal, 1965, 43, 546-550.

Cross, K. The junior college student: A research description. Princeton, N.J.: Educational Testing Service, 1968.

Dolan, D. Strategies for facilitating the development of student personnel programs at Chicago City College. Unpublished paper prepared for an NDEA institute at Michigan State University, 1969. Cited in Monroe, C. Profile of the community college. San Francisco: Jossey-Bass, 1972.

Ellis, A. Reason and emotion in psychotherapy. Secaucus, N.J.: Lyle Stuart, 1962.

Feder, D., et al. Administration of student personnel programs in American colleges and universities. Washington, D.C.: American Council on Education, 1958.

Gleazer, E. This is the community college. New York: Houghton-Mifflin, 1968.

Hertz, S., Gold, L., & Wallach, M. Credit for remedial courses? Community College Review, 1977, 5, 4-6.

Humphreys, J. Toward improved programs of student personnel services. Junior College Journal, 1952, 22, 382-392.

Jencks, C., & Riesman, D. The academic revolution. Garden City, N.Y.: Doubleday, 1968.

Knoell, D., and Medsker, L. From junior to senior college: A national study of the transfer student. Washington, D.C.: American Council on Education, 1965.

McConnell, T., & Raines, M. A report to the Carnegie Corporation of New York from the National Committee for Appraisal and Development of Junior College Student Personnel Programs. Washington, D.C.: American Association for Junior Colleges, 1965.

McDaniel, J. Essential student personnel practices for junior colleges. Washington, D.C.: American Association for Junior Colleges, 1962.

Medsker, L. The junior college: Progress and prospect. New York: McGraw-Hill, 1960.

Medsker, L., & Tillery, D. Breaking the access barriers. New York: McGraw-Hill, 1971.

Monroe, C. Profile of the community college. San Francisco: Jossey-Bass, 1972.

Moore, W. Against the odds. San Francisco: Jossey-Bass, 1970.

Nolan, E., & Hall, D. Academic performance of the community college transfer student: A five-year follow-up study. Journal of College Student Personnel, 1978, 19(6), 543-548.

Otto, H. Guide to developing your potential. New York: Scribners, 1967.

Patterson, C. Counseling and psychotherapy: Theory and practice. New York: Harper & Row, 1959.

Prince, J., Miller, J., & Winston, R. Manual for the Student Development Task Inventory. Athens, Ga.: Student Development Associates, 1976.

Raines, M. Junior college student personnel programs: Appraisal and development. Washington, D.C.: Association of Junior Colleges, 1966.

Reynolds, J. W. The future of the community college. In Current Issues in Higher Education. Proceedings of the 16th Annual National Conference on Higher Education. Washington, D.C.: Association for Higher Education, 1961.

Rosen, B. Open admissions at the City University of New York. Los Angeles: ERIC Clearinghouse for Junior Colleges, ED 050 676, 1970.

Thornton, J. W. The community junior college (2nd ed.). New York: Wiley, 1972.

Wrenn, C. Student personnel work in college. New York: Ronald Press, 1951.

3

STUDENT CHARACTERISTICS, DIVERSE GROUPS, AND COUNSELING

> The two-year community college more than any other post-secondary educational institution, seeks to project a student-centered image by attempting to meet the needs of individual students within a diverse student population.
>
> David L. Meabon, 1976

INTRODUCTION

The use for facts is action, so to review student characteristics before 1980 might seem a waste of time in a book aimed at action. But counseling and student personnel services were rapidly developing during the 1960s and were in a marked state of change, upheaval, and retrenchment during the 1970s. The implications drawn by student personnel workers from the facts presented to them during this 20-year period had a profound effect on developing the action responses made by student personnel workers in 1980. These action responses have become the programs now in operation by many community college personnel. Like it or not, settled programs have a strong tendency to influence the implications drawn from facts and exert limitations on further actions. Knowing a bit in 1980 about where previous perceptions have led might help overcome the impact of program inertia, as counseling services develop further and are asked to draw new implications and make new responses to new information.

THE PRE-1970 PERIOD

K. Patricia Cross said in a speech prepared for the annual meeting of the North Central Association, March 27, 1973:

Nationally almost nothing in higher education is the same as it was just one short decade ago. It is difficult enough just to do the old things better or to do them for more people or at less cost, but it is understandably bewildering to discover that the goals of the 1960's are no longer the goals for the 1970's.

The 1960s began with a clear mandate to identify talents and human resources. The nation was trying to keep up with the Russians, who had jumped out in front with Sputnik; America's president had vowed that Americans would get to the moon by the end of the decade. In 1958 Congress declared in Public Law 85-864 that a strong guidance effort was essential for the identification of talents and human resources, and for the most effective use of these resources:

We must increase our efforts to identify and educate more of the talent of our nation. This requires programs that will give assurance that no students of ability will be denied an opportunity for higher education because of financial need; will correct as rapidly as possible the existing imbalances in our educational programs which have led to an insufficient proportion of our population educated in science, mathematics, and modern foreign languages and trained in technology.

By 1960 the student personnel establishment, which began significant development only after World War II, turned its attention more fully to the identification of talent and career planning. The focus of this effort seemed to be on the "student of ability." This focus was a logical choice, since the prior history of higher education in this country was to train the mature, self-reliant problem solvers, who were for the most part intellectually and often socially elite young males. Selective admissions and demands for academic excellence were the norm in 1960.

By the end of the 1960s the focus had shifted to an emphasis on guaranteeing that no student would be denied an opportunity for higher education. The catchwords became "open admissions" and "equality of educational opportunity." In a single decade the elitist model of higher education had succumbed to a concern for educating the masses.

Personnel workers had to live through the pervasive philosophy of an educational establishment that saw national survival as dependent on the more or less ruthless application of a perceived natural law of selection. The functioning of this law in human terms would inevitably lead to the educating of a corps of elite leaders who would show the way and set the patterns that common people would then adopt and follow. This corps would also develop the natural resources from which all would profit. As concern for the development of all human potential began to grow, student personnel workers moved from contending with higher educators who believed that education should be governed by principles of capitalistic competition to sparring with these leaders for programs of counseling, remediation, and reentry. The fact that there was sparring gave evidence that there was a general shifting in the educational establishment away from the unalterable belief that the essence of a good education was the pursuit by a controlled number of students of a rigorous program of study—a program that these students either completed or failed on their own.

The end of the decade saw a groundswell of students seeking to enter some phase of higher education. More than 50 percent of all high school graduates were seeking to enter some type of college and there just were not enough Harvards or Stanfords or even Michigan States to go around. Further, there were increasing pressures to relax the procedural requirements of traditional education, which came from increasing numbers of adults and part-time learners attempting to gain entrance to college through nontraditional alternatives. There was a developing interest among women and ethnic minorities to gain equality, which pressed on the number of college openings and types of programs available. There was growing concern among the low achievers not to be denied their chance to improve their opportunities through postsecondary education. To many of these problems there was an available response in the nature of the community or junior college. This response saved many of the elitist institutions from the trouble of struggling with mass education.

In 1927 Frank Waters Thomas stressed the need for special help and advice for students whose lack of academic ability denied them admission to the standard college or university. The concept Thomas seemed to have in mind was that of rescuing the student in academic difficulty from the more highly selective admissions practices of more established institutions. But underlined in his writing was the notion that junior colleges could respond to the less academically talented, perhaps conserving the energy of the nation for the more important task of developing the talented elite.

Tyrus Hillway (1958) seemed to acknowledge a role of the two-year college as one of helping undecided students come to final decisions with regard to careers and further educational plans, thus playing a kind of conservator role for a more heterogeneous group of students than would enroll in four-year colleges or universities.

The U.S. community college was in place and ready to expand when college and university enrollments doubled in the decade from

1960 to 1970. Further, the community college developed in tune with the increasing faith the American public had developed in the power of education to open the doors of social and economic opportunity for the masses of the people, and seemed the most logical magnet for drawing the kind of student who, in fact, was the most likely to swell the college applicant pool.

The characteristics of the two-year college students enrolled at the end of the 1960s, outlined briefly below, mirror the real development the two-year college experienced during that decade.

CHARACTERISTICS OF TWO-YEAR COLLEGE STUDENTS IN 1970

It is probably true that community college students were such a varied group at this time that few generalities about them would appear useful. It seemed to be equally true that community college students as a group were about as heterogeneous as the communities in which the colleges were located. Despite the community biases and perhaps low utility of generalizations, data were kept and decisions were made on mean characteristics of community college students nationwide.

The vast majority of community and/or junior college students came from the lower-middle socioeconomic class and from skilled-labor families. Few of these students came from upper-class families or from families that could appropriately be called poverty families. The typical two-year college day student had a median age of 19; more than 85 percent of these students were less than 22 years of age. The adult student population was on the rise, but was largely to be found in evening, part-time programs. Actually, by 1970 about one-half of all students enrolled in community colleges were adult, part-time students.

Male students outnumbered female students. Minority student enrollments were much lower than they should have been, given their share of the national population. The majority of black students who entered colleges during the 1960s enrolled in predominantly black colleges, which tended to be noncommunity, four-year institutions. These figures are somewhat deceptive; although approximately 15 percent of all junior/community college enrollments nationally were minority students, minority enrollments could range from a few percent to nearly 100 percent of the student body at a given institution, depending on the area.

As to ability, the two-year college students were a select group, since nationally about one-half of the 18- to 21-year-old group was in college in 1969. But when comparing two-year college students with four-year college or university students, two-year college students scored much lower on a variety of ability measures. Over 50 percent came from the lower half of high school seniors.

It is interesting to note that Cooley and Becker (1966) found two-year college students more like noncollege youth in ability than four-year students, at the same time that they found two-year college students as a group more similar to four-year students on every index of socioeconomic status used in Project Talent—including mother's and father's education, father's occupation, number of books in the home, and whether the student had a room, desk, and typewriter of his own at home.

As a group, two-year college students were not found to be committed to intellectual values. They did not seek an intellectual atmosphere and often did not find one. They were much more likely to concentrate on practical and materialistic rather than intellectual and cultural activities. Their orientation was less likely to be humanitarian. In general, two-year college students were more cautious and controlled than four-year college enrollees. They were more apt to lack confidence in themselves, were less likely to be occupationally adventuresome, and were more concerned with ways leading to occupational success and financial security. Cross (1968) indicated that junior college students were more authoritarian and less autonomous. And the general consensus was that these students were less self-motivated and in greater need of guidance and control.

COUNSELING: 1970

By 1970 the arguments had been made on the need for professionally trained counselors on junior college campuses. Efforts were well under way to overcome faculty resistance to counseling. Most had learned that the release of faculty on a part-time basis to serve as counselors was a waste of resources. The battle to accord junior college counselors coequal status with instructional staff was being waged.

The majority of trained counselors in the junior college were still more comfortable working with the potential transfer student than the potentially terminal student. Counselors often prided themselves in being able to help able students enter senior colleges. When transfer seemed inappropriate, counselors often spent time attempting to cool off students by bringing their goals and expectations more into line with their measured abilities and expressed interests. Counselors were less well equipped to do effective vocational counseling or career development. Because of the large numbers of "undecided" or "vaguely decided" students who then, as now, enrolled in junior colleges, one would have expected counselors to concentrate on vocational counseling. But the general consensus at the end of the 1960s was that this type of counseling was very inadequate.

Counseling was for the most part provided only during the day, and thus did not reach the part of the student body that enrolled for evening classes. Counselors were experimenting with encounter groups and personal development approaches in 1970. But they were missing many of the needs of women attempting to return to college, after a break in schooling, often on a part-time or evening basis. The specific needs of minorities and foreign students were also not of paramount concern to the majority of counselors. And the pressures for outreach work by counselors often were dealt with by administrative juggling rather than changes in counseling approach or the development of new areas of counseling expertise.

Two things probably worked together throughout the 1960s to bring counseling to the point it reached in 1970. One was the struggle of counselors for legitimate standing, which led to an almost over-professionalization of the counseling role. Many counselors developed the attitude that dealing with such problems as choice of course or curriculum or even choice of a vocational objective was not the best use of a truly professional counselor's time. Many counselors came to believe that their time was better spent in helping students with in-depth investigations of personality problems. This attitude contributed to inadequate counseling services in many areas and the development of a type of counseling that served only a very small proportion of the student body.

The second factor was related to the basic personality characteristics of two-year college students. The vast majority of students declared themselves transfer students. This track was considered to have more prestige, and a student whose goals were vague was more likely to opt it. Counselors were faced with students who lacked confidence in themselves selecting a track that served to support this failing sense of self-confidence. If counselors were responsive to students' declared intentions, without understanding the motivations for these declarations, then a counseling program that concentrated on the transfer student and deeper personality confusions was a logical development.

There was, in 1970, a very strong need for research and evaluation data that would lead to decisions. All too often necessary data were unavailable and so decisions were likely to be made under conditions of stress without adequate consideration of the ultimate consequences to the students who were presumably to be served. Significant information about students was especially sparse.

CHARACTERISTICS OF TWO-YEAR
COLLEGE STUDENTS IN 1980

As a different kind of student began to enter an old world of education, schools began to develop and accommodate the needs of the students who were showing up at the front door. K. Patricia Cross, perhaps more than anyone else, has studied the characteristics of junior and community college students. Two elaborate studies (1968, 1971) of more than 70,000 junior and senior high school students and first-semester two-year college students have come to be regarded as central works on what she then classed as "new" students. The key categories of these new students were adults and part-time learners and low-achievement students. What is important to note is that in the early 1970s these groups numerically constituted the overwhelming majority of students new to postsecondary education. They simultaneously represented groups whose problems were educational rather than social. By 1980 the new or nontraditional student of the early 1970s had become or was rapidly becoming the traditional student on two-year college campuses.

In some way, 1970 was a watershed year. During the years 1965 through 1970, enrollment increases in two-year colleges continued at an annual percentage rate of more than 11 percent. In 1965, a rate in excess of 23 percent was recorded over the preceding year's enrollment. In 1971, the rate of enrollment increase slowed to an annual percentage rate of about 7 percent. From 1976 on, the percent of increase of enrollment in two-year colleges over preceding years averaged less than 4 percent. The growth in absolute numbers of students enrolling in two-year colleges in either full- or part-time courses for credit continued at a very steady pace during the 1970s. At the same time, two-year colleges were reporting huge increases in numbers of students participating in community education programs offered for no academic credit. By 1980 approximately 3.5 million students were enrolled in such courses offered through two-year colleges, compared with approximately 4.5 million students enrolled in courses for credit. The ten-year increase in continuing or noncredit education in community colleges has been approximately 500 percent. Two-year colleges enroll more participating adults in this learning category than any other segment of higher education (AACJC, 1980).

The American Council on Education Fact Book (Anderson, 1980) indicates that 39 percent of students enrolled in all types of postsecondary institutions are enrolled in two-year colleges. The Bureau of Census (1979) reports that three-fourths of the growth in two-year college enrollments during the 1970s was contributed by the 22- to 34-year-old population.

Age

In 1970 53 percent of two-year college students were under 20 years of age. By the end of the decade this percentage had decreased by more than one-third (Bureau of Census, 1979). The mean age of two-year college students enrolled for credit is now 27. Approximately 1.5 million people over the age of 34 are enrolled in college; more than 60 percent of this group are participating in undergraduate programs; and more than 80 percent are enrolled part time.

Older students are more likely to be high achievers than younger students. The mature adult appears to have a better problem-solving orientation and a great desire to be able to apply new knowledge immediately. The average adult learner in 1980 cites job or career transitions as the major reason for returning to schooling. If adult learners are attending school part time, chances are nine out of ten that they are also employed, probably full time. Even among full-time adult students, more than half are employed an average of more than 30 hours per week.

The average adult learner is not looking for a diploma or a degree. Older learners are most frequently looking for some response to transitions or particular needs in their lives. It seems likely that this demand for rapid, nondegree learning by adults will continue, as the occupational structure of the country continues to change as a result of job retraining needs, technological innovations, expanded social services, entry and reentry of women, longer life, and growth of leisure time.

Even now the typical noncredit or part-time credit student is a married female about 36 years of age who has had two years of college and earns a better than average salary (Participation in Adult Education, 1980). Approximately 12 percent of the adult population in the United States are enrolled in adult education courses. More than half of these students are women. The higher the level of education already achieved, the more likely the person is to be enrolled in adult education. And the more affluent, the more likely the person is to be so enrolled.

An age category that remains largely untapped by two-year colleges is the population over 55. Less than 8 percent of this group at present avail themselves of any formal educational opportunity. It is estimated that the age group between 65 and 74 will increase by about 35 percent by the end of the century.

Unfortunately, most student personnel workers are poorly educated about the stages of normal development of the mature adult. Largely unaware of the life needs of a population that spends briefer periods of the day or week on campus, these workers seem less able to respond to the personal, marital, and recreational needs of the adult. While some progress has been made in career areas, the older student still is the least well served. Staff members who are specialists in counseling the mature adult should have as their prime focus the planning and/or adapting of programs suitable for the needs of the adult learner, as well as the education of other staff members to increase their ability to be able to make knowledgeable responses to normal adult life crises.

Sex

In contrast to the student body of the 1960s, women have become the majority group among all undergraduate learners in the United States. Women now comprise more than 52 percent of the total head count and 54 percent of the part-time formal learning population (AACJC, 1980).

Women have been rusing into the labor market at record rates. Education is seen as an important aspect of this entry. At the same time, women continue to find marriage their most common life state and the majority of women choose to have children at some point in their lives. This fourfold adapting—wife, mother, student, and worker, which occurs simultaneously for many women—exerts an unusual strain. Women enrolled in formal educational opportunities need a great deal of support in order to succeed as learners as well as wives, mothers, and workers. Whereas men are usually supported by their wives in learning activities, women often cannot expect such support from their mates, since time taken for additional learning usually places additional demands on the male spouse.

The change in percentage of women enrolled in two-year colleges during the past ten years presents new demands on student personnel services to provide adequate support in the form of trained counselors sensitive to women's needs, peer support groups, childcare facilities, and adequate assistance in overcoming problems confronting women attempting to enter or reenter the world of work.

Minority Students

During the 1960s minority students were underrepresented in community colleges, compared with their numbers in the total population. By 1979 community colleges were enrolling more than 38 percent of the nation's minority students. According to Gilbert (1979), between 1970 and 1978 there was a 52 percent increase in minority enrollment. Black enrollment increased by about 30 percent and Hispanic by 65 percent. At present, one out of every four community college students is from a minority group.

In responding to the needs of minority students the attitudes and values of the counselor are very important. Counselor ethnicity is perceived by students as a significant variable in counselor selection (Gilsdorf, 1975). That there is need for compatible counselors is especially true for Chicano students, many of whom enter community colleges with definite identity crises. These students have been living in two cultures, believing that they must totally accept one and reject the other (Gonzalez, 1972).

It still remains largely true that black high school graduates come mostly from low or middle quartiles in socioeconomic status and ability, but have higher aspirations to postsecondary education than comparable whites (Clowes & Levin, 1980). While it is true that two-year colleges serve primarily the middle-ability strata of students, with four-year colleges serving primarily the upper strata and no college adequately serving the lowest stratum of society, blacks—who cluster in the lower status and aptitude groupings—cluster in the four-year colleges despite the rise in the number of blacks attending two-year colleges. The generally higher level of aspiration and concern for status on the part of black students appears to be an advantage, since, as a group, black students who aspire to a two-year degree and attend a two-year college complete and receive an associate degree at the same rate as do white students. Moreover, initial enrollment in a two-year college seems to have a less pronounced negative effect for blacks than for whites in ultimately obtaining a bachelor's degree (Clowes & Levin, 1980).

High-Risk Students

During the 1960s the major group served largely by two-year colleges were those students measured as achieving poorly in schools. It is not accurate, though a commonly held misconception, to equate this group with ethnic minorities (Cross, 1971). Even today, numerically, most students enrolled in remedial programs in community colleges are white.

The task of serving the high-risk student or the student who has not yet demonstrated at least average academic achievement is not a recent phenomenon in community colleges. By 1968, the courses offered most often in these colleges were remedial English, reading, and mathematics. Remedial courses, however, did not remedy student learning difficulties. Few students completed the remedial courses they were assigned and less than 10 percent persisted with the second semester.

Community colleges today are recruiting and admitting increasing numbers of students who are characterized as high risk.

These students are not only deficient in basic academic and study skills, but more and more of them may be characterized as having a "failure identity." Such students have little confidence in their ability to stay in college, let alone succeed. The failure-identity student not only expects to fail, but often actively behaves in ways that promote failure. These students are usually lost, not because the colleges are perverse but because most community college instructors and counselors do not understand high-risk students and few staff members possess the helping skills needed to stop the failure-producing behavior of these students.

Most students entering community colleges as their first attempt at postsecondary education lack adequate verbal skills. The reading level of average entering students today is between the eighth and ninth grade, even if they have finished high school. As a rough generalization, approximately 25 percent of all students entering community colleges are functionally illiterate—that is, reading below the fourth-grade level (Roueche, 1978). If community college students lack verbal communication skills, are reading below the ninth-grade level, lack solid study skills, motivation, and a belief that they can succeed, the odds are high that the students will not persist through one semester at a typical community college.

A special subset of the high-risk student population is the adult basic education group. These students are more often handicapped by a lack of confidence in their academic ability than younger students and need to be encouraged. They often have had past unpleasant experiences, including failure in school. As a consequence, these adult learners are frequently apprehensive about schools and school people. In addition, the adult feels a greater press of time than does the younger student. This press, often occasioned by the promise of a job or promotion if a high school diploma is earned, frequently leads to unrealistic expectations of progress on the part of the student, and serious concern about being asked to carry out what are perceived as irrelevant learning tasks.

Adults are often unfamiliar with the procedures and even the current vocabulary used in educational administration, and so frequently end up seeking help too late or in the wrong places. In addition to common problems such as lack of effective reading and study skills, vagueness of long-range goals, pressures of family life, and lack of contact with faculty and counseling personnel, the adult, high-risk student has unusual need for counseling (Grabowski, 1976).

Unfortunately, counseling for adults is at best inadequate. Despite the fact that counseling adults is the most rapidly developing area in the counseling field, there seems to be a lack of serious commitment by the educational community to provide such counseling. There is also a lack of adequate literature in this area and a paucity of counselors who are specifically trained to deal with the special problems of adults, especially the adult basic education student (Knox, 1979).

Foreign Students

During the 1960s little national attention was paid to foreign students in community colleges, even though select schools, such as Miami-Dade Junior College in Florida, reported that as much as 10 percent of their enrollment was comprised of foreign students. By 1971 Miami-Dade enrolled 5,000 foreign students, while 11 percent of all foreign students in the United States were enrolled in two-year institutions. The early 1970s saw the influx of great numbers of foreign students into community and junior colleges. By the mid-1970s their presence was finally beginning to receive the attention of policy makers, and by the late 1970s systematic and comprehensive approaches were being developed for servicing the international student in community colleges.

Because a number of problems are inherent in the transfer of foreign students to U.S. institutions, a variety of services need to be developed to respond to the needs of this subpopulation. Foreign students are often unfamiliar with the differences between higher education in this country and the educational systems in their home countries. The variety of course and curricular offerings can be bewildering. Matching personal interests and goals with institutional programs is difficult even for U.S. students. Degree requirements, program standards, and course content are frequently different from those to which a foreign student has been accustomed. Even when these students attempt to preplan their transitions to U.S. institutions and work to familiarize themselves with the system, they often do so with outdated information materials.

Foreign students are often confronted with financial problems. These include not only how to pay for one's education but such matters as fluctuating currency exchange rates, obtaining on-time payments of their government scholarships, and finding that the money available to them is inadequate to sustain them in certain areas of this country.

Perhaps the greatest obstacles for foreign students are language and cultural barriers. Inadequate skills in English usually provide the major stumbling block for foreign students in completing a program of study. Difficulty in adjusting to U.S. society, homesickness, climate changes, and even dating and friendship-building customs sometimes so overwhelm foreign students that they have little energy left for academic work. Foreign students are also frequently confronted with visa problems. Some, upon completing their programs of study, are not eager to return home.

Foreign students especially desire help in orientation to the academic setting and in the use of the English language. Adequate programs in both of these areas are lacking in the majority of two-year institutions, although progress has been made during recent years.

Many institutions have foreign-student advisors; but these staff members, while knowledgeable about practical problems of finances, visas, living arrangements, health services, and the like, seldom develop programs to prepare academic and professional staff to understand and meet the needs of foreign students. More than this, few institutions carry out a regular follow-up program of foreign students to determine the adequacy of the institutional services and programs that have been established.

Handicapped Students

Two-year colleges enroll a larger percentage of handicapped students than any other segment of higher education in the United States (Astin, 1980). Because of the diversity of impairments — hearing, orthopedic, speech, vision or learning disabilities, and the like—it is impossible here to detail all the needs of this subpopulation. Federal regulations have mandated that schools become accessible to the handicapped and, certainly in most jurisdictions, school districts are instructed to provide special educational services to students up to age 21.

Because of the diversity of agencies providing services for handicapped populations, it seems that each institution must have at least one staff member who is well acquainted with community resources and is skilled in assisting handicapped students in gaining access to these resources. Further, this staff member must have a thorough understanding of the various laws affecting handicapped populations, various federal, state, and local programs recently established to assist handicapped students, and an understanding of the obligations of the college to adapt to the needs of these students.

One category of handicapped student attending community and junior colleges in large numbers is the learning–disabled student. This class of handicapped student is particularly poorly served, since these students often present characteristics similar to the low-achieving student. Two-year colleges seldom have adequate assessment programs to identify the learning–disabled student. Moreover, even with a functioning assessment program, few colleges have developed even preliminary means for responding to the needs of the learning-disabled student. While it is true that there is a long way to go to respond adequately to the needs of the visibly handicapped, only the barest beginning has been made to respond to those whose handicap is hidden.

Transfer and Reverse Transfer Students

Since 1970 the percentage of students with previous college experience has tended to increase, while the percentage of students preparing for transfer has decreased. Reverse transfer is about as popular as transferring from two- to four-year colleges. Surprisingly, data show that the number of students who transfer from four-year to two-year schools is approximately equal to the number who transfer from a two-year to a four-year college. Financial need appears to be a major reason for transferring from a four-year to a two-year school, and desire to reach an educational objective is the major reason for transferring from a two-year to a four-year school.

Transferring students now comprise about 20 percent of credit students who initially enroll in two-year colleges. Whereas in 1970 community colleges typically had a three-to-one ratio of students enrolling in transfer programs, by 1973 more than half of the students graduating were receiving degrees. By the second half of the decade awards in occupational areas outnumbered those in arts and sciences and general areas by a ratio of three to two.

Students who complete two years of junior college and transfer to a senior college have a better chance of obtaining a bachelor's degree than those who transfer before they complete two years. Community and junior college transfers do about as well in senior colleges as those who enrolled in senior colleges during their freshman year, though they tend to take slightly longer to complete their study programs. Probably the most outstanding experience of students transferring to senior colleges, according to a study by Knoell and Medsker (1965), is that they appear to suffer some transfer shock. This is evidenced by an initial drop in grade-point average during the first semester after transfer. After 30 semester hours, however, the transfer students studied were obtaining higher grade-point averages than those students who had maintained continuous enrollment in four-year colleges.

In general, community colleges continue to meet the goal of providing adequate transfer programs. Loss of transfer credit seems to have considerably declined, and articulation problems between junior and senior institutions appear to be more the fault of the senior institution than the junior. Transferring students are very similar to students who originally enroll in four-year institutions in their personal and family characteristics, except that they tend to come from lower income groups. In general, if community college counseling has succeeded anywhere, it has been with the transfer students.

Counselors in community colleges are still faced with the problems of transferring that were so common during the 1960s. Counselors must still understand requirements of senior colleges, so that the work students put in during their first two years of schooling will not appear wasted. But counselors today must be equally familiar with the needs of students reverse transferring from four-year institutions. Many of these students are, in reality, rethinking their career goals. The reverse transferring student is often transferring away from the arts and sciences and general programs and toward the occupational curricula. Estimates are that approximately 45 percent of the men and women who reverse transfer are either planning to enter a new field or did not have definite vocational plans. And large numbers of reverse transfer students are very bitter about their experiences in their four-year institutions.

Nearly one-third of transferring students complain of getting no assistance in making their transfers. This is a serious indictment of counselors who a decade ago were often so proud of their success in the area of transferring. Maybe counselors are no less skilled in this area today; it might be that they are being asked to do too many tasks and there are too few counselors. It might also be that senior college counselors are the ones not providing adequate service to those who are transferring out of their institutions. Whatever the difficulties, problems with academic transfer programs are likely to decline over the next two decades for two reasons: the size of the traditional college-going age group will decrease, and four-year institutions will try much harder to recruit students planning to obtain a bachelor's degree (Cohen & Lombardi, 1979). Likely to increase are the problems of finding appropriate university majors for vocational-technical graduates who want more education and job preparation than their two-year college program provided (Walsh, 1978). Furthermore, counselors need to realize that in the years ahead transfer students will have a much greater variety of institutions into which to transfer.

Career and Technical Students

During the last half of the 1970s the community college has taken on the image of the practical person's school. Increased concern about job marketability has sent students throughout education scurrying to curricula that appear to provide better marketability.

Today for the first time, 80 percent of the full-time students attending two-year colleges cite ability to get a better job as the primary reason for attending.

Counselors probably find their greatest challenge in counseling career or technical students. Fortunately, counselors have begun to rise to the demand for more and better career and vocational counseling. Some perceive career counseling as the most needed counseling service in the community college. There is hardly a director of student personnel services not interested in hiring counselors skilled in career and vocational counseling.

The task of career or vocational counseling is no easy one even for the best trained of counselors. The area is complicated by inadequate information about rapidly changing jobs and economic circumstances; by the lack of adequate understanding of specific manpower needs of the job market area served by the school (which might actually cover a range of several hundred miles); by questions of availability of suitable training programs offered by the school, staffed by competent instructors who keep programs abreast of market and student demands; by student demands that affect curricula, not based on reasoned market judgments but often on biases of students not adequately informed about the rapidly changing world of work; and by the nature of the students enrolling in career and vocational courses and the biases of others about these students.

Even though some schools have attempted to respond to the complexity of career and/or vocational counseling through the use of computers, the utility of such information resources is limited by the information programmed into them. Regrettably, few programs have been developed to respond to the specific market demands of a given school. Counselors are usually left to work miracles on their own and all too often their biases seriously limit the horizons of the students they counsel. The result can often be that students are channeled into career choices because the counselor perceives the training to be available or the career in current demand.

Biases about career and technical students also serve to limit horizons. It is still common to view students enrolled in occupational curricula as less able than academic or transfer students. Available evidence shows, however, that academic students are only slightly higher in ability than occupational students, a difference even further reduced when the factor of age is computed into the equation. Medsker and Clark (cited in Stewart, 1966, pp. 46-52) concluded that the range of ability is about the same for both groups. There is some evidence that students who are successful in high-level, two-year technical programs have the intellectual ability to be successful in four-year programs, but students who are enrolled in lower-level trade-industrial programs would probably not be successful.

There has also been a continuing bias that occupational students are simply dropouts from academic curricula. This impression seems to have been largely spawned at a time when 75 percent of students declared for a transfer curriculum. The reality seems to be that occupational students are simply persons with different interests and aptitudes and that the curriculum each chooses is the result of a systematic process on the part of the individual. It is true that on the basis of interest scores alone, exclusive of measures of intelligence, large numbers of occupational students can be classified into broad clusters of curricula.

The general conclusion should be that in counseling students counselors should pay less attention to measured intelligence and more attention to such factors as student background, parental interests and attitudes, vocational interests, and perception of the job market area into which the student hopes to settle. It would further seem advisable for counselors to spend a great deal of time keeping up with the job demands in their areas, perhaps through the use of a resource committee developed to advise on such matters, as well as their own reading, research, and field casework. And, finally, it would be very helpful for the counselor to find a crystal ball to use to predict changes in the economy, in the world political scene, and in technological advances at least five years in advance.

REFERENCES

AACJC. 1980 Community, junior and technical college directory. Washington, D.C.: American Association of Community and Junior Colleges, 1980.

Anderson, C. (Ed.). A fact book for academic administration. Washington, D.C.: American Council on Education, 1980.

Astin, A. W. The American freshman, national norms for fall, 1979. Los Angeles: UCLA, 1980.

Clowes, A. A., & Levin, A. How do two year colleges serve recent high school graduates. Community College Review, 1980, 7(3), 24-35.

Cohen, A. M., & Lombardi, J. Can the community colleges survive success? Change, 1979, 11(8), 25.

Cooley, W. W., & Becker, S. J. The junior college student. Personnel and Guidance Journal, 1966, 44(5), 464-469.

Cross, K. P. The junior college student: A research description. Princeton, N.J.: Educational Testing Service, 1968.

Cross, K. P. Beyond the open door: New students to higher education. San Francisco: Jossey-Bass, 1971.

Gilbert, F. (Ed.). 1979 Minority report: Data and dialogue. Washington, D.C.: American Association of Community and Junior Colleges, 1979.

Gilsdorf, D. L. Minority counselors: are they really needed? Paper presented at the 31st Annual Convention of the American Personnel and Guidance Association, New York, March 1975. (ED 110 910)

Gonzalez, C. Counseling the Mexican-American student: A position paper. Unpublished paper, 1972. (ED 101 259)

Grabowski, S. M. Educational counseling of adults. Adult Leadership, 1976, 24(7), 225.

Hillway, T. The American two-year college. New York: Harper Brothers, 1958.

Knoell, D. M., & Medsker, L. L. From junior to senior college— a national study of the transfer student. Washington, D.C.: American Council on Education, 1965.

Knox, B. E. Counseling needs of ABE students. Community College Review, 1979, 7(1), 56-64.

Meabon, D. L. What every community college trustee should know about student personnel services. Washington, D.C.: Association of Community College Trustees, 1976. (ED 125 724)

Participation in adult education, 1978. Washington, D.C.: National Center for Education Statistics, Advance Report, February 1980.

Roueche, J. E. Let's get serious about the high risk student. Community and Junior College Journal, 1978, 49(1), 28-31.

Stewart, L. H. A study of certain characteristics of students and graduates of occupation-centered curricula. Final Report, Project 5-1052, Office of Education, Department of Health, Education and Welfare, 1966.

Thomas, F. W. The functions of the junior college. In W. M. Proctor (Ed.), The junior college: Its organization and administration. Palo Alto, Calif.: Stanford University Press, 1927, pp. 11-25.

Walsh, E. M. Articulation problems of vocational-technical students. Community College Review, 1978, 5(3), 50-54.

4

ORGANIZATION AND ADMINISTRATION OF STUDENT AFFAIRS

> The student is the heart of the total
> educational enterprise.
> Washington State Student
> Services Commission

INTRODUCTION

Student personnel programs have been closely related to other facets of U.S. higher education since they were established. Initially, the responsibility for student personnel services was distributed over the entire faculty. The faculty held the common view of the college student as an immature adolescent in constant need of supervision. More than this, student conduct that breached morals or the law was considered to reflect as much on the schooling institution as on the student. This was especially true of the early colleges, which accepted as their prime obligation, the perpetuation of the values of the religious or political community that founded them.

It was out of this heritage that student personnel services emerged. Initially student personnel specialists, distinct from the faculty or other administrators, were exclusively concerned with the purely physical needs of students, such as housing or recreation. But even these concerns could not be entirely separated from teaching, at least with regard to maintaining the degree of decorum deemed necessary for sober scholars.

As college enrollments increased and as specialization became inevitable, personnel work developed as a professional task distinct from teaching functions. In the early part of the twentieth century, student personnel work came to be accepted as consisting of those services responsible for student regulation and control. Student personnel workers became the principal agents of the administration in the enforcement of the rules and supervision of student affairs (deans of men and women).

After the Second World War, with the rapid increase of student populations that were more heterogeneous in nature, and the widening range of occupational choices for which students could be trained, demands grew for assistance in selecting, entering, and succeeding in college. Student personnel programs quickly became a collection of offices scattered around campuses, offering services responding to physical, academic, financial, and psychological needs. The need for coordination of this "selective services" approach led to the development of student affairs administrative structures.

ADMINISTRATIVE DEVELOPMENTS BEFORE 1960

The period after the Second World War until the late 1950s saw a great struggle to shift emphasis from the group to the individual in U.S. colleges and to establish personnel services as a professionally distinct grouping, while not completely separating these services from the instructional program. One of the first steps in this process was to establish a program with a full-time director. By 1950 about one-fourth of the public junior colleges were employing full-time guidance directors (Hillmer, 1950). And other junior college administrators had begun to realize the need for well-planned guidance programs, although such programs had not yet been implemented. The major difficulties in implementing coordinated personnel services at this time appeared to be threefold: cost, the lack of adequately trained personnel, and the lack of appropriate models and other information for organizing and administering student personnel programs.

The administrative structures for personnel services that developed in community colleges during the 1950s tended to follow models that centered control under a single head. There was a need to bring services that had developed separately into a cohesive and interacting union. There was a gradual development of student personnel services from a fragmented, part-time, or nonexistent staff base into a more cohesive and centralized unit following models commonly in place at the time for general university administration.

Not all programs of personnel services developed in the same way or from a similar philosophic base. Many programs during the 1950s attempted to integrate guidance and classroom instruction by having teachers ply both arts. As the 1950s began, more than half of all junior colleges used faculty members as part-time advisors or counselors. Others, admittedly a small number, developed strong staffs and programs. Only one-third of the colleges employed specially trained personnel as counselors or advisors.

Prior to 1960, student personnel services struggled for organization. Many schools did no better than pull together a few services under the dean of students. A few schools still provided counseling as a service of the administrative head of the institution. For most institutions organization of any kind was considered an improvement. Organizational trends paralleled a move for more professional workers and a growing emphasis on the student as an individual with unique talents and needs.

ADMINISTRATION DURING THE 1960S

The struggle for administrative change did not cease at the end of the 1950s. The development of programs that mediated between the needs of students and the pressures of institutions continued. Program development differed, depending on the size of the institution. Smaller institutions tended to develop less formal organizations for student personnel services, but so did institutions that were feeling a budget pinch, or those opting to allocate funds for development to accommodate rapid expansion, or those whose chief administrators maintained the philosophy that counseling responsibilities should be assigned to all members of the faculty.

Among those institutions that were organizing a formal administrative structure of student services, some were beginning to experiment with alternatives to the rigid line-staff model. An institution here and there began to talk about structuring services into clusters of related, mutually interdependent activities in order to improve horizontal communication and cooperation while maintaining a maximum amount of coordination. The emphasis even among the more experimental organizational configurations, however, was to pull together all nonacademic and nonbusiness functions of the college under a single individual who headed a division called student personnel services. This emphasis continued the serious problem of disassociating the instructional program from student personnel services. It also caused many faculty to continue to view the student personnel program as an unnecessary bureaucratic adjunct to the true mission of the college.

Some, such as McConnell (1960), suggested downplaying the autonomy and separate organizational status of student personnel services in order to keep the gulf between student personnel and academic staff as narrow as possible. Although McConnell appeared to opt for this strategy, he believed that it would be undermined by the student personnel people who intensely wanted to acquire status for themselves and their profession.

Of course there were other strategies for narrowing the possible gulf. These strategies included the work of the chief institutional administrator in unifying the instructional, business, and student personnel programs; the involvement of the institution's board of trustees in more than the business affairs of the college; the employment of highly qualified student personnel staff who could maintain the respect of the academic staff; and the willingness of the student personnel staff to experiment with and evaluate the services they delivered to a changing population in order to demonstrate how effectively these professionals could assist both students and teaching staff.

Perhaps the strategic requirement for development of student personnel services during the 1960s was to organize in such a manner that this staff could permeate the entire campus. Serious responses to the question of the most effective organizational model, however, had to wait for the decade of the 1970s. During the 1960s, student personnel workers were mainly concerned with establishing the need for professional counselors, obtaining legitimate standing for them in community colleges, reducing faculty resistance to student personnel work, and establishing at least a basic administrative structure during a time of rapid expansion and sometimes great unrest.

During the latter part of the 1960s and early part of the 1970s student personnel workers were placed unwillingly in the national limelight. The most dramatic changes effected by these years of campus unrest was the demise of college structures and procedures resting on the concept of in loco parentis. Students' rights as citizens came to be increasingly recognized, due process became a watchword in matters of student discipline, and students were given a greater participatory role in the governance of educational institutions.

The person on most campuses who suffered the greatest conflict in role and function was usually the student affairs administrator. In the past these administrators had attempted to thread the lines between students, faculty, and administration, trying to explain and interpret one to the other. As a result of the student unrest, students began to insist that student affairs administrators should represent their interests. But as chief student affairs administrators exercised more administrative functions and assumed titles such as vice-president, presidents came to regard these administrators as part of the central university team and not the students' advocates.

The result of the conflicts on campuses at this time, as far as administration of student personnel programs was concerned, was that the decade of the 1970s began with many more organizational

problems than solutions. There were several alternative models
for student personnel services administration being discussed. But
in community colleges the centralized line model of student personnel services administration was followed 90-95 percent of the time.
Changes in established administrative modes would be difficult at
best.

ADMINISTRATIVE DEVELOPMENTS DURING THE 1970S

By the early 1970s student personnel service structures were
established in most community colleges and further organizational
changes were under way, though more slowly than at comparable
nonresident four-year institutions (Crookston, Atkyns, & Franek,
1974).

During the early 1970s several forces worked to shape management models and strategies at junior and community colleges.
These forces included the concept of the college as a community and
a part of a larger community; the insistence that students be involved in the planning and management of their college lives; caution
among chief university administrators and student personnel specialists not to let control get too far out of their hands; and the fact
that junior college students were generally less articulate, more
conservative, and less likely to take strong positions on issues
than their four-year counterparts. One result of these forces was
that the predominant administrative structure of student personnel
services continued to be the centralized model. Under this model,
related student personnel functions are grouped under a chief administrator who in all likelihood supervises most, if not all, of the
services traditionally classified as student personnel. The administrator then, for the most part, reports directly to the chief administrator of the college. This structure generally puts student
personnel functions on a par with instructional functions. It is a
tight-ship, low-trust model.

These centralized models emphasize visible lines of authority
through which the chief administrator defines roles and practices.
Management is carried out through calendars and schedules, specific orders, and formal inter- and intragroup relationships. Such
a model also tends to foster private staff communication, suspicion,
and low participation in problem-solving activity (McDaniel &
Lombardi, 1972).

A countertrend was also developing during the early 1970s.
This trend, generally referred to as decentralization, represented
an effort to facilitate closer working relationships between the
teaching faculty and student personnel staff. Although the primary

administrative responsibility remained in the hands of the chief student personnel administrator even in schools moving toward more decentralized models, the movement toward decentralization indicated a wish among some to attempt a higher-trust or more campus-involved organization. This movement was probably indicative of an easing among student personnel workers and their need to prove themselves as professionals. This trend was also facilitated by a student drive for a more participatory voice in their lives as students and members of the community.

O'Banion (1972a) saw most organizational experimentation taking place during the 1970s in the area of decentralization of counseling services. His own strongly stated belief was that if student personnel programs were to have a major impact on community colleges, counselors would have to leave the comfort and isolation of the counseling center, and student personnel programs would have to become involved in the curriculum, instructional processes, faculty activities, decision-making processes, and in the community (O'Banion, 1972). The question was clearly stated: "Should the counselor be literally moved out of the counseling office and housed with faculty members?" (O'Banion, 1972a, p. 182). A few experiments did exactly this and moved counselors into academic divisions. Some were placed under the administrative leadership of the division chairman. But for the most part, student services stayed in their own part of the campus while student personnel workers exercised the roles of either service or maintenance people or counseling office therapists.

STUDENT DEVELOPMENT MODEL

The major advance in the early to mid-1970s was the development of an alternative model for the student personnel professional. This model was generally called the student development model and people who followed it were alternatively called student development specialists or human development facilitators or some variant of one or the other. The major shift of this model, when contrasted with student personnel services, was from a group student-growth or services approach to an individual student-growth or personalized education approach. The movement was on, at least in theory, for each student to have an individually designed curriculum, and student development specialists were to have the knowledge and skills necessary to assist individual students in every other facet of behavioral development.

The student development model is based on the belief that people have an innate growth principle that makes them capable of

self-realization and fulfillment in both personally and socially responsible ways. This model implies that educational potential
exists in every aspect of an institution's programs and activities.
As a process, student development is the strategy or procedure
the institution deliberately formulates to create opportunities for
the development of each student. Student development is an outcome when students do, in fact, achieve skills and an understanding
of themselves and of the world in which they live and work (Meabon,
1976).

In order to carry out the student development model, student
development specialists must accept the premise that a student's
education affects and is affected by all aspects of the student's life.
As a result, these specialists must be able to assist students with
questions ranging from "Who am I?" to "What is the best combination of learning experiences that will lead me to my vocational
goal?" The student development specialist must also be able to
help faculty, administrators, even boards of trustees, in identifying institutional objectives and actions that will provide for and
structure the behavioral development of each individual student.
What the student development model seems to demand is a master
of all trades. O'Banion (1972b) indeed outlined an idealized prototype of the kind of person needed to facilitate the student development model, drawing heavily on characteristics espoused by pre-
vailing humanistic psychologists as describing a healthy personality.

Given the right kind of staff, O'Banion was correct in pro-
jecting the appropriate organizational structure as being a decentralized administration-by-participation model. But by the mid-
1970s community college innovators were all too aware of the
problems associated with this model. It appeared that a democratic staff could not exist as an island in an ocean of bureaucratic
controls. Battle lines were drawn between the military-industry,
line-of-command pattern of most colleges and the participative
pattern hoped for. Further, there existed a great gap between
rhetoric and practice, which made change more difficult. Administrators generally agreed with high-trust principles: wide participation in decision making, face-to-face relationships, mutual
confidence, open communication, and internal control of performance. A much smaller number practiced them.

The demand on both student personnel chiefs and staff of the
decentralized student development model appeared to be too great
to allow easy implementation. At any rate, while it is a model that
many conceded had theoretical merit, it was seldom implemented
in its entirety. In the realm of higher education, this less hierarchical model not only required changing the way in which schools
are governed by redistributing power among all members of the

school community, but restructuring the very systems of higher
education themselves. Further, in times of scarcity, a hierarchical administrative structure seemed necessary to regulate the dis-
tribution of limited goods and services. And finally, schools continued to function on centralized models on the assumption that such
models are the natural and inevitable reflections of the bureaucracy
that regulates the rest of society.

ENTRY INTO THE 1980S

There remains a need for new management structures in community and junior colleges in the 1980s. The student development
model is certainly a ground-breaking approach. At least philosophically there seems to be wide agreement that the quantitative,
technical, lower-trust, less human management techniques need
some modification, if indeed they have not already served their
purpose (Manilla, 1979). The student development and decentralized
signposts mark the way for other qualitative approaches that should
be considered in the future.

The fact that quantitative approaches to decision making and
military-industrial organizational models still predominate among
community and junior colleges, even in divisions of student development, does not negate the fact that pressures are building for
shifts toward more decentralized participatory systems (Marks,
1978). Greater emphasis is being placed on the leader's qualities
than on the system of leadership used by an institution or even on
demonstrated skills (Eaton, 1978; Marsee, 1979).

Students are responding better to the decentralization of some
services (Selgas, 1977). Community colleges are generally re-
assessing their goals and priorities during a time of reduced public
support, marked enrollment shifts or declines, changing consumer
interests, reductions in staffs or shifts from more full-time to
more part-time staff members, high inflation, insecurity about
state and federal financial support, increased autonomy problems
because of increased external controls, and increased need for data
and flexibility in order to respond to change.

The question for the 1980s is how to manage the functions
generally carried out by student personnel services programs.
These functions now generally include those in the following list:

I.   Functions that inform
     A.   Preadmissions information. Dissemination of information
          by printed material, counselor visits, consultation with
          potential students and their families, telephone contacts,
          conferences, correspondence and use of the public media.

    B. Orientation. Providing for the academic, social, and attitudinal orientation of students to the institution.

    C. General information. Providing information for explaining educational and occupational opportunities; providing information pertaining to certification, testing, and general college functioning.

    D. Interpreting college policy. Providing information about college regulations, goals, aims, and methods.

II. Functions that control

    A. Admissions. Providing for the orderly entry of students into the institution.

    B. Registration. Providing a systematic method for enrolling students in classes.

    C. Student withdrawals, transfers, and graduation. Providing for the orderly exit of students from the institution.

    D. Student records. Maintaining accurate records of students while they are enrolled in the institution and once they have left the institution.

    E. Academic and social regulation. Providing due process for the reasonable protection of students' rights and those of the institution against undue infringement.

III. Functions that evaluate

    A. Applicant appraisal. Providing for transcript and test interpretations, individual case studies, and the interviewing of prospective students.

    B. Testing services. Providing measurement of intellectual, interest, personality, values, and vocational factors.

    C. Health appraisal. Canvassing of health and physical well-being of students and staff, and development and review of health records.

    D. Research and follow-up. Developing local normative data and conducting other research on special topics of interest; follow-up of transfers, withdrawals, and graduates.

    E. Program and staff evaluation. Providing evaluative information for the improvement of student services including student evaluations of program and staff.

IV. Functions that facilitate

    A. Individual counseling. Counseling services provided to individual students, their spouses, and where appropriate, their families regarding such items as clarifying values, attitudes, interests, and abilities; formulating vocational-educational plans; identifying and helping resolve problems that interfere with the student's progress; identifying re-

ferral sources for problems beyond the capability of the
professional staff or mission of the institution.

B. Group counseling. Providing a forum to help solve personal concerns, develop new learning, increase human
awareness, and facilitate human development through group
process.

C. Educational advising. Providing information regarding
selection of curriculum and courses, including occupational
requirements, transfer requirements, and the availability
of the wide variety of services and agencies useful in fostering the student's academic progress.

D. Staff development. Providing wide-ranging and coordinated
opportunities for professional growth for the college staff,
consultants for special areas of interest and need, resources for staff development conferences, attendance at
professional meetings, professional literature, and research support services.

E. Special programs. Providing classes, tutoring, and other
forms of programmatic assistance in study skills, remediation, career exploration, interpersonal communication,
self-understanding, and other forms of personal development.

F. Health service. Providing assistance in improving health
knowledge, attitudes, and habits, and developing strategies
for maintaining optimal personal and environmental physical and mental health.

G. Financial aid. Providing information relative to obtaining
financial assistance necessary to pursue one's education.
Providing individual counseling about student expenses;
providing general information on managing one's finances
and obtaining financial aid; developing sources of student
aid; conducting studies on the impact of aid programs on
the institution; managing scholarship awards.

H. Career placement. Providing employment placement
services for students and alumni; fostering work-study
opportunities, maintaining effective relationships with in-
dustrial, commercial, governmental, and educational
enterprises, and other cooperating agencies; maintaining
follow-up records of alumni.

I. Services to special student groups. Providing for the advising of special student groups regarding educational,
social, attitudinal, financial, and legal problems; assisting
in the development of programs for special student groups.

J. Faculty consultation.

V. Functions that involve
   A. Activities. Assisting in the development of cultural, so-
      cial, educational, and recreational experiences for stu-
      dents and the community.
   B. Campus governance. Assisting in the meaningful involve-
      ment of students in the governance of the institution.
   C. Student government. Assisting in the development of a
      student government that feels a responsibility and has the
      authority to respond to student concerns; providing train-
      ing in interpersonal communications, leadership, and
      fiscal responsibility.

VI. Other functions
    The functions listed above are common to almost all stu-
    dent services programs. There are other related functions
    that may or may not exist at a given institution or may or
    may not be carried out by student services. Where these
    functions are included administratively in student services,
    appropriate staffing and funding must be provided. Such
    functions might include food services, residence halls,
    bookstores, traffic management, campus security, and
    cocurricular activities such as student newspapers or
    intercollegiate sports.

Jonassen and Stripling (1977) asked practitioners at all of
Florida's public community colleges to rank the functions carried
out at times by student personnel workers. After three rounds of
ranking, the following priorities emerged, in descending order:

1. Administrative organization
2. Student counseling
3. Career information and decision making
4. Student advisement
5. Faculty consultation
6. In-service education and staff development
7. Change agents
8. Student development
9. Financial aids.
10. Precollege information
11. Program articulation
12. Information center
13. Personnel records
14. Student registration
15. Group orientation
16. Paraprofessionals and peer group counseling

17. Educational testing
18. Services to special population groups
19. Program evaluation
20. Placement
21. Curriculum development
22. Community services
23. Applicant consultation
24. Applicant appraisal
25. Cooperative education
26. Student induction
27. Teaching
28. Student self-government
29. Cocurricular activities
30. Academic regulation
31. Health appraisal and services
32. Athletics
33. Social regulation
34. Child care

If cuts in programs or administrative reorganizations are called for, this listing appears helpful in establishing administrative priorities. Further, it seems that practitioners are aware of the need for change and are prepared to accept new responsibilities required by a changing student population and developing institutional and faculty needs. The Jonassen-Stripling list shows a greater emphasis on student development and a decrease of emphasis on student regulation. There is also ample evidence that student personnel practitioners want to become more involved in the total administrative organization and decision-making process of their respective institutions.

It does not appear that with an installed bureaucracy many institutions are going to succumb to developing pressures to move dramatically from a low participatory to a high participatory model of governance in the near future. The results thus far have indicated that unless a junior or community college adopted a high participatory governance structure at the time it was founded or as a result of unusual internal turbulence, a lower participatory/higher bureaucratic model was maintained.

There is a need to redesign organizations, especially student personnel organizations, to be more responsive during the 1980s both to their environments and their people. Further, it appears that for the near future a new, responsive organization must be one that can be integrated with existing bureaucracies. The solution seems to be, for existing junior and community colleges, a parallel-structures model based on a student development philosophy.

This model is developed around flat and flexible but formal, problem-solving governance organizations that supplement bureaucracy and exist side by side with it, but do not replace it.

The 1980s will demand that community colleges respond to external environments of high uncertainty, rapid change, inflationary pressures, regulatory constraints and an antigrowth mentality. Internally, as has already been indicated, there are shifts in student populations, shifts in the expectations of existing college labor forces, demands for more voice in the total administrative and decision-making process of the college by faculty, staff, and students, continued movement toward collective bargaining, demands for more opportunity for career progress and, in general, for a greater sharing of power.

The centralized line model of administration is largely inflexible. Any of a number of decentralized models are difficult to implement and, depending on the type, can become nearly as inflexible administratively as a centralized line model. The best solution seems to be to permit existing bureaucracy to function where it is functioning well, and to develop a different structure capable of dealing effectively with the tasks and conditions for which bureaucracy is not suited. The structural form that seems to be able to accomplish this is what has been called the parallel organization (Miller, 1978).

The parallel organization is an attempt to institutionalize a set of externally and internally responsive, participatory, problem-solving structures alongside the conventional line of organization that carries out routine tasks. The parallel organization is not the same as the advisory committee activity that frequently exists in colleges, nor is it a completely new structure developed to replace the old one. The parallel organization is a second, equally formal organization that provides an additional management structure, supplementing that which already exists. This parallel structure has two distinct sets of advantages: it provides a means for managing change by providing flexibility and responsiveness, and it provides a source of opportunity and power above and beyond the sources in the bureaucratic structure. It is thus potentially able to enhance individual satisfaction and effectiveness in the very act of coping with new pressures.

In outlining this administrative model, there is no attempt to downplay the need for the highest possible level of worker; indeed, O'Banion's ideal prototype, previously mentioned, would be the hoped-for student personnel worker. It is suggested, however, that even the best workers can be made more effective as a function of the positions they hold within the system; as their levels of access to advancement and challenge and the chance to increase competence and skills are enlarged as a result of their positions; and as their access to resources and capacity to mobilize them in order to accomplish tasks efficiently are better provided by their positions. Further, it is a known fact that workers who are denied opportunity devalue their skills, lower their aspirations, and often resist change and innovation.

PARALLEL STRUCTURES IN STUDENT AFFAIRS

The development of parallel managerial structures must begin with the existing bureaucracy. At least the major sources of power—boards of trustees, presidents, and heads of student personnel services—must be convinced that such structures have the ability to improve communication, morale, and delivery of services, and high level linkages must be forged.

Second, broad developmental and organizational objectives must be established. For example, objectives might be to increase the effectiveness, creativity, and sense of opportunity and power of student personnel workers, and increase the capacity of student personnel workers to respond to change and thereby offer more appropriate student services.

Third, the mechanisms for shifting to a parallel organizational structure must be provided. These will include financing; a commitment to employees that time spent involved in such a structure will be worthwhile and rewarded (this commitment must rest on the belief that employees involved in such a structure will gain skills, improve their morale, and develop more creative responses for the organization through this involvement with the parallel structure); and implementation authority for line personnel.

Then initial planning and education can begin. Planning will have to take into account where problems exist, what information will be needed to facilitate change, what problems will be encountered that will retard the establishment of new change structures, and how needed information can best be obtained. Then the information will have to be obtained, and understanding and support for the parallel organizational structure concept will have to be generated through providing forums for educational discussion (a form of structural intervention). If the focus is on the restructuring of student personnel services, it will be necessary to develop an advisory group that can touch all bases in the college and supply knowledgeable counsel for decisions needed to implement actions, authority for cross-campus involvement, and high-level sources of recognition and reward.

A steering committee will be needed as one key layer of the parallel structure and will be especially important in determining what information may be needed for continued change, in addition to that available through usual line structures. Further, the steering committee must know how to incorporate various sources of data, how to obtain more data when necessary, and how to analyze them, and must implement data feedback to every constituency. Data input, analysis, and dissemination are of importance for a quick assessment of problem areas. The value of the parallel structure lies in having a cooperative structure in place to formulate action responses to arising difficulties, empowered to implement these responses. The greatest roadblock for a parallel structure in the process of being developed is the task of convincing college staff and students that such an organizational structure will provide something useful, that there will be follow-through, and that actions generated will not be sabotaged by existing bureaucratic structures.

Figure 4.1 shows a possible parallel structure operating alongside a typical bureaucratic line organization. The steering committee and advisory group can be variously formed. Though representative of the various levels currently existing in the college's bureaucracy and the various broad constituent groups, members of both the steering committee and advisory group should be drawn from volunteer pools. The steering committee is likely to be or become the management group of the parallel organization.

Task forces generally emerge out of identified needs and data feedback meetings. These task forces can be composed quite differently, depending on the nature of the problem or problems identified and the levels and areas represented by the various problems. Task forces are to explore the problem or problems of concern to them, analyze data, collect more data, and formulate and propose action plans. The work of each task force is to be reported to and discussed with the steering committee.

The strategy of the parallel organization is to create for experimental action as well as career development a setting that is flexible, yet connected to existing college structures. The action plans of the task forces must be seen as relevant to the whole organization, so that whatever lessons are learned or actions taken can ultimately be incorporated into the bureaucratic structure. Task forces ordinarily present their findings and plans across the flat parallel organizational structure and through the vertical bureaucratic structure. Task force presenters may not be on the same bureaucratic level as some members in the receiving hierarchy, but are elevated to a credible level because of their place in the parallel organization.

FIGURE 4.1

Parallel Organization Structure

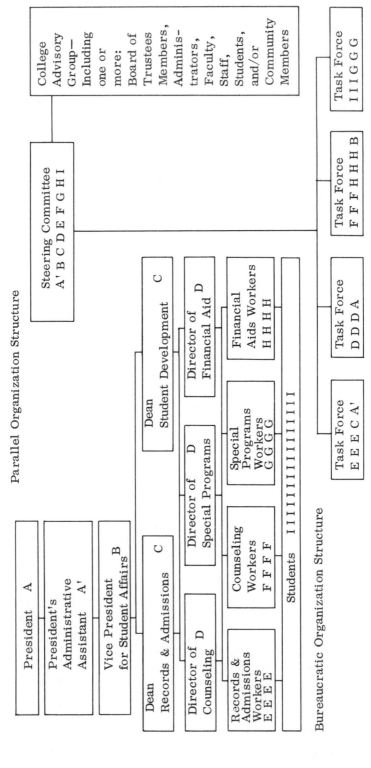

Bureaucratic Organization Structure

Note: Letters indicate the component elements.
Source: Constructed by the authors.

Using the parallel-organization structure, problems internal to the Student Affairs Division, for example, but cutting across subdivisions, might expeditiously be identified and analyzed and action plans drawn. An identified group would also be in place to foster the implementation of the plans drawn and reformulate plans if the results obtained were not those expected. The same type of structure could be used across the campus or system to resolve problems that exist on a much broader base. The full implementation of the student development model, for example, on junior or community college campuses, might be best dealt with through the establishment of a parallel organization structure.

Task forces are part of the implementation process. They must be free to make key decisions about how to organize themselves, how to involve and inform other workers, and how to continue, for example, a flow of services to students while in a major transition period.

As problems in the organization continue to be identified by the bureaucratic line hierarchy, or the parallel organization steering committee, or by the task forces emerging from the general staff or students, a structure for responding to these emerging needs is in place to generate a response without stopping the routine operation of the college. Further, such an organization should improve managerial capacity, increase and broaden planning skills, and increase job motivation, while helping to correct stereotypic views of workers across units.

In general, a parallel organization structure should improve communications by involving workers in planning for and resolving the problems caused by a rapidly changing world causes. Such an organization should help workers gain a larger view of the institution and the difficulties encountered by supervisors, through engaging people in spotting emerging problems. It should help workers be aware of data and learn how to collect and analyze it.

Activity on task forces and the steering committee should afford participants an opportunity to improve and demonstrate their problem-solving and managerial skills. Interface of the parallel organization with the bureaucratic structure should help those in the traditional line hierarchy become aware of the extent of the personnel resources and interest available in an existing staff.

Through the use of parallel structures many of the problems that demand a reconceptualization of staff involvement, such as shifting counseling to evenings, or to individual academic divisions or providing counseling for part-time and/or older students, or for the community, can be developed by the very people who will make the action responses work. Further, the action plans will seem less like assigned or expected duties for those involved in developing them. Instead, participants will gain the benefits of working out creative solutions to thorny problems and seeing their solutions implemented successfully.

It is possible for a mechanistic and an organic organization to exist side by side, each carrying out different but complementary tasks. The two kinds of organizations are not necessarily opposites, as suggested by those who have drawn distinctions between centralized and decentralized organizations. The military-industrial line organization is the maintenance-oriented, operating hierarchy; it defines job titles, pay grades, a set of reporting relationships, and related formal tasks. The main function of such a mechanistic organization is the maintenance of the organization.

The organic organization is change-oriented. People are grouped together temporarily in a number of different ways appropriate to problem resolution tasks. These people are not limited by their positions in the hierarchy. A different set of decision-making channels and reporting relationships are opened and the organization as a whole is more flexible. The main task of the parallel organization is the continued reexamination of routines, exploration of new options, and the development of new procedures and approaches. This organization seeks to institutionalize change. As the utility of new procedures and approaches is demonstrated, these can be transferred into the bureaucratic organization for maintenance and integration.

AREAS OF FORESEEABLE ADMINISTRATIVE CONCERN

Since change is seen as the single most important characteristic of the future, in what areas must the administrator or change team be especially vigilant? There seem to be six broad areas of major concern: staff utilization; institutional research, planning, and evaluation; financial planning and administration; marketing; individual-college-life linkages; and community responsiveness.

Staff Utilization

Reductions in force, retraining programs, and flexible use of staff on hand are issues with which general college and student personnel managers must be concerned. Existing budgets must be reviewed in order to provide retraining programs for lateral transfer to avoid layoffs when a reduction in force is mandated, or to maximize use of a largely tenured faculty when changing market demands cannot be responded to by increasing staff. Even when lateral transfer is not called for, current budgets must provide for professional development programs that emerge from a clear understanding of the relationships among professional development, planning, management, and evaluation systems. Colleges can no longer rely on individual initiative and indirect sources of reward to foster professional development. Now administrators must plan and finance staff development to prepare existing staff as resources for programs deemed necessary for the future of the organization.

Institutional Research, Planning, and Evaluation

It is evident that boards of trustees, academic managers, and staffs must respond to new and flexible ways of governing their organizations during the 1980s. Careful institutional planning based on research can increase institutional effectiveness if managers will make the changes the research and planning indicate. Institutional research is no longer a luxury but a vital base for cooperative planning to deal with reduced resources. Student personnel administrators have a special obligation to maintain an accurate understanding of student need by keeping abreast of the data made available to them by the regular institution research sources, as well as data they request from their staff or the data staff teams generate or obtain while developing new change strategies.

Financial Planning

Colleges have generally experienced diminishing financial resources. There is not an academic institution in the country that has escaped the ravages of inflation and the energy crisis. Most academic institutions have also been affected by a post-Proposition 13 mentality. It is a prudent administrator who plans for across-the-board reductions in financial support to continue. Such planning must heighten concern with educational mission, functions, and governance structures—a positive result of financial curtailment, in the opinion of the authors.

Student personnel administrators must consider the effect on students of such institutional economy measures as reduction in numbers of noncredit courses, the lessened commitment to the open-door policy of admissions, and an end to no-tuition policies. These administrators must also be aware of the demands for services to be delivered by an increasingly limited staff to an increasingly varied student population attending the college during a longer span of hours.

Because increases in tax sources can no longer be counted on to finance even basic services, community colleges must develop fund-raising abilities. Unfortunately, community colleges are entering this aspect of academic life at a distinct disadvantage compared to those institutions that have long histories of refining their fund-raising capacities. Student personnel staffs must begin to practice grantsmanship, if this is not already an established practice. Fiscally responsible administrators must become familiar with the advantages and disadvantages of zero-based budgeting. And administrators must learn that reduced fiscal support does not necessarily lead to program evaluation or to better program planning and more efficient allocation of limited resources.

Marketing

Community colleges, perhaps more than any other type of academic institution, must be aware of the opportunities and pitfalls presented by the reduction in the traditional student pool and the potential increase offered by the nontraditional student pool. During a time of potentially declining enrollments, recruitment and retention become critical matters for institutions whose financial base is directly or indirectly tied to the numbers of students it services. Junior and community colleges generally must become more consumer-oriented. The measure of success of a consumer orientation and marketing strategy is attendance. Attendance depends not only on offering meaningful educational experiences but on well-coordinated student services. Student services personnel already know that they are forced to market their own products in order to be able to demonstrate their utility to the institution as a whole. As a result, increasing numbers of student personnel workers find themselves engaged as instructors of human development courses, hoping they can put on an instructional show interesting enough to open the way for students to use the other student services available. Student services administrators must come to understand the marketing role of their staffs in enrollment, attendance, and retention of students. It is usually up to the academic divisions to put together attractive academic programs. But it is just as frequently the responsibility of student services staffs to advise academic divisions on the nature of student academic needs; cut down registration red tape; provide adequate media coverage of outstanding programs; provide supportive services for a variety of student anxieties; assist students in weathering financial storms in order to maintain enrollment; and coordinate placement and follow-up activities for every academic division in order to help the divisions generate programs that are responsive to both student and employment markets.

Individual-College-Life Linkages

The student development model sets student services as the key link in the individual-college-life linkage. Student affairs administrators must find ways to foster their staffs' involvement in every facet of college life. This involvement includes not only helping each student design the most satisfying educational plan possible, but helping students follow these plans as fully as possible, helping academic divisions supply the necessary growth experiences to service a diverse student body, helping the work world adapt to the students the institution educates, while helping students adapt to the world of work and helping the community welcome and support "lifelong learning."

Community Responsiveness

Of all existing educational institutions, community colleges are probably the most appropriate for the development of innovative programs. Community colleges have shown flexibility in program content, teaching methods, use of community sites for instruction, innovative outreach, and recruitment methods. But community colleges cannot be complacent. Despite their general responsiveness to the market conditions of the 1970s, community colleges have not tackled their responsibility to raise the general level of expectations, cultural maturity, and values of all the people. Accepting this responsibility will mean acknowledging that Americans are still a long way from being an educated people. One out of every five has never been beyond grade school, and large groups of people are still denied adequate education. The student affairs administrator is challenged with how best to attract and provide for student populations that have thus far found continued education displeasing, unaffordable, inconvenient, or denied. It rests largely on the student affairs staff to help orchestrate education that can be responsive to the high-risk, low-achieving student, to the poor, the handicapped, the elderly: It is often up to this staff to provide services to the community that unfortunately are not always seen as educational, including community counseling, consultation, and family advisement.

In the 1980s student services administrators will have to find ways of building and guiding services to students, the institution, and the community for 14-16 hours a day, six and sometimes seven days a week, with a staff that will not grow. Student services staffs will be called on to exhibit skills in which they are not trained, often skills they do not believe they can come to possess. The society will demand responses to increasingly complex problems for an increasingly complex population.

The only hope for a better future response is to make the most effective use of every resource, of each person's time and talents. The organizational plan, therefore, must involve each facet of the organizational community in maximizing the use of resources with as much creativity and flexibility as human beings can muster. Such utilization cannot rest on one person. The entire staff must accept the broadest of institutional mandates as its mission and work cooperatively to generate active responses. There is evidence that community college staffs are ready and willing to take up such a challenge.

REFERENCES

Ayers, A. R., Tripp, P. A., & Russell, J. H. Student services administration in higher education. U.S. Department of Health, Education and Welfare, 1966.

Blasser, W. W., & Crookston, B. B. Student personnel work: College and university. Encyclopedia of Educational Research (3rd ed.). New York: Macmillan, 1960. 1415-1427.

Crookston, B., Atkyns, G. C., & Franek, J. S. Administration of student affairs at community colleges as compared with urban-commuter institutions. Technical Report No. 2 Detroit, Mich.: National Association of Personnel Administrators, February, 1974. (ED 091954)

Eaton, J. S. Studies in possibilities: Academic leadership. Paper presented at the 58th Annual Convention of the American Association of Community and Junior Colleges, Atlanta, April 1978. (ED 154896)

Foresi, J. Administrative leadership in the community college. Jericho, N.Y.: Exposition Press, 1974.

Hillmer, M. A. Present status of administrative organization of student personnel programs public junior colleges. Junior College Journal, 1950, 21, 143-144.

Jonassen, E. O., & Stripling, R. O. Priorities for community college student personnel services during the next decade. Journal of College Student Personnel, 1977, 18(2), 83-86.

Manilla, S. J. Governance and leadership in the 80's: Role of planning, management and evaluation in decision-making. Paper presented at the 59th Annual Convention of the American Association of Community and Junior Colleges, Chicago, April 1979.

Marks, J. L. On decision-making processes and structures. Unpublished paper, 1978. (ED 162690)

Marsee, S. E. Some thoughts about leadership. Unpublished paper, 1979. (ED 162684)

McConnell, T. R. The relation of institutional goals and organization to the administration of student personnel work. In M. L. Snoke (Ed.), Approaches to the study of administration in personnel work. Minneapolis: University of Minnesota Press, 1960.

McDaniel, J. W., & Lombardi, R. A. Organization and administration of student personnel work in the community college. In T. O'Banion & A. Thurston (Eds.), Student development programs in the community junior college. Englewood Cliffs, N.J.: Prentice-Hall, 1972.

Meabon, D. L. What every community college trustee should know about student personnel services. Washington, D.C.: Association of Community College Trustees, 1976. (ED 125724)

Medsker, L. L. The junior college. New York: McGraw-Hill, 1960.

Miller, E. C. The parallel organization structure at General Motors: An interview with Howard C. Carlson. Personnel, 1978, 55(4), 64-69.

O'Banion, T. Exceptional practices in community junior college student personnel programs. In T. O'Banion & A. Thurston (Eds.), Student development programs in the community junior college. Englewood Cliffs, N.J.: Prentice-Hall, 1972a.

O'Banion, T. Junior college student personnel work: An emerging model. In T. O'Banion & A. Thurston (Eds.), Student development programs in the community junior college. Englewood Cliffs, N.J.: Prentice-Hall, 1972b.

Selgas, J. W. Student services: An evaluation over time, 1972–1976. Research Report #16. Harrisburg, Pa.: Harrisburg Area Community College, 1977. (ED 148408)

Williamson, E. G. Student personnel services in colleges and universities. New York: McGraw-Hill, 1961.

5

INDIVIDUAL COUNSELING
APPROACHES

> The client and counselor both grow through
> individual counseling.
>
> B. Siegelwaks (1981)

A considerable portion of any counselor's time is devoted to individual counseling. This is where, traditionally, the vast majority of training, experience, and research is directed. Although the community college counselors may face caseloads considerably larger than those of their colleagues in other settings, the importance of continuous development of effective individual approaches to client problems is a necessary counselor commitment.

This chapter will present what is believed to be an effective model for individual counseling in the community college, describing specific approaches to facilitate the elements of the model. Also presented are selected examples and practice exercises to familiarize the student with these approaches and the way in which each relates to the overall individual counseling model.

INDIVIDUAL APPROACHES AND THE
PROCESS OF COUNSELING

Professional journals, counseling textbooks, and professional development workshops abound with new and varied techniques for individual counseling. It is difficult at times to separate the efficacy of new individual approaches from the possible charismatic effects of the individual espousing the approach. Furthermore, many techniques are developed and researched on a very limited number of clients with limited outcome criteria. While these procedures certainly do not invalidate any approach, they do impose certain limitations on interpreting and applying the procedures for use with the specific subpopulations of the community college. Counselors, with limited time and organizational resources, find themselves in a different position, sifting through this abundance of information for approaches that can be useful in their day-to-day counseling efforts.

It could also be argued that, until very recently, the research and training efforts of the profession have not adequately dealt with the specific and unique problems associated with applying the available counseling technology to the community college. It is the intention here to present and demonstrate useful approaches, counseling technology, so to speak, to skill-building efforts in the primary areas of function for the community college counseling—vocational, educational, and personal growth and development.

SOME BASIC FACTORS IN INDIVIDUAL COUNSELING

At the outset it may be useful to discuss certain factors in community college counseling that are basic to the ideas to be presented in this chapter.

Therapeutic Conditions of Empathy and Respect Comprising Core Ingredients Essential to a Facilitative Client-Counselor Relationship

Rogers (1951), Carkhuff (1969), and other humanistically oriented writers (for example, Carkhuff & Truax, 1967; Combs, Avila, & Purkey, 1978; Patterson, 1974) have aptly demonstrated that without these conditions present in the counselor-client interaction process, constructive client growth and development is difficult if not impossible to attain. Although the counselor's ability to demonstrate empathic understanding and to communicate respect to the client may not be the definitive, necessary, and sufficient conditions for effective helping, they are crucial to the establishment of a unique relationship—specifically a counseling relationship, which is basic to the entire counseling process. Without these conditions, the effectiveness of any technique or approach will be lessened. One is hard-pressed even to envision a disrespectful and nonempathic counselor significantly employing any approach to helping.

The Need for Some Degree of Client Self-Awareness or Self-understanding for Meaningful Client Growth

Regardless of the nature of the client problem—educational, vocational, or personal—some degree of insight into one's own behavior is needed for meaningful change to occur. Without this insight, behavior or behavior change in the context of the problem presented has insufficient meaning to ensure the necessary commitment or motivation to continue the process. Granted, for certain clients with a relatively good grasp of their personalities and problems, specific approaches can deemphasize this element of the helping process. For these clients, the overall approach to helping will be more technique-oriented with considerably less self-exploration. This is generally the exception, however. With most individuals, failure to consider the "person" in the context of the problem will not initially help clients to help themselves.

The opposite is also true and deserves some mention, since it is not uncommon to find counselors placing so much emphasis on insight that little time is left to help solve the problem. In fact, for some students with very specific problems—for example, improving study skills, gaining specific information or knowledge about a given area, losing weight, and so on—overemphasis on self-awareness may be seen as a waste of valuable time and counterproductive to their immediate motivation to bring about change. With community college students this is often the case. Not surprisingly, their criterion for continued counseling is improvement in their problem areas. The balance between the amount and depth of self-awareness is a judgment made by all counselors at some point early in the counseling process. The importance this judgment can have is reflected by its presence in almost all theoretical approaches to counseling (for example, Carkhuff & Berenson, 1976; Ellis, 1962; Krumboltz & Thoresen, 1976; Patterson, 1974; Perls, 1973).

Community College Counselors as Agents of
Change for Students, through Intervention

Counseling, by its definition and purpose, explicitly or implicitly suggests change. All counseling approaches, irrespective of the theoretical rationale, are specifically designed to produce change. Thoughts, feelings, attitudes, behaviors, actions, and perceptions are all subject to some degree of modification as a function of the counseling experience. Counselors by their intervention are the agents of change. If the counselor is competent and effective, the change manifested by the client will be meaningful and appropriate. The overall purpose of this chapter is to present ways in which the counselor can accomplish this role as an agent of meaningful and productive change.

The Counselor's Behavior, Both Verbal
and Nonverbal, as the Vehicle for
Constructive Intervention and Change

Hackney and Nye (1973) devote considerable attention, as do most writers on the subject (for example, Eisenberg & Delaney, 1976; Ivey, 1971), to the importance of basic verbal and nonverbal communication techniques. If any aspect is the common thread between the various techniques and approaches to counseling, it is the basic verbal and nonverbal interaction skills. Without some level of expertise in these skills, few if any individual approaches can be effectively employed.

The basic elements of the model for individual counseling at the community college level and the approaches that derive from it presuppose minimum competencies for interaction skills. (For those readers who desire additional reading and skill development in basic verbal and nonverbal skills, the annotated bibliography at the end of the chapter provides specific reference to several excellent texts and programmed instruction manuals.)

A MODEL FOR INDIVIDUAL COUNSELING

On the basis of the factors presented in the foregoing section, the authors have formulated a hierarchical decision-making model for counseling in the community college. It is based upon certain explicit notions of the writers as to what counseling is and how it should be done. From a global perspective the model views counseling as a problem-solving endeavor in which the client learns useful decision-making skills that can be generalized to any problem. The model views each of the elements as related to subsequent elements in a hierarchy where the outcome or attainment of the objectives for each element serve as input for the next element in the hierarchy (see Figure 5.1).

Models of decision making or problem solving are not new to the field of counseling. They have been variously employed to build appropriate skills for a wide variety of client problems and subpopulations (Gelatt, 1962; Krumboltz & Thoresen, 1976; Tolbert, 1974).

The authors feel this model is uniquely suited for individual counseling with community college students primarily because of its flexibility of application, a characteristic essential to individual counseling with the heterogeneous subpopulations and problem types found at the community college level. Within this framework, the counselor can emphasize those elements that require attention and deemphasize those that do not.

FIGURE 5.1

Hierarchical Problem Solving

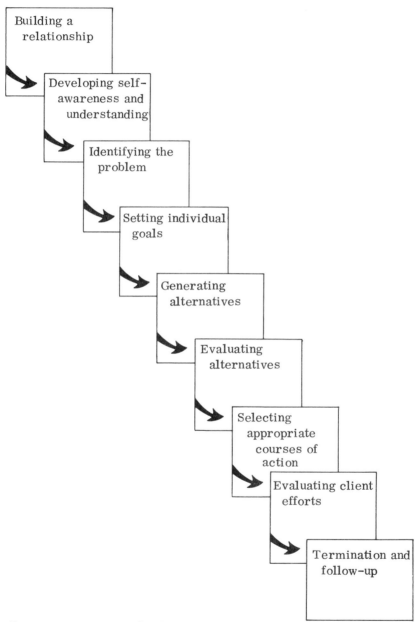

Source: Constructed by the authors.

Regardless of the theoretical orientation of the counselor, the characteristics of the clients, or the type of problems encountered at the community college, the hierarchical model presents much flexibility as a model for counseling and can easily integrate the individual approaches from various theoretical positions that are presented later in this chapter.

One final note of caution: the model in Figure 5.1 should be viewed as an increasing hierarchical process and not a series of discrete, independent elements unrelated to each other. The approaches counselors use, such as those presented in this chapter, must be part of this overall process; otherwise, individual approaches become simply trial-and-error efforts that ultimately will prove counterproductive to the community college student.

HIERARCHICAL PROBLEM SOLVING

If counseling is viewed as a series of related tasks or elements, each building upon the preceding in a hierarchy toward the final resolution of a particular problem, one can appreciate the complex and evolving structure of the counseling process. With this view, the individual approaches used to bring about this evolvement can be seen in their appropriate perspective.

This section will briefly present the nine segments of the model and discuss their importance to the overall counseling process. As mentioned earlier, this model is quite applicable to the community college and the wide diversity of student problems it encounters.

Building a Facilitative Relationship

Building a facilitative relationship is the first and most important element of the counseling process. Without this foundation to build upon, future problem-solving efforts will be minimized. The importance of a warm, trusting relationship between client and counselor has been well established in the counseling literature (Carkhuff, 1971; Okun, 1976). For community college students the facilitative relationship is even more crucial to counseling success, as it greatly contributes to motivation and commitment to change—two important factors in this client population. Development of a facilitative relationship begins with the initial contact between the client and counselor. It is at this point that a facilitative and receptive climate must be established, so that the client feels free to discuss personal concerns in an open and forthcoming manner.

While this element begins with the first client-counselor contact, it may in fact begin long before the client ever meets the counselor. Initial client expectations and perceptions of the counselor or the client can greatly affect whether a relationship will even begin. Most community colleges are relatively small geographic areas with considerable student-to-student interactions so, if negative or erroneous perceptions of the service or agency prevail, they will greatly inhibit potential counseling contacts. Research has shown that initial client perceptions and expectations are powerful determiners of counseling outcomes (Goodstein & Grigg, 1959; Paradise, 1978; Shapiro, 1972; Wilkins, 1973). Considerable attention should be given, then, to the initial client contact and the facilitation of a counseling relationship, if future counseling success is to be attained.

Developing a facilitative relationship is accomplished by using active verbal and nonverbal interaction skills that demonstrate trust, empathy, understanding, and respect: specifically, listening and responding to the verbal and nonverbal messages of clients as they discuss the problem situation. Ivey (1971) has called this responding "attending behavior" and has developed elaborate training exercises to enhance necessary interaction skills.

Table 5.1 presents certain of the more common verbal and nonverbal techniques essential to relationship building.

TABLE 5.1

Basic Counselor Interaction Skills

Verbal	Nonverbal
Reflection of feeling	Good eye contact
Clarification	Facial and body animation;
Summarization	for example, smile, head
Verbal reinforcers; for example,	nodding, posture
Yes, I see, OK	Posture and mood
Reflection of content	Confident and empathic
Interpretation	demeanor
Nonjudgment responding	
Language level appropriate	
to the client	
Open invitations to talk	
Moderate rate of speech,	
tone of voice	

Source: Compiled by the authors.

Using these techniques appropriately should help to convey the conditions necessary for building a facilitative relationship. Almost all counseling approaches, including those presented later in this chapter, assume appropriate levels of expertise in these interaction skills.

The community college student is not likely to have a clear understanding or knowledge of counseling or the counseling process. In addition, distorted or inaccurate expectations may also be present. Clarifying exactly what counseling is all about at the very beginning can resolve any potential problems. It has been found that structuring—specifically explaining what counseling is about and what can be expected from it—can be particularly useful to clarify initial expectations and perceptions that may be counterproductive to counseling. The use of contracts, explicit or implicit agreements as to what is expected from both counselor and client, is another useful approach for this purpose. These approaches will be discussed in greater detail later in this chapter.

Developing Self-awareness and Understanding

As a facilitative relationship is being developed, the next element of the hierarchical process is emerging: the development of self-awareness and understanding.

The presence of facilitative conditions allows clients to discuss their concerns in an open and nonthreatening environment. With the help of the counselor, clients begin to see themselves with greater understanding and awareness. Issues that were difficult to define become more concrete and clearly perceived. Areas that were confusing take on new meaning as insight into one's behavior is developed. A clearer understanding of the problem in the context of its occurrence happens as a direct result of these earlier efforts toward self-awareness. Thus, the necessary requirements for the next element of the hierarchy coalesce—that of identifying the problem or concern.

It should be mentioned that this element of the hierarchy will continue throughout the process. Ideally, clients should continue to learn about themselves throughout the entire counseling experience. For many clients, developing self-awareness is their sole purpose for coming to counseling. For others, it is just a necessary step in helping to deal with a specific concern or problem-solving task. It is generally a good rule of thumb to spend only the time with this element that is necessary to help students adequately and accurately identify problems in the context of their occurrence, and understand the meaning and ramifications of the problem situations and their own efforts to change.

Self-awareness can be a lifetime task if one wishes to pursue it. Many community college students may see this element as a waste of time—time better spent in trying to solve the problem. When this is the prevalent attitude, it is wise to discuss it and explain its importance and relevance to the rest of the process. If self-awareness itself is not the goal of counseling, it should be treated only as one of the elements in the hierarchy.

Identifying the Problem or Concern

In terms of understanding the problem situation it is important to help the client move from nebulous and abstract descriptions to more clear and concrete ones. As the process develops, issues, feelings, attitudes, thoughts, and so on that have been discussed need to be made more specific. Specificity is required so that concrete goals can be established to resolve the problem.

Many community college students will come to counseling unable to accurately or specifically define their problems. Others may have their concerns defined, but in terms so abstruse that it is difficult to apply any specific intervention strategy; for example, "I don't feel good or happy anymore," or "I'm too shy around boys." Problems defined this vaguely make setting goals difficult if not impossible. Indeed, a considerable part of counseling is always devoted to helping clients clarify and understand the feelings, perceptions, and overall meaning of their problems as they relate to them as persons.

Haley (1969) advances a convincing argument for accepting the client's presenting concern as the main focus for counseling and the authors would certainly agree with and encourage this position. The vast majority of community college students who come to counseling have a well-defined awareness of why they are there; however, it is generally incomplete in scope. For meaningful decision making and successful action to occur, an accurate and realistic picture of the overall situation must be present. Helping the student to identify and clarify the problem does not imply that there exists some other real problem that only a trained professional could decipher.

A word of caution in relation to this element of the hierarchy— nothing can turn off students more quickly than the notion that their expressed problems are merely symptoms or cover-ups of some other deep-seated problem. A good standard to follow is to focus on helping students with what they want help with, not on what the counselor believes they need help with. It has been suggested many times (for example, Combs, Avila & Purkey, 1978; Patterson, 1974) that clients know their situations better than anyone else, and that the counselor's role is that of a facilitator of clarification and understanding.

Counselors can greatly aid problem identification by encouraging specificity and concreteness in discussion related to the problem. This greater specificity can increase the general level of self-awareness as well as contribute to a clearer definition of the goals or objectives of the experience.

Setting Individual Goals

One of the easiest things a counselor can do to ensure successful outcomes in counseling is to help the client set individual goals. Although this is the simplest technique to incorporate into the counseling process, it is many times the most easily overlooked. Writers in the area (Eisenberg & Delaney, 1976; Gottman & Leiblum, 1974; Krumboltz, 1966) have long argued that clear and specific goal setting should be an integral part of counseling.

As Urban and Ford (1971) suggest, specifying goals helps to define the nature of the change and establish criteria against which the effectiveness of counseling can be judged (a later element of the hierarchy). The individual goal provides direction and focus for the remainder of the counseling experience, and contributes as well to continued motivation and commitment.

It is not that counselors have no well-defined plan as to the direction and focus of the counseling, although some do not. It is more that this direction and focus should be a mutually agreed upon plan of action such that client and counselor are explicitly aware of the desired outcomes of their efforts.

Goals can be short- or long-term, a single-outcome objective or a hierarchy of simple goals building toward one complex end product. All goals, however, should be mutually agreed upon, relevant to the issues at hand, realistic and attainable, specific and clearly stated, and defined in such a way that the effectiveness of the intervention strategies or efforts at change can be readily assessed.

When goals are well stated, they provide the opportunity to generate and evaluate alternative courses of action. Below are some examples of goals stated in different ways.

Stated Poorly	Stated Well
I want to improve my self-concept.	I want to increase the amount of time I spend thinking good things about myself.

I want to figure out what to do
with my life.

I want to be able to decide
whether to attend more college or find a job.

I want to do better in school.

I want to improve my study
skills.

Goals can be set informally within the context of the dialogue
between the client and counselor or they can be formally stipulated
in written terms. It is generally a good approach to establish written outcome goals for the community college student. The appearance of goals and behaviors in writing seems to add an additional
positive dimension to the individual's overall commitment (Homme
& Tosti, 1971). The use of written contracts will be further discussed later in this chapter.

Once individual goals are set, it may be necessary, at some
point, to modify or change them. This is to be expected, especially
if client efforts to change are unsuccessful. Evaluation of the appropriateness of the intervention strategy or the appropriateness of
the goals may lead to the conclusion that certain modifications are
in order. Reviewing with the client the characteristics of goals
(presented earlier in this chapter) should be the first step toward
modifying or changing the goals or the intervention strategies. Obviously, if the individual's goals change, it is likely that the intervention approaches might also require change.

If the client succeeds in attaining his goals, two outcomes are
possible: termination of the counseling process (with the exception
of any follow-up efforts by the counselor) or the establishment of
additional goals.

Generating Alternatives

Once the problem has been identified and appropriate goals
have been set, the next element involves generating alternative
courses of action to resolve the situation. Many community college
students cannot envision the many alternatives that are open to them
to resolve their problems. Students with problems tend to have a
rather myopic view of their situations and the possibilities. In addition, the process of selecting acceptable intervention strategies may
not be possible, since most students will not be aware of the possible
counseling approaches available to help them.

The option to choose between appropriate alternatives provides
students with an opportunity to regain control of their situations. It
must be remembered that for some individuals, coming to counseling

can be perceived as an admission of some loss of control or power over one's life. Helping students to generate alternatives demonstrates that individuals do have control over their lives. It is also a good strategy, where specific intervention alternatives are present, to help the students feel they are part of the process that generates these options. When they have been part of this process, greater commitment and motivation for implementing the approaches should be present.

The emphasis in this element of the hierarchy is not merely on generating alternatives specific to the individual problem, but rather on how to make effective decisions overall. Being able to generate viable alternatives to any situation is an important life skill for the community college student.

Evaluating Alternatives

Once the alternative courses of action are identified, the client, with the help of the counselor, evaluates the alternatives and selects the appropriate courses of action to achieve the client's individual goal. This involves critically examining the consequences— the pros and cons of each alternative.

By this stage in the process, counselors have a good understanding of their clients and their situations, and the clients have, or should have, a greater awareness of themselves. Only with this prerequisite knowledge is accurate evaluation of the alternatives possible. When difficulties occur in this element of the hierarchy, it may be an indication that previous elements have not provided sufficient input to the process. In that case it may be necessary to return to earlier elements to resolve these issues.

Open and candid dialogue on evaluating consequences will help provide the framework for accurate evaluation. Realistic evaluation of the consequences is necessary if accurate evaluation is to be accomplished. Tolbert (1974), in his discussion of decision making, suggests identifying both possible and probable outcomes. The evaluation of alternatives should consider what is possible and what is probable. Estimating what can happen and the probability that it will happen are both essential to the examination of the consequences of each alternative.

In a sense the counselor, through an accepting and understanding approach, can help the student to evaluate what is in reality a value question. Personal values, as Tolbert (1974, p. 172) points out, become one of the most significant aspects in this element. "Counseling can help the counselee make his values explicit. They will emerge in the discussion of options."

Another key role for the counselor in this element is providing sufficient and realistic information on which to evaluate possible alternatives. Information on specific strategies, intervention techniques, or just basic information related to resolving the concern will be important determiners in weighing the alternatives that have been generated. In the example below, Joe is seeing a counselor about the possibility of transferring to a four-year college or dropping out because of poor grades and a lack of finances.

Counselor:	It sounds like you're having a difficult time evaluating the consequences.
Joe:	What do you think about transferring to the State University?
Counselor:	Well, there is some information you should know. To transfer to State, you'd need to have a C+ average at a minimum. Do you think this is a possibility?
Joe:	I wasn't sure what the grade requirement was. . . . What about the tuition costs? I mean being away from home. I might not be able to find the kind of job I have now.

Sometimes, in an effort to develop and foster insight and awareness, counselors forget that providing information is a major function of the community college counselor. Conveying and evaluating accurate and valid information for making educational, career, and personal decisions is possibly the most significant role for counselors working with community college students. All too often counselors, wanting to be quasi psychotherapists, neglect their information-providing role with their students. While this may seem to be quite a strong statement, this neglect nonetheless contributes to an overall lack of effectiveness in counseling outcomes. The model presented here requires that the necessary information be present in order to generate, select, and evaluate the alternatives in the decision-making process.

Selecting Appropriate Courses of Action

The responsibility for selecting the appropriate course of action in resolving a problem rests solely with the student. The counselor's role is to facilitate this choice.

If the choice is for some type of therapeutic or counseling intervention strategy (for example, assertiveness training, study-skills training, workshops, and so on), all involved parties must be fully aware of and understand what is to be expected. Here clarifications and explanations of any intervention and its relationship to the individual goals are essential. Selection of appropriate courses of intervention must not regress to trial-and-error efforts at solving problems. When the intervention becomes trial and error, it is a sign of inadequate problem solving and inappropriate decision making.

The key word in this element of the hierarchy is action. All the products of the previous elements should combine to produce some type of student action toward resolving the problem. In this element of the hierarchy, the necessary raw materials are present to select a meaningful and viable course of action. Many students may be satisfied with their increased self-awareness, but feel powerless or apprehensive about taking that first step of action ("I know now why I am shy around girls, but doing something specifically about it is another thing.")

If the individual approaches necessary to bring about change are appropriately presented and discussed, misperceptions clarified, fears are allayed, and encouragement is provided, the probability of successful action toward a goal will be greatly enhanced.

Avoiding decisions and delaying appropriate action can be, in itself, self-rewarding, in that it postpones the necessity of taking steps to resolve a problem. Deciding not to decide, however, is not the type of problem-solving skill that will benefit the client. When and if this occurs, a return to earlier elements of the hierarchy is in order.

As some students approach the point where action must be taken, they evaluate the overall situation and drop out of counseling. Premature termination is a persistent problem for all counselors, the community college being no exception. It can be minimized only if it is anticipated by the counselor, and usually by this stage of the process sufficient clues are present to detect any decrease in motivation and commitment to change.

Evaluating Client Efforts

All counselor efforts must be evaluated in some form to determine their appropriateness and effectiveness. Individual evaluation by client and counselor should be a continuous, ongoing effort throughout the elements of the hierarchy. Evaluation criteria should reflect the specific outcomes based upon the goals that the client wishes to achieve. For example, suppose a student has stated that his goal is to have a better relationship with his parents. This goal may be achieved by a variety of individual approaches. How it is judged effective may involve examining the following evaluation criteria:

A decrease in the number of arguments or disagreements between
   the client and his parents
An increase in the frequency of time spent discussing relevant
   issues and problems with parents
The self-reported improvement in the quality of the relationship
   between client and parents.

The counselor and the client can determine the nature and
scope of the evaluation as well as what the evaluation criteria will
be. Evaluation data can come from a variety of sources: self-
report of the client, observation, feedback from significant others,
improvement or change on test results, and so on. Without clear
and specific criteria, evaluation will be indirect and inexact, thus
leading to the possible inappropriate use of intervention or problem-
solving strategies that prolong or prematurely terminate the counseling process.

Termination and Follow-up

As Okun (1976) and others point out, there are three types of
termination that can occur:

1. When both the client and the counselor feel that the individual goals have been achieved. This is successful termination
and can provide the participants in the process with a rewarding
feeling for their efforts. In this situation, both client and counselor
should know when the last session will occur in order to resolve any
issues or feelings associated with the termination of counseling.
When does this last session occur? If the previous elements of the
hierarchy have been completed, successful termination should occur
when the individual goals that were set have been attained.

2. When the counselor must initiate termination for some
reason. Usually this will be for purposes of referral to another
counselor or agency. This occurs whenever counselors believe
they can be of no further assistance to the client, but that someone
else can. This situation will likely present itself during earlier
elements of the counseling process.

3. When the client prematurely terminates. Premature termination can occur at any time and is a common problem in the community college setting. Not having the opportunity to finish what has
begun can be a frustrating and demoralizing experience for any counselor.

The reasons for premature termination are many and varied,
reflecting inadequacies and shortcomings on the part of the client,

the counselor, the agency, or the general setting. The exact reasons will always be difficult, if not impossible, to determine. Self-evaluation with regard to possible reasons for client termination is a necessary and difficult task. Open and honest self-evaluation of efforts can provide an impetus for possible improvements, whether for the individual or the institution.

When goals have been achieved and termination is nearly completed, the counselor should leave the client with the knowledge that the door to the counselor is always open. This conveys continued interest in the client, should the need arise. All too often termination is handled too quickly and mechanically—"We have attained our goals; now you can stop coming here."

The termination of counseling can involve many complex feelings and considerations that need to be dealt with as part of the process of this element. A certain degree of concern must be devoted to ending the counseling relationship, just as in any relationship. In certain situations ending can be as critical as beginning. Simple questions can help explore these issues:

How do you feel about having achieved these goals we set?
I'm wondering how you're feeling about not having to come in anymore?
How does it feel to be all finished?

Any issues or feelings that result from such inquiry should be discussed and resolved prior to the last session. It is a useful technique to have the client consider any thoughts about termination prior to the last session. Usually this can be accomplished as a suggestion for the last interview:

Counselor: Next week will be our last meeting and I'd like to have you think about how that makes you feel. There's usually going to be some important things to discuss along with a sort of wrap-up of what we've accomplished and what it will mean after you stop coming here. So for next week, you might want to think about those things.

Counseling follow-up is probably the area most neglected by counselors. Checking to see how clients are doing and if there are any new developments is a useful adjunct to overall counseling efforts. Conveying the idea that the counselor wishes to be of help not only when the client is being seen but after the regular appointments have terminated can greatly improve the effectiveness of the counselor and the program. Community college students, in particular, respond quite favorably to any form of follow-up inquiry following termination. Even just suggesting that the door is open if the need arises can be a helpful follow-up approach. Many times evaluation conducted during follow-up efforts can provide valuable feedback that was not present during regular counseling.

Follow-up need requires only a simple inquiry of the person's current situation. It can occur by telephone, by formal letter, by informal note. The authors have found the best method of follow-up to be the use of an informal note to the student via campus mail, wherever possible (rather than sending it to the student's home address). This method is the least formal and maintains the confidentiality of the client's visits. The tone of the note should be cordial and friendly. It should simply inquire as to how things have been going, and demonstrate continued interest in the client.

A typical follow-up letter might read:

> Dear Sally,
> Just a little note to see how you are doing with your new major. It has been about two months since we finished our counseling and I was curious to see if your enthusiasm with your new studies is still high. Please feel free to drop me a note here at the Center or stop by whenever you'd like to talk. Once again, best of luck with your new plans.
> Sincerely,
> John Q. Counselor

This type of follow-up is simple to initiate and can provide an additional dimension to the overall counseling program. The time for initiating follow-up will vary, but generally speaking, with community college students, four to six weeks following termination is ideal for follow-up action.

On occasion, community college counselors have been known to complain that once students terminate, they never hear from them again. In most cases this is due to the counselor's failure to initiate any follow-up procedures. Follow-up is not difficult, requires very little counselor time, and can be beneficial to all concerned with the total counseling process.

Some Concluding Remarks

The hierarchical problem-solving model for individual counseling, derived essentially from certain basic assumptions relating to the process of counseling, has been presented for community college counselors. This model is felt to be the most viable and adaptable for working with individual clients. The authors have deemphasized techniques and individual approaches that can be used to facilitate each of the nine elements of the hierarchy, reserving them for later in the chapter, since many have multiple purposes that span several of the elements.

There are a few points of summary in relation to the model that should be reemphasized before proceeding to specific individual approaches.

1. Each element of this model, or any model for counseling, should be based upon certain basic assumptions relating to the role and function of the counselor, and all techniques and approaches that are used should be a direct extension of the counselor's effort to implement the stage, components, or elements of the model. That is, techniques and individual approaches are not ends in themselves; they are just means to implement the goals of any counseling model.

2. The time span for each element of this model, as well as the process itself, will vary greatly from client to client, depending on the nature of the problem and the present state of the client's self-awareness. For some clients, this may be only one or two sessions; for others it may be several. Skilled community college counselors must gauge their efforts to meet the needs of the students. Certain students will not want to spend much time on insight-related activities, others will. One simple rule to follow is that the student is the client and not the model. One must, however, always keep the elements of any approach to counseling in perspective—that is, counseling should be viewed as a process, not a series of discrete, trial-and-error efforts to solve problems.

3. Action is the key to change. Effective change will always require some client action. The obvious precursor to this is some necessary level of motivation and commitment to change.

4. Each of the first nine elements of the hierarchy provides the raw materials for the next level: each building upon the skills and resources of the previous elements; each dependent upon the previous in order to advance toward subsequent elements; and each adding new information to achieve the final conclusion of the counseling process—the resolution of individual counseling goals.

INDIVIDUAL APPROACHES

The individual counseling techniques discussed in this section are presented to facilitate the use of the elements of the counseling process presented earlier in this chapter. An attempt has been made, where appropriate, to incorporate some skill-building exercises for certain of the techniques and approaches.

One note of caution before proceeding: too many current counseling theories are not really theories of counseling, but rather compilations of techniques and approaches that try to maximize the effectiveness of a specific position and overlook or neglect the underlying model upon which the technique is based. Therefore, many of the available techniques do not truly define any theoretical orientation or position. This should explain the wide and rich variety of individual approaches that are presented to make the hierarchical model useful in community college counseling.

The use of any specific technique is far from a definite personal statement of one's theoretical orientation, but it should directly reflect some element of the model under which the counselor is operating. With this in mind the following individual approaches are presented.

Structuring

Structuring refers to the counselor's explanation to the client of the nature, role expectations, and goals of the counseling process. For the community college student, it can be considered an orientation to counseling in general.

It is wise not to assume that every community college student is a sophisticated and knowledgeable consumer of psychological services. Few students, in their initial contact with counselors, will be aware of what is expected of them or what to expect from the counselor. Apprehension, caution, and anxiety are usually present under these circumstances, none of which is conducive to effective counseling. Providing structure to the situation will help to alleviate some of the counterproductive feelings and misapprehensions that may be present (Brammer, 1973; Ladd, 1971; Myrick, 1968). Most importantly, structuring can clarify the client's responsibility early in the process by showing that the counselor will help, but that it is the client who will ultimately solve the problem.

Structuring, when used appropriately and not in a rigid and condescending manner, can enhance the development of a counseling relationship. In fact, the use of structuring should be considered whenever there is a need to discuss or clarify the counseling process for the client.

Brammer and Shostrum (1968) note that a lack of structure can arouse anxiety and perhaps lead to failure. This is very possible with community college students. The authors' work has suggested that these students require a certain level of structure and anything that can be done to explain or clarify the "rules" of counseling will usually facilitate the desired outcome. Many community college students are very direct and practical in their thinking. Once they are aware of what is involved, they are usually apt to be cooperative and willing participants in the process.

Structuring can be used to clarify the ground rules for counseling with community college students. Some examples of structuring are given below.

Setting Time Limits

Counselor: Well, John, I'm glad you came in to see me about this. We have about an hour to talk so maybe you can begin by telling me how I can be of help.

or

Counselor: We'll only have about four weeks until the end of the semester, so we should plan on getting into these strategies right away.

Client and Counselor Roles

Joe: My buddy Frank told me how you helped him and I thought you could help me the same way.

Counselor: Well, I should mention that for this to be effective, a lot will depend on your initiative and responsibility for bringing about the changes you'd like to see.

Joe: What do you mean?

Counselor: Well, my role is really more to help you help yourself. Some of the decisions that need to be made, only you can make. I'll be here to help you learn how to make them. But what is finally decided will be your decision.

or

Sally: I remember when you talked to our orientation class, you said if we had any problems we couldn't handle, we should come to see one of the counselors. I'm not sure this is something anyone can help with.

Counselor: We can help students with almost any problem. If we can't do it ourselves, we can find someone who can help. Maybe you can tell me a little about what brings you here and we'll see if we can help you with it.

School Policy and Procedures that
Govern Counseling Activities

Christopher: I'm failing two courses and I thought that maybe if I came here I could explain why and get a course drop approved since you handle academic problems.

Counselor: We do help solve academic problems, but we can't approve course drops after the deadline has passed. What we can do is make a recommendation to the dean if it seems justified, but we'd need your approval to discuss your difficulties.

Confidentiality

Frank: I thought what we say is just between us. You know, sorta confidential. So why do we need to tape record it?

Counselor: Well, Frank, what we say is between you and me. However, you should also know that if something comes up where I feel another student or you are in danger or great trouble then I couldn't, in good conscience, keep it a secret. I'd have to try to help the best way I could. Do you understand that?

Frank: Well, what about the taping?

Counselor: The tapes are for my use. To help me review what we do here and try to do a better job of helping you. Sometimes when we hear what we say at a later time, it has a different meaning or more meaning. No one else hears them and I usually erase them after I review them. Oh, and you are free to hear them again if you wish. How do you feel about that suggestion?

Explaining Possible Courses of Action

Margaret: How long will it take if I join this self-awareness group you mentioned last week? I really don't want to start something that I won't have time to finish.

Counselor: Well, the group generally meets for two hours a session and it should last the entire semester. Being in the group will be a little different than your coming to see me because there'll be other people trying to accomplish the same thing as you and participation is very important.

Sam: The interest test you mentioned seems like a good idea, but I don't like taking tests.

Counselor: These tests are a little different, Sam. There is no right or wrong answer. They'll just ask you to indicate the kind of things that you find interesting. They won't provide any indication of your ability in any area, but they'll indicate how similar your interests are to people already in those job areas.

Sam: How accurate are they? I mean, will they tell me what major I should be in?

Counselor: They won't show anything that certain. All they can do is provide some additional information so your decision making will be based upon greater knowledge. Sometimes they're helpful and sometimes they're not. Are there any other questions you have about the tests?

The examples demonstrate that clear, matter-of-fact responses that serve to clarify, explain, or expand the student's knowledge of what the process is all about can provide the best-structured framework from which to facilitate the counseling process. Not every rule, role, or issue need be made explicit. Starting with language that is familiar to the students and showing empathy for their concerns are the best facilitators of a relationship for counseling.

One word of caution: too much structuring can have negative consequences. The student may interpret the efforts as ultimatums or demands and this potential misperception should be avoided. The structuring should not be so detailed as to confuse the student with an overemphasis on how everything is to be done to the total neglect of the student as a person.

Exercise

For the following client responses, write an appropriate counselor response utilizing the necessary structuring discussed earlier. Later you can compare and discuss your responses in small groups.

1. Jane: Hi, I'm Jane Walker and I'm not really sure I should be here. I don't have an appointment, but I need to talk to someone right away.

Your response: _____

_____

_____

What type of structure, if any, does your response reflect?

_____

_____

2. <u>George</u>: How do I know that this approach you mention will work?

Your response: _____

_____

_____

What type of structure, if any, does this response reflect?

_____

_____

3. <u>Margot</u>: Before I tell you why I'm here, how long will it take? I mean, will I have to keep coming here?

Your response: _____

_____

_____

What type of structure, if any, does this response reflect?

_____

_____

4. <u>Jimmy</u>: Well, I want someone to tell me what to do about transferring to another school. That's why I came here.

Your response: _____

_____

_____

What type of structure, if any, does this reflect?

_____

_____

5. <u>Mark</u>: You mentioned at the orientation that all counseling is confidential. Before I say anything I need to know if that's true.

Your response: _____

_____

_____

What type of structure, if any, does this reflect?

_____

_____

6. <u>Anna</u>: How come the biology instructor sent me to see you? I know I'm not doing well in the course, but that's my business.

Your response: _____

_____

_____

What type of structure, if any, does this reflect?

_____

_____

Identifying Irrational Thinking

To develop some degree of self-awareness and an ability to identify and understand the problem, the impact of cognitive behaviors should be examined. This examination can greatly enhance the validity of the first several elements of the hierarchy.

Ellis (1962, 1974, 1977) and his supporters over the years have focused on the cognitive processes that contribute to the many problems individuals develop. He believes that people tell themselves irrational thoughts and that these irrationalities contribute to self-defeating behaviors. Most clients, when discussing their situations, will demonstrate cognitive reasoning in relation to their problems that is clearly illogical. When the counselor can identify the illogical reasoning and, perhaps, demonstrate how it is affecting the situation, greater awareness and movement toward resolution can be expected.

The counselor's verbal skills in being able to identify and clarify the irrational reasoning and illogical thinking that is found in client problems can be a real asset, whether the problem is academic, vocational, or personal in nature. One need not try to cognitively restructure the client's thinking, although counselors should be able to identify and integrate the information and ideas presented, in order better to help their clients understand their current situations.

Ellis (1962) has presented several irrational ideas that he believes produce self-defeating behaviors. The following list, based on his work, can be viewed as general themes of an irrational or illogical nature that appear common among the present problems of community college students.

- It is a dire necessity to be loved or approved by everyone for everything I do.

- Certain behaviors are wrong and evil and people who perform these acts should be punished.

- It is terrible and catastrophic when things are not the way I want them to be.

- Much human suffering is externally caused and is forced upon people by others.

□ If something is or may be dangerous, one should be terribly concerned with it.

□ It is easier to avoid than to face the difficulties of life.

□ One should be thoroughly competent, adequate, and achieving in all possible aspects of one's life.

□ Because something once strongly affected one's life, it should continue to affect it.

□ One has virtually no control over one's emotions and cannot help feeling certain ways.

Ellis believes that these irrational beliefs help to maintain or exacerbate the individual's problem, and his approach is directed toward identifying the irrational thoughts and restructuring the individual's thought processes with rational thoughts. This "cognitive restructuring" (Ellis & Greiger, 1977) involves helping the client to rethink and reverbalize the irrationalities.

If one listens to clients discussing their problems, one can hear such common irrational statements, which are so much a part of the repertoire of beliefs of so many (for example, "He makes me so mad," "That's the way I am," "If only things could be the way I want them"). Helping the client to see the irrationalities and how they are contributing to the problem is an initial and necessary step toward resolving the problem.

Exercise

The following are excerpts of typical community college student problems. In each example, identify the irrationalities found in each and write a response in your own words to each excerpt. You may wish to refer to the list of irrational ideas that was presented earlier. This exercise should help you to facilitate client self-awareness by identifying and responding to the client's irrational statements.

1. About two years ago I fell in love with Michael. He told me that he loved me too. It was so beautiful. Life took on real meaning. Then it ended. It was awful and since then I won't let myself trust anybody again.

Irrationality: _____

_____

Your response: _____

_____

2. I don't understand why I fail so much. I try very hard to do good in everything. It's as though my efforts don't count. There are forces working against me. I really believe that sometimes. I'm always failing at something.

Irrationality: _____

Your response: _____
_____

3. People don't have any say over how they feel. If that was different, everyone would always be happy. It really depends on how other people treat you. When they treat me good, I'm happy. When they don't, I'm not.

Irrationality: _____

Your response: _____
_____

4. It just didn't work out the way I wanted it to. Sally had to go and ruin the whole party. I wanted the dancing downstairs and the food upstairs. She ruined my whole party.
Irrationality: _____

Your response: _____
_____

5. I live my life to please other people. I figure that's what we're here for. I try so hard and still the people I know—well, most of them—almost all of them—just don't give a damn for me. The harder I try the less people like me.
Irrationality: _____

Your response: _____
_____

6. I know she doesn't like me and never will, but I can't help feeling the way I do. There was never anything between us, and I know it's silly but I can't help liking her the way I do. You really can't control love I guess.

Irrationality: _____

Your response: _____
_____

Going from the Abstract to the Concrete

Helping clients to be more specific in their description of problem situations can facilitate better awareness and aid in accurate problem identification. Eisenberg and Delaney (1976) provide a simple verbal interaction to move clients from the vague and abstract to the specific and concrete, which they call Counselor Tacting Response Leads (CTRLs).

Clients can be vague or overgeneralize when discussing their concerns (for example, "This whole business bothers me," "People can't be trusted to do anything"). Initially this vagueness is an acceptable way for clients to express themselves, but after the process begins, the focus should be on identification of the problem and the context in which it occurs; more specificity is required.

CTRLs can help clients to be specific, clarify what they mean by what is said, and contribute to later goal-setting behaviors. They can also be used to mildly confront the client about some inconsistency that has been stated.

Specificity
Client: I'm not doing too well in my major.
CTRL: What exactly do you mean by "not doing too well?"

Goal-setting
Client: I would like to be able to have a meaningful relationship.
CTRL: Maybe you could describe what you mean by meaningful relationship.

Clarification
Client: Things never go right in math class.
CTRL: Tell me about what happened the last time they didn't.

The CTRLs used above help the client move from the vague to the concrete by encouraging specificity and can be useful whenever specificity is required.

Exercise

For the following client statements, respond with a CTRL that will encourage greater specificity.

1. He really bothers me.
CTRL: _____

2. I wish this thing would just go away.
CTRL: _____

3. My mother and I just never get along.
CTRL: _____

4. Every time I go to automechanics class, Mr. Johnson jumps all over me for nothing.
CTRL: _____

5. This school isn't any fun at all.
CTRL: _____

6. The things he does just aren't fair!
CTRL: _____

The Autobiography

The autobiography can be a useful individual technique to encourage self-exploration and understanding in community college students. It can provide useful information for self-awareness and problem identification. The technique is little used by counselors today (Shertzer & Stone, 1974), which is unfortunate because the approach has unique value in that it allows students to tell their own stories in their own words.

The autobiography itself can be structured or unstructured. The unstructured autobiography is totally open-ended. Individuals are instructed to write about themselves without regard to any specific questions or topics. What is written will generally be what is personally important. The structured autobiography requires the student to address certain issues or answer certain questions. Annis (1967) suggests two additional categories: comprehensive, covering a wide range of topics over a long period of time, and topical, focusing on specific topics, experiences, time periods.

The authors suggest that the autobiography can be a useful adjunct to counseling, is topical, structured, and used to help clients gain greater insight into their situations. The structure should be explicit, with questions and areas a priori delineated by the counselor for the student to write as homework. It can also facilitate discussion during sessions in which the client is not very verbal.

This approach can be used with student problems of any type and only requires the counselor to be able to generate relevant questions for the student. For example, an individual who really felt that he had no skills to offer the job world sought career counseling. He was so set in his beliefs that it was very difficult to help him explore any possible courses of action. It was also obvious that these feelings were affecting his self-esteem, especially since he had recently finished his Associate of Arts degree. He was asked to write

a biographical sketch describing his accomplishments and achieve-
ments—going back as far as he could remember. No matter how
trivial it seemed, he was requested to write it down. This information was used to help him identify any consistencies in the achieve-
ments and accomplishments he had attained throughout his life. The
information from the sketch and the discussion of it was later used
in relation to his current interests and abilities. It turned out he
was very enterprising and became interested in starting a business
of his own.

If the use of autobiography accomplishes only one task—that
of allowing clients to sit back and take stock of their lives on any of
a number of significant dimensions—it will be worth the effort. Most
individuals in counseling, regardless of the reason, do not have a
good grasp of all that they have accomplished in their lifetimes.
This method allows them actually to see the sheer magnitude of all
that has been noteworthy.

The following guidelines should be kept in mind when using the
autobiography.

□ Provide structure in the form of topical areas or questions to
  be addressed that are relevant to the client's problem. An out-
  line is sometimes useful for this purpose.
□ The topical areas are the key to the success of the approach.
□ Give the student an idea of how long the written work should be,
  as well as any other special instructions.
□ Have the student do the autobiography for homework between
  sessions, where appropriate and meaningful.
□ Go over the autobiography with the student to discuss relevant
  points or issues at greater length.
□ Use caution in making interpretations from the autobiography.
□ Although several writers have suggested interpretative schemes
  for the autobiography (Allport, 1942; Baldwin, 1942; Shertzer &
□ Stone, 1974), there is little research evidence to suggest the
  validity of possible diagnostic or interpretative uses. As a facilitator of exploration and self-awareness, however, it is a useful
  counseling tool.

As Baird (1954, p. 39) pointed out almost 25 years ago, "It
is a low-cost technique that helps the student to organize and interpret his experiences in such a way as to see the personal significance
and know himself better."

Exercise

For the following student problems, generate the necessary
questions or topical areas that should be given to the student as

structure for the use of an autobiography. Discuss your answers in small groups.

1. John can't seem to get interested in any courses. It appears that he is indecisive about making any choices between college majors. While he does well in his courses, he finds them terribly dull.

2. Sally is a nonverbal client. She doesn't seem to want to talk about her problem of nonassertiveness, and furthermore, she doesn't feel comfortable discussing personal issues.

3. Alice has trouble with her parents. She can't seem to spend more than an hour with them without getting into an argument. She is very defensive about her relationship with them and when asked about situations or events, becomes very vague.

4. George wants to learn how to relax while taking tests. He is very achievement-conscious and feels he has to get the best grade in the class. Whenever he takes a test, he feels so much pressure to do well that he can't think of the material. Regardless of this situation, he still maintains a straight A average.

5. Kathy and Joe are two newly married students who attend the community college on a part-time basis. They claim that the pressures of school, work, and the home are causing damage to their relationship. They want to improve their relationship and continue with school. They both report that the biggest problem for them is the perceived academic competition they sense in each other.

6. Martha's boyfriend has recently stopped seeing her because of her possessive behavior. She was not very surprised, as she states, because this has happened several times before with other guys. She feels that maybe she can't get along with any man because of her high expectations.

Determining Antecedents and Consequences

In order to identify accurately and understand the issues, ramifications, and possible causes of an individual's problem, an examination of the context in which the problem occurs is essential. Context refers to the relationship between the environmental influences that affect behavior and the individual's definition of the behavior as a problem.

Social learning theory (for example, Bandura, 1971; Mischel, 1971) provides many useful insights into the issues of problem identification and resolution. Most prominent among these insights is the principle that antecedent events and predictable consequences are major factors in the environment that exerts control over behavior.

When the behavior is defined by the student as a problem, certain identifiable antecedents and consequences can be determined to help account for the behavior (problem). If the community college counselor can utilize this in helping the student to identify the existence of possible antecedents and consequences, not only will greater understanding of the problem develop, but possibilities for intervention may be planned to help the individual gain control over the situation.

Antecedents, whether external (such as an odor, sound) in the environment or internal (for example, thought, feeling) within the individual, are cues that precede and possibly trigger behaviors (Thoresen & Mahoney, 1974). Consequences, which follow a behavior, can be reinforcing, punishing, or neutral events, either external in the environment (such as praise, money) or internal (for example, thoughts and feelings, such as "I am a good person," "What an idiot I am!"). If change in a behavior is to be accomplished, a break in the relationship between the behavior and its antecedents and/or consequences is necessary (see Figure 5.2). For behavior to change, intervention either at point X or point Y or both must happen. In actuality, since most behaviors are quite complex, many of these behavior chains can be intertwined and interrelated. Although it may appear, at first glance, an impossible task to identify all relevant antecedents and consequences, it is not really so difficult in most cases. Surprisingly, efforts along this line will move clients to greater understanding of their situations and lead to the planning of effective intervention strategies for change.

FIGURE 5.2

Behavior Chains

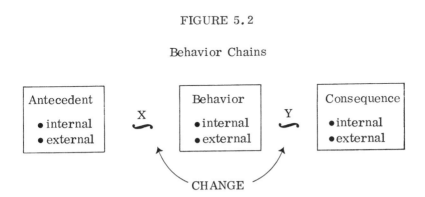

Source: Constructed by the authors.

Thoresen and Mahoney (1974) suggest that no behavior (or problem) will exist at all times in every situation. Shy students will not be shy with everyone at all times, just as failing students will not be failures in all areas of their lives. A functional analysis of the behavior will help identify the situations in which the problem occurs and provide considerable information to remedy it. This analysis of antecedents and consequences can be accomplished by the student with the assistance of the counselor and the resulting information can be discussed in the counseling session. The counselor can facilitate self-awareness by drawing out the student on relevant antecedents and consequences that are present, both positive and negative. Also possible antecedents and consequences, not identified by the student, can be suggested by the counselor for discussion.

A note of caution: since almost all behavior is multicausal, a simplistic approach may erroneously lull the counselor into a false sense of competence in handling behavioral problems. Most counselors should expect to find a multiplex of both positive and negative consequences for most problem situations, together with many antecedent conditions that contribute to the behavior. Although this approach to problem solving is no panacea, it can provide a starting point for problem identification and action. A brief example can best illustrate this.

> I hate studying. I'd rather do anything than study. I get bored and frustrated and even nervous and I just hate it. So, I start to study in the student lounge, which is where I usually study, and when one of the guys comes around and says that he wants to do something, I just lose all my motivation and go. It feels good to get away. I don't feel like a slave to school, but my grades aren't doing too well and that makes me feel guilty about the whole thing.

Antecedents	Consequences
dislike for studying	feeling of freedom when
pressure from school	not studying
possible anticipatory	ambivalent feelings,
thoughts of boredom	guilt and pleasure
always in places with	bad grades
distractions	

As can be seen in the example, several different factors are probably operating as antecedents and consequences in this situation and quite possibly could warrant further discussion with the student.

Also, note should be taken of both positive and negative consequences that have been identified. Generally this ambivalence between positive and negative consequences can be found in many problem situations. With follow-up discussion these factors can provide information useful to effective intervention.

Exercise

In the following problem situations, identify the antecedents and consequences that may be present.

1. <u>Richard</u>: There is nothing I love as much as smoking dope. I hang around people who take life easy and get high a lot. I like those kind of people. I wake up in the morning and the first thing I want is a few long hits. If ever I'm out of stuff, I get all strung out—you know, I get all nervous and I'm not able to think or do anything. In the past, when I lived at home, it was no problem, but now that I'm here, I've been missing a lot of school and my parents are hassling me about it.

Antecedents   Consequences

2. <u>Jane</u>: I know I talk too much in classes. People think I'm aggressive and that I talk about irrelevant things. I love to debate and argue to test people on what they know. It gets me involved in the class and I really feel good afterward. I feel like I've proven something. You know I try to listen to the news on the radio all the time and read the papers every day, just so I'll be well informed. I think everyone ought to be well informed, but the people in my class don't. They just hassle me about it. No one's friendly at all.

Antecedents   Consequences

3. <u>Mark</u>: I don't think I have a hangup about sex, but I do get very nervous around women. I know exactly what'll happen, cause it happens the same way every time. I get worried about what to say and do and it's so obvious that I feel like a fool. That's why I try to avoid having to talk to them, if I can. I'd rather be with the guys. They don't make me nervous, but my friends kid me about it a lot and that's bothering me too.

Antecedents   Consequences

Using Contracts

A contract is an agreement, written or oral, that specifies the responsibilities of all parties involved. Contracts can be of two types: process and outcome.

Process contracts, usually unwritten, are the agreements between client and counselor to engage in counseling for a stipulated duration. Generally, when the client first comes to counseling, an agreement is made whereby the individual will continue to see the counselor for several sessions before any decision to terminate is made. This commitment to counseling initially helps to minimize premature termination. Usually a verbal contract can be initiated at some point in the initial session. For example, the counselor might say, "Well, John, I think we can be of help and I would suggest that it might not be a bad idea to agree upon our getting together for two more sessions to work on the problem. After that time, we can see where we are and where we're headed and if you want to continue with counseling or not. How does three sessions sound?"

Outcome contracts refer specifically to stipulating the goals that are to be achieved and the behavior that is to be accomplished by each involved individual, counselor included. In addition, the contract can specify which actions are to be rewarded and what that reward will be (Mahoney & Thoresen, 1974). Using written forms for contracting provides additional motivation and commitment and eliminates any inconsistencies over what is to be expected. Kanfer and Karoly (1972) further suggest that the explicitness and clarity of the contract, together with the mutuality of control in the helping relationship (the counselor's role in upholding his or her end of the contract), increases the probability of contract fulfillment.

Motivation and commitment are two factors that greatly contribute to successful counseling with community college students, and contracting is a useful approach to facilitate those factors. Outcome contracts should be directly related to the individual's goals; be clear and precise; be written in positive terms; involve both student and counselor responsibilities and expectations; stipulate what will happen when the individual carries out the agreement and what actions will occur if the contract is not followed; and be dated and signed by all participants. An example of an outcome contract for a student who wishes to spend more time studying will demonstrate these points.

Outcome Contract

Date_____

Outcome goal: to spend two hours each school day studying until my grades increase to a B average.

I agree to spend two hours each school day studying. If I spend two hours studying on Monday to Friday, I may have Saturday and Sunday off as a reward. If I do not spend all five days studying, I must also study on the weekend for three hours each day. If I break the contract, my counselor reserves the right to stop seeing me. If I continue with this contract, my counselor will continue to provide tutoring in the subject areas for which I need extra help.

signed_____
                                            Student

_____
                                            Counselor

Contracts can be quite useful in negotiating compromises between a client and a third party who is not involved in counseling. At times, when another party is directly involved in the problem, but for some reason cannot or will not become involved in the counseling, a compromise in the form of a contract can be used to help the student achieve a workable agreement, as shown in the example below.

Date_____

Outcome goal: To decrease the frequency of arguments with my roommate over the use of our apartment.

I agree to allow my roommate to have guests over to visit at any time during the time of Wednesday to Sunday, provided I receive four hours notice. In return, he will allow me undisturbed quiet for studying Monday and Tuesday and three hours on all other days of the week.

If he breaks the agreement, I can use his car to drive to school the following day. If I break the agreement, he can use my stereo for two days.

signed_____
                                            Student

_____
                                            Roommate

_____
                                            Counselor

With a little creative thought, many ingenious applications can be made. Homme and Tosti (1971) and Mahoney and Thoresen (1974) provide a more complete discussion of behavioral contracting.

Exercise

For the following situations suggest a contract that could be used to facilitate the achievement of successful outcomes.

1. Joe is trying to lose weight because his friends have been making fun of him. He realizes that he eats too much and decides to see a counselor, since he feels it's a matter of will power.

2. Mary is very upset because she misses her boyfriend who is always at college. She receives few letters from him and this makes her worry, so that her performance in school has been declining since she last saw her boyfriend.

3. Hank is on the baseball team and spends a considerable portion of his free time practicing various sports. He's very athletic, but is having difficulty passing two required courses. If he can't bring his grades up to passing by midterm, he'll not be allowed to play on the school team. He comes to the counselor for help.

Goal Setting

As discussed earlier in this chapter, goal setting is a technique that allows the student and counselor to be aware of exactly what their purposes are in counseling. It provides direction and focus to the entire counseling process. The goals, derived essentially from the identification of the problem, should contain certain important elements:

They should be mutually agreed upon. If the student and counselor cannot agree on the problem, it is quite unlikely that there will be agreement on any goals. When the counselor and the client are in agreement as to the exact purpose of counseling, however, motivation and commitment can be expected.

They should be directly relevant to the client's problem and the client's reasons for coming to counseling. The goals should be those that satisfy the client's needs, not the counselor's needs or those of any other involved individual.

They should be realistic and attainable. If it is quite unlikely that they can be achieved, or if they are so unrealistic that their attainment is implausible, then working toward them is a futile and self-defeating task. For example, the student with low grades and little academic motivation should not have medical school as a goal.

They should be specific and clearly stated, so that everyone is aware of exactly what is to be worked upon. All interested parties should know exactly where they are in relation to goal attainment. This offers little room for inconsistencies or misunderstanding.

They should be defined in such a way that the effectiveness of client effort can be readily assessed. When this is the case, the time of termination of counseling will be apparent to all parties; that is, they will know, in advance, when counseling will be completed. They will also be able to tell whenever a given approach or technique to achieve the goals is not working.

Overall, the goal should spell out exactly what the counseling experience is to accomplish. The best approach to take is to go from the problem statement to identification of goals by discussing with clients what they would like to accomplish or how they would like to see the situation work out.

Exercise

For the following student problem statements, write a specific goal or goals to be attained. Remember the criteria for goals that were stated above.

1. I feel so alone here! I just can't make any friends.
Goal: Initiate some social interaction with potential friends each day.

2. I find it impossible to study. I just can't get anything done.
Goal: _____

_____

3. I'm afraid of making a fool of myself in phys. ed. class. I'm not good at sports and never will be.
Goal: _____

_____

4. I'm not doing anything these days except partying. I feel my life is going nowhere.
Goal: _____

_____

5. Every guy I go out with just uses me. I can't seem to get into a legitimate relationship. I feel that men just want me for sex.
Goal: _____

_____

6. I can't stand the classes I'm taking. I'd rather do something. I'm tired of just reading about being a nurse.
Goal: _____

_____

7. I'm trying to be a full-time student, but my kids and my husband are so demanding. I feel like I'm going to break into two parts.
Goal: _____

_____

8. If I can't get an "A" average, I'll have no chance of getting into State. Then I'll never be with my boyfriend, Terry.
Goal: _____

_____

Exercise

On the basis of the criteria for well-written goals, analyze what is wrong with the following and restate them in better terms.

1. Goal - To be a more effective person.
   What is wrong with this goal? _____

   Can this goal be rewritten? _____

2. Goal - To increase my number of dates with girls.
   What is wrong with this goal? _____

   Can this goal be rewritten? _____

3. Goal - To decide what to do with my life.
   What is wrong with this goal? _____

   Can this goal be rewritten? _____

4. Goal - To do better in school.
   What is wrong with this goal? _____

   Can this goal be rewritten? _____

5. Goal - To get along better with my roommate.
   What is wrong with this goal? _____

   Can this goal be rewritten? _____

6. <u>Goal</u> - To increase my self-concept.
   What is wrong with this goal? _____

   _____

   Can this goal be rewritten? _____

   _____

Generating Alternative Courses of Action

As discussed earlier, many students have a difficult time seeing that there are alternative courses of action open to them. They
feel, when confronted with a problem, that there are no options,
that they are without a choice, and that they are not in control of the
situation. Gelatt (1962) concluded some time ago, and it is undoubt-
edly still quite true, that two of the most frequent problems are the
inability of students accurately to assess the probability of given alternatives and their lack of knowledge of the complete range of possible alternatives.

If counselors can help clients see the alternatives that are
available and help students learn to generate alternatives for any
problem or situation, then students will begin to see that they do
have choices, for without alternatives, no choice is possible (Tolbert, 1974). When choices are present, as they usually are, the
student has options and opportunity for action.

The counselor's role, it should be remembered, is not to generate alternative courses of action, but to help the student to do so.
Some students may need more help than others, but unless the counselor can facilitate the student's learning of the process, overall
knowledge of decision making will be limited.

In order for the counselor to generate alternatives the counselor must have a relatively good knowledge of the student and the
problem situation. The advantage, of course, is the objective view-
point that allows the counselor to see certain things that may be
overlooked by the student.

To demonstrate generating alternatives, consider the following vignette of Jane and her relationship with her mother.

My mother refuses to realize that I've grown up. She
gets on me like I was still in high school. I don't think
I deserve it and it drives me crazy. She has no right
to talk to me the way she does. I keep a job and go to
school at the same time. I even pay for room and
board. Maybe I let it bother me too much, but I hate

being asked where I'm going and being told what time to
come home. I just think she's unreasonable and I wish
I could do something about it.

A few of the possible courses of action for Jane include the following:

She could support herself outside the home by taking her own apartment.
She could explain her feelings about her life style and independence
to her mother.
She could compromise her independence a bit and work out some
agreement that both could accept.
She could concentrate on being less bothered by her mother's behavior.

Exercise

For the following problem vignettes, generate possible courses
of action in response to the problem statement.

1. The Case of Claire
   I get very depressed not having any real friends I can talk with.
   I had some friends in high school, but none of them came here.
   Nobody I meet seems at all interested in the things I like. I
   can't seem to talk to anyone for more than two minutes. No one
   seems at all interested in making friends. They just come to
   class and go home when it's over. You never see anyone around
   at any other time. I'm kind of shy so it's hard to call people up
   at home. Besides I wouldn't know what to say. I don't want
   them to think I'm trying too hard or I'd do anything to get someone to be a friend.

   Alternatives:

2. The Case of Alice
   Things aren't going too well in school. I'm in the nursing program and I just got my midterm grades. It doesn't look too
   good. I always wanted to be a nurse and really worked hard in
   high school. I know the program is hard, but I thought once I
   got here, I was home free. I do the assignments and I'm real
   good in hospital, but I just can't seem to do well on the tests.
   My whole family is real proud of me and they expect me to be a

nurse. I just can't let them down. I can't let myself down either. I don't know whether I should stick with it or drop out or switch to something easier.

Alternatives:

Evaluating and Selecting Alternatives

Once the alternatives have been generated, the difficult task is to evaluate them in order to select the appropriate course of action. The process of evaluating involves estimating the likelihood of possible and probable outcomes. Bross (1954), in his extensive discussion of decision making, states that the process of deciding requires a predictive system for assessing possible alternative actions, the possible outcomes, and the probabilities, together with a value system for weighing the desirability associated with the outcomes.

Kepner and Tregoe (1965), in their approach to decision making, consider an additional factor that should also be part of the overall selection of best alternatives, which involves assessing and controlling the adverse consequences of the choice. This factor is sometimes overlooked by counselors who focus their efforts on logical decision making—that is, the choice—but neglect to help the student deal with any adverse consequences resulting from that choice. Dealing with any adverse consequences will be part of the counselor's discussion of the pros and cons of each alternative. Efforts to minimize or control these conditions should be an integral part of the problem-solving process at this stage of the hierarchy.

Helping the student to list the pros and cons for each alternative is the simplest approach. It should be kept in mind, however, that the student's values will be part of this determination whenever selection of possible and probable outcomes is to be made. Thomas (1956) has aptly pointed out that probabilities will have totally different meanings for different individuals, so that even an alternative with a low probable consequence may have a high valence for the problem-solving process. He refers to this as the "positivistic fallacy"—that of equating the desired with the desirable. When possible alternatives are evaluated in terms of possible and probable outcomes, the same probability could have considerably different relevance for different individuals.

In practice, evaluating alternatives requires the client to list the pros and cons of each alternative. Generally, this is done as a homework assignment and brought to the next session, where, together with any additional outcomes the counselor has added, they are discussed and rank-ordered in terms of the value the subject places on each. This is done to help the student select the appropriate alternative.

Students in this selection must be aware of their responsibility for the decision. The student does the selecting and assumes responsibility for that selection. This fact, which is so important, should be discussed early in the process of counseling, so that the temptation to have the counselor select or suggest will not interfere with the student's ability to learn the necessary decision-making skills. Whenever counselors assume the role of making decisions, they cannot win; if the counselor is correct, the student has not learned anything from the process; if the counselor is wrong, the student has someone to blame for an incorrect decision. The question of responsibility for decisions is basic to the overall assumptions of the counselor's role in the helping process.

All that is necessary with this approach is to help the student identify pros and cons of the alternatives and help develop some methodology to prioritize them. An example of identifying the pros and cons will demonstrate this counselor skill.

Barbara: I wonder about moving in with Jim. I think my parents would really be upset about it, but we really wouldn't be doing anything different than we are right now except that we'd be officially living together. I see nothing wrong with it myself, but my parents wouldn't understand. I'm afraid that if I don't move in with Jim I'm going to hurt the relationship, but if I do move in, it will probably hurt the relationship I have with my parents. I love them both.

Pros   This is something she wants to do.
          It will promote a better relationship with Jim.

Cons   It will endanger her relationship with her parents.

Exercise

Two problem vignettes are presented. For each vignette, list possible pros and cons for alternatives that may be present in each case.

1. George: I'm really tired of being in school. I hate this place the same way I hated going to high school. This is just a super high school anyway. I only came here because my mother wanted me to. She's been working

two jobs so that I could come and I don't want to see her killing herself just for this. I'd rather be out there working so she could stay home. I could probably make more money fixing cars than she could with her job. Besides, I know more about cars than Mr. Jones, my advisor, anyway.

Pros

Cons

2. Mickey: I'm afraid to make the decision to marry Jenny. I mean, I do love her, but I just don't think I'm ready yet. I told her that it might be better to wait till I finish school, but she says she can support us with her job. Actually, she makes a lot of money so that's no problem, but I really don't know if I'll like the idea of being supported by a woman. She said that I have to decide now or else I can forget about us. Sometimes I want to do it and then sometimes I think it'll be a big mistake. Either way I lose something.

Pros

Cons

Utilizing Occupational and Educational Information

One of the most obvious but least developed functions of the community college counselor is the conveying of information relating to educational, personal, and vocational development. Valid, accurate, current, and understandable information plays a crucial role in the problem-solving process. Unless information is made available, it is unlikely that meaningful decisions will be made.

Considering the vast amount of information relevant to vocational, educational, and personal problem solving that is available, it is quite impossible for community college counselors to have a thorough knowledge of specific information. Counselors, however, should have a thorough working knowledge of available informational resources as well as a working skill in finding the answers to questions, when necessary. This is not to say that counselors should function as reference librarians to their students. On the contrary, it is always the best approach to direct the students to the correct sources and let them find the necessary information. One author is reminded of his third-grade teacher who directed students to a rather imposing dictionary to look up unfamiliar words so that they would never forget them. Her approach does not differ from that suggested here.

While specification of the limitless informational resources available—leaflets, brochures, monographs, booklets, books, government reports, audio-visual material, and computer informational systems—is beyond the scope of this book, there are available several excellent references that accomplish this very task. Readers are encouraged to review these sources before any attempts are made to develop a knowledge of the available informational resources.

Occupational Information (4th ed.) by Robert Hoppock, published by McGraw-Hill (1976), is a classic reference on occupational information.

Career Information in Counseling and Teaching (3rd ed.) by Lee Isaacson, published by Allyn and Bacon (1977), is a comprehensive textbook covering all phases of career counseling. Special chapters on the utilization of information are provided.

The Information Service in Guidance (3rd ed.) by Norris, Zeran, Hatch, and Engelkes, published by Rand McNally (1972), is a treasure chest of knowledge relating to available educational, personal, and vocational information and can serve as an excellent reference manual for those individuals developing an information resource center.

Counseling for Career Development by E. L. Tolbert, published by Houghton-Mifflin (1974), provides several chapters on information and informational systems that are currently available, together with descriptions of computerized and other innovative informational systems.

Just looking at the editions published in the above list suggests one of the most perplexing problems of using information: Is it current and up-to-date? All information should be periodically reviewed to assess whether it is still current and valid. One author vividly remembers chuckles of laughter coming from several students who were browsing through some career monographs. While the monographs in question contained useful information, the photographs they contained were considerably out-of-date and the clothes worn by the individuals in the photographs evoked considerable attention. Even when something like this is explained to the student, a certain lack of confidence in the information will be present—and information, unless it is used, is relatively worthless.

Criteria for Evaluating Information

Information materials and resources should be evaluated on the basis of the following questions:

Are they accurate and valid?
Are they biased in their presentation?
Are they well written and understandable?
Are they expensive?
Are they current and up-to-date?
Are revisions in the materials likely?
Do the materials provide additional sources of information?

The above questions are important considerations for the community college counselor in developing and maintaining an information resource center. The National Vocational Guidance Association (NVGA) publication, Guidelines for the Preparation and Evaluation of Career Information Media (1971), is a basic source for all those who use vocational, educational, and personal information.

A considerable amount of information is available free of charge and in many cases the information is excellent. It must be remembered, however, that this information may be used for public relations, recruiting, or advertising purposes. Hoppock (1974) warns of the hazards in using free information, which may lead to misperceptions by naive readers. Careful evaluation, however, will minimize this, thereby providing useful information for students at little or no cost.

Information in Counseling

Retrieval of information is a problem for counselors or students. Community college students, as a group, have considerable need for basic information related to a wide variety of personal, educational, and vocational concerns. Often, however, they do not possess the skill to explore and find the required information. Any efforts that counselors can provide will contribute to the necessary information needed for effective problem solving. Sometimes a simple suggestion like checking the school library or writing a letter to a professional organization for information can be overlooked in the haste to provide actual counseling for the student. Developing information-seeking skills can be most beneficial for the student. In many ways, just exploring for information can have positive benefits. The exploration itself will usually acquaint the student with new and hopefully useful supplementary knowledge.

Most career decision-making programs specifically utilize this aspect—the student's individual exploration of vocational information. For example, Dwight (1975) presents a model for a career decision-making course taught by Essex Community College in Maryland, which involves, among other things, the students learning to make assessments of local and national manpower trends. While it is not the primary focus of the program, exploration of information sources is the critical component of the course. Similarly, Pearson (1975), in his approach, self-identification of talents, discusses the usefulness of exploration for career choice.

Acquiring Materials

Brief mention has been made of obtaining free materials that are available from private industry, business, and commerce organizations, professional and trade organizations, and the largest information disseminator—the government. In addition, the U.S. Government Printing Office sells some of the most inexpensive and well-prepared materials available.

Taylor (1973) describes an excellent idea for keeping current information available to students. At Thomas Nelson Community College in Hampton, Virginia, contact with a nearby U.S. Army base produced a cooperative agreement between the school and the base's Pre-Discharge Education Program on using available information. Cooperatively using available resources by such agreements as Taylor's or by consortia arrangements is an excellent way to increase available information, materials, and services at little or no extra cost.

Vocational Counseling Approaches

The approach presented at the beginning of this chapter, hierarchical problem solving, is directed specifically, as earlier indicated, to decision-making skills—in this case, vocational decision-making skills. Further explication of this approach, at this point, would be somewhat redundant; however, several other approaches that can be integrated with hierarchical problem solving will be briefly discussed.

Stewart and Winborn (1973), in their approach to decision making, present a model called systematic counseling, which represents a synthesis of learning theory, systems analysis, and educational technology. The detailed approach is comprised of 12 major subsystems that contain a total of 85 functions that counselors commonly perform during the course of the counseling process. Detailed descriptions together with methods and materials can be found in Stewart et al. (1978). Similar detailed approaches for decision making in vocational counseling and developing can be found in Gelatt (1962), Tolbert (1974), and Krumboltz and Thoresen (1976). Gelatt, Varenhorst, and Carey (1972) have developed a student and leader manual to decision-making skills, titled Deciding, which can be a useful resource for decision making.

An interesting approach to evaluating vocational alternatives is provided by Housley (1973). In a research study, he attempted to determine whether individuals are more concerned with positive, seeking-out activities or are really concerned with avoiding negative, unpleasant activities in tentative selections of career choice. His thesis of vocational choice by rejection of possible alternatives is based upon the premise that, vocationally speaking, people are more certain of activities they dislike than of those they like. Using this approach to eliminate alternatives is similar to using inverse priority, but may allow the student to be more certain of the value of each alternative before attempts are made to select among them.

Another innovative approach to predicting job preferences, using a decision-making model, has been researched by Swinth (1976). It is called the "discrimination net survey," and requires individuals to describe their decision processes in the form of a decision tree, using job attributes they consider important, as the basis for branching a decision map. Any job, to be considered acceptable, is tested against the most important attribute; for example, job is in operations analysis, or salary is contingent upon merit, not seniority, and so on. By using a process of ranking acceptable paths or directions, a job that has the appropriate combination of attributes will exit on an "accept path"; if not, it will be rejected somewhere along the way. Construction of the net is the end product of an elaborate system of work values and priorities the individual believes to be important. Once constructed (the difficult part), however, it is a relatively simple task to follow the path to a decision. Research studies suggest its potential for job selection decisions by systematically weighting and prioritizing job attributes and work values.

SOME CONCLUDING REMARKS

This chapter has outlined some basic individual approaches to community college counseling, which follow a hierarchical problem-solving approach. The hierarchical model presented is a generic model since it can be applied to a variety of individual concerns. It is hoped that counselors and community college students will ultimately learn the basic model rather than any specific techniques or cookbook approaches, since the model maximizes transfer to many problem areas. Later chapters will present additional approaches to group work and outreach programs.

SUPPLEMENTARY RESOURCE BOOKS ON
BASIC VERBAL INTERACTION SKILLS

Benjamin, A. The helping interview. Boston: Houghton-Mifflin, 1974; a classic little book on interview skills, which is well written. It integrates the interview skills with the overall helping process.

Brammer, L., and Shostrum, E. Therapeutic psychology (2nd ed.). Englewood Cliffs, N.J.: Prentice-Hall, 1968. This is a comprehensive textbook covering therapeutic approaches. Several chapters are devoted specifically to verbal and nonverbal counseling techniques. It is written from the perspective of a counseling psychologist and a clinical psychologist.

Gazda, G. Human relations development (2nd ed.). Boston: Houghton-Mifflin, 1976. This is a beginning "how to" book on human relations training. Although the emphasis is on educators, the basic communication skills are those of counseling.

Hackney, H., and Nye, S. Counseling strategies and objectives. Englewood Cliffs, N.J.: Prentice-Hall, 1973. A compact, well-written text on basic techniques from a behavioral approach in a programmed text format; a useful self-pacing introductory manual.

Ivey, A. E. Micro-Counseling. Springfield, Ill.: Thomas, 1971. This book attempts to break the counselor's verbal interaction skills into discrete modules for learning purposes. The approach, as well as the text, have been well received and are well researched.

Long, L., Paradise, L. V., and Long, T. J. Questioning: Skills for the Helping Process. Monterey, Calif.: Brooks/Cole, 1981. This book presents a detailed discussion of the use of questions in the counseling process. Included are comprehensive skill-building exercises and a thorough presentation of problem-solving techniques.

Okun, B. F. Effective helping: Interviewing and counseling techniques. North Scituate, Mass.: Duxbury Press, 1976. This book presents a variety of theoretical approaches and techniques in an unbiased manner. The examples and exercises are probably the best available in a book of this nature.

REFERENCES

Allport, G. W. The use of personal documents in psychological science. New York: Social Science Research Council, 1942.

Annis, A. P. The autobiography: Its uses and value in professional psychology. Journal of Counseling Psychology, 1967, 14.

Baird, C. R. The autobiography. Education Digest, 1954, 19, 39-43.

Baldwin, A. L. Personal structure analysis. Journal of Abnormal and Social Psychology, 1942, 37, 163-183.

Bandura, A. Social learning theory. New York: General Learning Press, 1971.

Brammer, L. The helping relationship: Process and skills. Englewood Cliffs, N.J.: Prentice-Hall, 1973.

Brammer, L., & Shostrum, E. Therapeutic psychology. Englewood Cliffs, N.J.: Prentice-Hall, 1968.

Bross, I. Design for decision. New York: Macmillan, 1953.

Carkhuff, R. Helping and human relations, Vols. I and II. New York: Holt, Rinehart and Winston, 1969.

Carkhuff, R. The development of human resources. New York: Holt, Rinehart and Winston, 1971.

Carkhuff, R., & Berenson, B. Beyond counseling and therapy (2nd ed.). New York: Holt, Rinehart and Winston, 1976.

Carkhuff, R., & Truax, C. Toward counseling and psychotherapy. Chicago: Aldine, 1967.

Combs, A., Avila, D., & Purkey, W. Helping relationships (2nd ed.). Boston: Houghton-Mifflin, 1978.

Dwight, A. H. A model career decision-making course. Community and Junior College Journal, 1975, 45, 23-24.

Eisenberg, S., & Delaney, D. The counseling process (2nd ed.). Chicago: Rand-McNally, 1976.

Ellis, A. Reason and emotion in psychotherapy. New York: Lyle Stuart, 1962.

Ellis, A. Humanistic psychotherapy. A rational-emotive approach. New York: McGraw-Hill, 1974.

Ellis, A., & Grieger, R. Handbook of rational-emotive therapy. New York: Springer, 1977.

Gelatt, H. B. Decision-making: A conceptual frame of reference for counseling. Journal of Counseling Psychology, 1962, 9(3), 240-245.

Gelatt, H. B., Varenhorst, B., & Carey, R. Deciding. New York: College Entrance Examination Board, 1972.

Goodstein, L. D., & Grigg, A. E. Client satisfaction, counselors, and the counseling process. Personnel and Guidance Journal, 1959, 38, 19-24.

Gottman, J. M., & Leiblum, S. R. How to do psychotherapy and how to evaluate it. New York: Holt, Rinehart and Winston, 1974.

Hackney, H. L., & Nye, S. Counseling strategies and objectives. Englewood Cliffs, N. J.: Prentice-Hall, 1973.

Haley, J. The art of being a failure as a psychotherapist. American Journal of Orthopsychiatry, 1969, 39(1), 691-695.

Homme, L., & Tosti, D. Behavior technology. San Rafael, Calif.: Instruction Learning Systems, 1971.

Hoppock, R. Occupational Information (4th ed.). New York: McGraw-Hill, 1976.

Housley, W. F. Vocational decision-making: A function of rejecting attitudes. Vocational Guidance Quarterly, 1973, 21, 288-292.

Isaacson, L. J. Career information in counseling and teaching (3rd ed.). Boston: Allyn and Bacon, 1977.

Ivey, A. Microcounseling: Innovations in interviewing training. Springfield, Ill.: Thomas, 1971.

Kanfer, F. H., & Karoly, P. Self-control: A behavioristic excursion into the lion's den. Behavior Therapy, 1972, 3, 398-416.

Kepner, C. H., & Tregoe, B. B. The rational manager. New York: McGraw-Hill, 1965.

Krumboltz, J. D. Behavioral goals for counseling. Journal of Counseling Psychology, 1966, 3, 153-159.

Krumboltz, J., & Thoresen, C. Counseling methods. New York: Holt, Rinehart and Winston, 1976.

Ladd, E. T. Counselors, confidences, and civil liberties of clients. Personnel and Guidance Journal, 1971, 50(4), 260-261.

Mahoney, M., & Thoresen, C. Self-control: Power to the person. Monterey, Calif.: Brooks/Cole Publishing, 1974.

Mischel, W. Introduction to personality. New York: Holt, Rinehart and Winston, 1971.

Myrick, R. D. An investigation of client orientation models in counseling. Unpublished doctoral dissertation. Arizona State University, 1968.

Norris, W., Zeran, F., Hatch, R., & Engelkes, J. The information service in guidance (3rd ed.). Chicago: Rand-McNally, 1972.

National Vocational Guidance Association. Guidelines for the preparation and evaluation of career information media. Washington, D.C.: NVGA, 1972.

Okun, B. F. Effective helping: Interviewing and counseling techniques. North Scituate, Mass.: Duxbury Press, 1976.

Paradise, L. V. Client reluctance and counseling effectiveness. Paper presented at the Annual Convention of the American Educational Research Association. Toronto, 1978.

Patterson, C. Relationship counseling and psychotherapy. New York: Harper and Row, 1974.

Pearson, H. G. Self-identification of talents. Vocational Guidance Quarterly, 1975, 24, 20-26.

Perls, F. The gestalt approach and eye witness to therapy. Palo Alto, Calif.: Science and Behavior Books, 1973.

Rogers, C. Client-centered therapy. Boston: Houghton-Mifflin, 1951.

Shapiro, R. J. Resistance revisited. American Journal of Psychology. 1972, 26(1), 112-122.

Shertzer, B., & Stone, S. Fundamentals of counseling (2nd ed.). Boston: Houghton-Mifflin, 1974.

Siegelwaks, B. Personal communication, January 1981.

Stewart, N. R., & Winborn, B. A model for decision-making in systematic counseling. Educational Technology, 1973, 13, 13-15.

Stewart, N. R., Winborn, B., Johnson, R., Burks, H., & Engelkes, J. Systematic counseling. Englewood Cliffs, N.J.: Prentice-Hall, 1978.

Swinth, R. L. A decision process model for predicting job preferences. Journal of Applied Psychology, 1976, 61(2), 242-245.

Taylor, H. T. Community college counselors get current information. Vocational Guidance Quarterly, 1973, 22, 146-147.

Thomas, L. G. Prospects of scientific research into values. Educational Theory, 1956, 6, 200.

Thoresen, C. E., & Mahoney, M. Behavioral self-control. New York: Holt, Rinehart and Winston, 1974.

Tolbert, E. L. Counseling for career development. Boston: Houghton-Mifflin, 1974.

Urban, H. B., & Ford, D. H. Some historical and conceptual perspectives on psychotherapy and behavior change. In A. E. Bergin & S. L. Garfield (Eds.), Handbook of psychotherapy and behavior change. New York: Wiley, 1971.

Wilkins, W. Expectancy of therapeutic gain. Journal of Consulting and Clinical Psychology, 1973, 40(1), 69-77.

6

GROUP COUNSELING
APPROACHES

Groups can be for better or for worse
Bates and Johnson, 1972

The effective use of groups by college counseling personnel has been growing rapidly throughout the decade of the 1970s. For many reasons counselors are becoming aware of the importance of group approaches for the achievement of their goals and objectives. This awareness is especially important to community colleges where the effective utilization of counseling resources is always a critical concern.

At present the use of group approaches is steadily increasing, and counselors are expecting even greater emphasis on group approaches in the future. Litwack (1978), in a national survey of 426 two-year colleges, polled over 6,000 counselors on their various responsibilities. Group counseling was rated eleventh on a list of 25 current responsibilities. When asked about their future responsibilities, however, the counselors rated group counseling fourth, behind vocational counseling, personal-social counseling, and consultation—the top three current responsibilities. Similar findings on the importance of groups have also been reported by other surveys of community college counseling (Hinko, 1971; Miller, 1979). They found groups being offered in such diverse areas as assertive and leadership training, career exploration, divorce adjustment, returning women's groups, and test-anxiety groups. It is interesting to note that the most frequent problems of community college students, according to the Miller study (1979), were academic difficulty, vocational concerns, interpersonal problems, and anxiety—those very concerns that group approaches seem so well equipped to handle. So it would appear that counselors have eagerly begun to respond to the need for more efficient methods of meeting the needs of large numbers of students when too few professionals are available—an early plea from Morrill, Ivey, and Oetting's (1968) benchmark report on the college counseling center.

This chapter will discuss a basic model for group counseling on concerns that are commonly seen by the community college counselor. There will also be presented certain specific group approaches that have been found useful in dealing with the main concerns facing the community college student.

THE GROUP IN COUNSELING

Group as opposed to individual counseling is a unique interactional phenomenon. Remarkable in its own right as a method of choice for many of the developmental problems facing students, it offers the additional advantage of being efficient in use of resources. As interest in groups has flourished, so too has the proliferation of group approaches. Marathons, encounters, T-groups, growth groups, and so on have all attracted both interest and uncertainty. Often enthusiasm and zeal by practitioners—some competent and some not so competent—have contributed to the justly deserved criticisms and concerns as to exactly what group counseling is and how it should be used. This, coupled with presently available data on the potential negative or detrimental effects of group experiences (Eddy & Lubin, 1971; Lieberman, Yalom, & Miles, 1973; Shostrum, 1970), should serve as a caution to those who approach groups with the conceptualization that group counseling is merely an extension of individual counseling. Nothing could be farther from reality.

To begin with, definitions of group have been advanced by most of the leading group authorities (for example, Cohn, 1964; Gazda, Duncan, & Meadows, 1967; Mahler, 1969). Terms such as group guidance, group counseling, group therapy, group psychotherapy, though admittedly difficult to separate, do represent essentially different helping efforts provided by oftentimes different professionals in different helping situations. For the most part, however, community college counselors are usually concerned with the first two terms—group guidance and group counseling. As will be seen, throughout this chapter these two terms will be used synonymously under group approaches, since it is difficult, if not unnecessary, to separate the guidance/educational element from the counseling element in group work.

The definition most closely conveying the essence of group counseling for the community college, as the authors see it, was advanced more than 15 years ago by Cohn, Combs, Gibian, and Sniffen (1963). They see group counseling as

A dynamic interpersonal process through which individuals within a normal range of adjustment work within a peer group and with a professionally trained counselor, exploring problems and feelings in an attempt to modify their attitudes so that they are better able to deal with developmental problems. (p. 355)

Several points of emphasis should be noted from this definition. Group guidance and counseling focus on individuals within a normal range of adjustment, not on clinically or emotionally disturbed individuals. This latter group is generally considered to fall within the scope of group therapy. By and large, community college counselors do not, and probably should not, be offering group therapy, but should be able to identify and make appropriate referral for these individuals. Also critical to this definition is the emphasis on developmental problems. It is toward these developmental problems, faced by students throughout the range of adulthood, that counselors should be focusing their efforts.

Within this definition is the notion of group guidance, providing specific information and educational functions, as it relates to certain specific problem-oriented topics—for example, how to find a good job, how to write a resume, information about sexual concerns, how to study, and so on. All too often some writers (Collins, 1964; Mahler, 1969) have maintained that a distinction exists between group counseling and group guidance, with guidance being seen as information presented to clients in large groups, sometimes with discussion, sometimes not. This, it would seem, is an unnecessary and misleading dichotomy, since it is difficult if not impossible to separate the guidance/information elements from any counseling group.

The definition should, however, clearly reflect the fact that community college counselors are not group therapists dealing with the types of problems that do require intensive and extensive effort to understand and solve. These are best left for the individuals clinically trained to handle them and are almost exclusively not part of the counselor's designated duties and responsibilities. Later in this chapter, in the section on appropriate screening procedures for starting groups, this issue will be discussed further.

To demonstrate the relevance of the definition to the practice of group counseling, Conyne, Lamb, and Strand (1975), in a national survey of groups offered by college counseling centers, found that the majority of groups offered could be characterized as developmental or adequacy-enhancing. They were designed with a personal growth-guidance focus and geared for relatively well-functioning individuals to enhance their present assets and skills to cope with future situations. Thus, the developmental approach to group experiences, as defined above, appears most relevant to the work of the community college counselor.

Goals and Functions

The factors in individual counseling that were discussed in Chapter 5 are equally applicable for group counseling. In fact, most of the goals and objectives for individual counseling are quite readily conducive to group experiences. Some counseling goals, such as solving problems dealing with interpersonal functioning, may be even more effectively achieved by use of groups. Researchers and writers have commented extensively on the goals of group work. By and large, the following are believed to be the major functions of the group experience for the community college student:

To provide an opportunity to examine, in an open and facilitative atmosphere, thoughts, feelings, beliefs, and behaviors

To achieve a greater understanding of their behavior and how it affects and is perceived by others

To provide and receive verbal and nonverbal feedback from peers with common concerns

To enable clients to become more confident in their skills and abilities and to give and receive support and encouragement for their efforts to bring about change and resolve problems

To provide clients with an individual learning experience about their and other group members' behavior, so that some degree of transfer will occur on future personal interactions

To help clients learn to be more open and honest with themselves and less defensive in their interaction with others, as they progress through their growth and development

To provide an open forum for the clients to learn from the experiences—both good and bad—of other members of the group

To encourage clients to learn a process for resolving problems and issues that they may be facing or may face in the future.

It should be reemphasized that for the majority of problems faced by the community college counselor, a well-planned, systematic program of group experiences has the potential to be more efficient and effective, will reach out to a far greater number of students, and will facilitate greater attainment of overall counseling goals than utilization of only individual counseling. Group experiences can be and have been utilized for the basic problem areas of community college students, including

- career and vocational counseling
- coping skills training
- orientation to the community college
- study skills and motivation training
- skills for the transfer or potential transfer student
- self-awareness
- assertiveness training

Their specific utilization will be discussed later in this chapter, along with some not-so-basic problem areas that have used group experiences.

There are, however, certain circumstances, usually defined by the status of the client, under which a group experience would not be in the best interests of the client or the group. In general, it has been noted that individuals at the extremes of any behavioral or attitudinal dimensions should be excluded from group experiences (Hansen, Warner, & Smith, 1980). Individuals who are aggressive or extremely hostile in their interpersonal interactions would probably not benefit from group approaches. Similarly, individuals extremely withdrawn or passive might become worse in reaction to group experiences (Yalom, 1975). In general, any individual whose behavior is so deviant or potentially deviant from that of the other members of the group will consume so much of the leader's time and energy that the group experience will be of little value to the other members or the individual. These persons are best handled by individual counseling.

Mahler (1969) best summarizes the purpose of group in his statement:

> It is evident that the major potentialities of counseling are common to both group and individual counseling. By determining the purpose and needs of an individual requesting help, and by designing the group counseling program to achieve specific goals, the counselor can provide valuable opportunities for people to learn and grow and live more effective lives. (p. 21)

Important Factors in Conducting a Group

There are several important factors in conducting any group in the community college setting. They should be examined and discussed as part of the initial planning for any group that is being considered.

Purpose

The basic purpose of the group is probably the single most important factor to consider in initial group planning. All too often, groups are eagerly formed without any clear or organized purpose in mind. The counselor decides that test anxiety is a problem for students, so a test-anxiety group is formed; or that a large number of students are requesting assistance because of transfer shock, so a transfer-shock group is formed—clearly not the best approach to take. This is not to say that these types of groups are not appropriate to offer. They are needed, but the types of groups to offer and how they should be conducted should be determined by the basic purpose of the overall group program.

If the counselors are not aware of the types of student concerns present in the college, then the first step should be centered around finding out what group services should be offered. The next step is to determine what groups could be offered. Here, staff training and competence, student interest and needs, time demands, and the goals and objectives of the counseling service should be considered. Types of groups offered at the community college will usually fall into one of three broad categories: developmental/growth-enhancing, remedial/problem-centered, and outreach-oriented.

Once the types of groups to be offered are identified, the specific purposes of the groups should be well planned and discussed. Objectives for the entire course of a group should be developed in advance. In general, groups conducted in the community college will be structured, task, or problem-centered, rather than the traditional, free-flowing process groups that are more common to group therapy, encounter groups, or sensitivity groups. It is always good practice for the leader or leaders to have some specific objective or purpose in mind for each session. This is beneficial for the leaders and for the members, especially in this setting, because there are usually time limits on the extent and duration of the group. This type of planning in regard to the purpose of the group will contribute to the leader's maintaining control of the group and help facilitate its basic purpose. For the members to know exactly what they are doing, and what they are going to be doing during the sessions will also contribute greatly to their motivation and commitment.

Selection of Participants

A great deal has been written concerning the homogeneity of group members with regard to age, sex, personality differences, ability levels, and so on (Diedrich & Dye, 1972; Dinkmeyer & Muro, 1979; Garfield & Bergin, 1978; Napier & Gershenfeld, 1973).

It would seem that the community college would be a relatively homogeneous population with respect to these variables, but that is not usually the case. Most community colleges will consist of relatively diverse subpopulations, and factors such as those mentioned need to be considered in relation to the purpose and goals of the group, as part of the selection process. For example, a group being planned for returning students might consider the following questions. Would it be better to keep returning men and women separate since they have uniquely different problems? Would it be better to have separate groups for younger and older returning students, since their developmental needs are quite different? One could probably continue to generate a list of questions about the participants, taking into account many other potentially important variables beyond those mentioned earlier. The key is, of course, that these are the considerations that need to be addressed in the initial planning regarding the purpose of the group and the selection of participants.

In general, groups usually work quite effectively in the community college setting when they are heterogeneous in terms of these factors. The diversity of membership contributes to a more valuable experience through greater exposure to other members who are different in make-up, but may be facing the same problems. It should be noted, however, that heterogeneous groups may not always be the best approach. Community college students, whether young or old, in general seem to feel more comfortable with people their own age. If this feeling is prevalent, it may interfere with the purpose of the group.

One last and perhaps the most overlooked consideration on selection for a group is the issue of screening members. Every group should begin with the appropriate screening of members to insure that their initial expectations, perceptions, and individual goals for participation are in congruence with the purposes of the group. This is best accomplished by an interview in which the counselor can discuss and clarify these issues. It will help insure that potential group members are in the appropriate group and it can screen out those individuals who could best benefit from either individual counseling or a referral to more appropriate therapeutic help.

Mistakes of screening can contribute greatly to an ineffective experience for the entire group, as well as to the possibility of casualties. Lieberman, Yalom, and Miles's (1973) extensive research on the group experience has shown that individuals with overly high expectations together with low self-esteem run the greatest likelihood of becoming casualties—actually becoming worse as a function of their group experience. Individuals who will not profit from the experience or will be a negative influence on the group should be identified at this stage.

In the community college setting, where groups are likely to be somewhat structured and limited in their duration, screening becomes an even more critical issue. Also, success of the group will be enhanced when members know what is expected of them and what they can realistically expect from the group experience (Johnson, 1963; Yalom, 1975). The screening interview will help identify some sense of the members' motivation to complete the group sessions, as well as indicate their likelihood of becoming active participants.

Many community college students may have overinflated expectations that a particular group will solve their problems, and with overtaxed staffs and large student bodies, it is easy to envision how groups can be seen as a panacea. A good screening interview addressing the following questions will resolve this issue.

How did you find out about the group?
What do you know about group counseling already?
Have you had any previous experiences in groups?
What do you expect to accomplish in the group?
Are you willing to meet for X number of times until _____?
What types of problems or concerns do you have with discussing personal information in front of others?
How comfortable would you feel if acquaintances are members of the group?
How would you feel about setting some individual goals for your experience before beginning?

This is a sampling of the types of issues that should be addressed during the screening interview. In a sense, this interview serves much the same purpose as an intake interview. Counselors develop an initial understanding of the students and their situations, with the hope of making a judgment as to the appropriateness of group as the method of choice. Sometimes students will sign up for a group as a ploy to mask certain more difficult, sensitive, or severe problems. The interview, regardless of the seeming innocuousness of the particular group, should be completed in order to help identify these individuals. It is easier for all concerned if this is accomplished during screening rather than once the group has started to meet.

One final point: the screening interview should be conducted by those counselors who plan to lead the group. Also, if coleaders are to be used, both coleaders should be doing the screening together. This requires some additional time, of course, but it will facilitate the decisions as well as contribute to initial rapport with the leaders, since the student will have already had time to meet and get to know both coleaders.

Exercise

Try this group exercise with your fellow counselors on conducting a screening interview for a group dealing with test anxiety and study skills. Break into triads, with one person conducting the interview with another person, and the third serving as an observer. Rotate the counselor's role until all have had an opportunity. You may wish to change the type of group, as well. When each has had a turn at the interview, discuss the observations and feedback. Now, try it again as coleaders conducting a group. Follow the same procedure this time, except that two counselors will do the screening interview on the third. When all have finished, discuss the differences in the two interviews.

Size of the Group

The desirable number of members is always a consideration. The ideal number must be balanced against student needs and interests, staffing concerns, and the type of group. As a rule, as the depth of expected involvement of the members increases, the size of the group should decrease. Structured groups—for example, for test-taking skills—with a high guidance or educational component could be larger in size without reducing their effectiveness, but groups requiring more personal involvement—for example, social competency groups—are most effective with a smaller size. Generally, seven to ten members seems to be the group size suggested most often (Corey & Corey, 1977; Hansen, Warner, & Smith, 1980). Too few members, especially with absences, will cause the group not to be a group, just as too many will cause disruptive subgroups to form (Hare, 1962).

As mentioned earlier, it may be advisable to increase group size to perhaps 12-15 members when there is a strong informational component to the groups—for example, job-hunting strategies. This will usually work well, especially if discussion in smaller groups is provided. Once again the size, 7-10 plus or minus a few, will depend on the type of group, level of personal involvement expected, and the basic purpose of the group.

Duration and Frequency

Groups conducted in the community college are generally time-limited in duration; that is, they have a set beginning and a preestablished end, usually centered around the academic calendar.

They will usually be conducted during some time frame within an academic semester. Generally, 8-12 weeks is the ideal duration. It is usually not good for group continuity and continued membership to extend through semesters, and long-term groups, by and large, are not best suited for the community college. The duration is best determined, however, by the initial purposes and objectives of the group.

The time frame for the group is related to the issue of open or closed groups. The closed group will meet for a predetermined number of sessions or until the group decides to terminate—ideally with the concurrence of the leader. An open group, on the other hand, continues to function without a predetermined ending time. As members leave the group, new members replace them. The open-type approach is more commonly found in clinical settings and for use when little structure or task objectives are part of the purposes of the group. By and large, however, closed, time-limited, structured group experiences are most suited to the developmental needs of the community college student.

The number of meetings each week is also an issue, but no conclusive research exists on the optimal number. Intensive, crisis-oriented, therapeutic groups may meet every day or several times each week, but for the types of groups and client population served by the community college, once a week appears to be the most useful and manageable.

Scheduling will always be a problem for members in this setting, so leaders should be aware of class schedules, extramural activities, working times, and so on, when they schedule their groups. Also, additional scheduling problems can be avoided if groups are scheduled in advance of announcing them. This will aid potential members in their planning for participation. Attempting, however, to accommodate all the prospective members of a group in setting a time will be an impossible task and more than likely the semester will end before the sessions can get started.

Setting and Length of Session

It is always important, as with any type of counseling, to have an appropriate place for counseling to take place, free from interruption and disturbance, with sufficient privacy to encourage open and frank discussion. With too small a group room, participants will not be able to sit comfortably and see all members that are present. With too large a room, participants may feel lost. A room sufficient to accommodate the participants, whether the counselor chooses to have them sit around a large conference table or in chairs grouped in a circular arrangement, is usually most facilitative.

The length of time for each session should be determined by the purpose of the group. Generally, for community college work, one hour to one and a half hours seems to be the most common period. This will allow for time to get "warmed up," and yet not be so long that members begin to lose interest in the discussion or need to take breaks that could limit the continuity of the session.

One final point on the time involved: the meetings should end promptly at the appointed time. Groups have a tendency to bring up significant material just before it is time to end the session. This can readily be avoided if the leader or leaders start toward closure 10-15 minutes before termination. It is usually good practice to end on a positive note, and planning the ending of the session will definitely contribute to a good closing. When leaders end sessions promptly, members are encouraged to bring significant material to discussion when there is still sufficient time for discussion.

The same holds true for starting the sessions. They should begin on time rather than wait for individuals. In this way, members will not be rewarded for being late and sufficient time for the meeting will not be reduced. It is difficult sometimes for counselors to be explicitly consistent in timing their sessions, but it is quite important in this setting. Groups do have a way of running over the time.

Exercise

Consider the following factors important to conducting a group: purpose, selection of participants, size of the group, duration and frequency, and setting and length of session. Break into groups of three counselors and plan a group for each of the following situations. Write down your plans and discuss the issues with small-group members.

1. A group experience for returning housewives is to be planned to help them adjust to the community college situation.
2. A group is to be conducted for students with weak social competency skills—for example, difficulty in talking to the opposite sex, difficulty in talking to instructors, general shyness, and so on.
3. An academic orientation group is to be conducted for liberal arts students planning to transfer to the state university after completing the final year of the associate degree.
4. A group on job-interview skills is being planned for technical students.

After completing the planning for these groups, take note of how many decisions had to be made even before the group was to meet.

HIERARCHICAL PROBLEM SOLVING IN GROUPS

The hierarchical problem-solving model presented in Chapter 5 for individual counseling is an excellent approach to providing the structural base for group counseling efforts. It quite readily lends itself to the basic problem areas faced by the community college student:

- Orientation to college life
- Career and vocational planning
- Job-seeking and marketing skills
- Academic and study skills
- Social-competency skills
- Self-awareness
- Assertiveness and coping skills

While the nine elements for the process are essentially the same for both individual and group counseling, the procedures for using them differ greatly in the individual counseling session and in the group counseling session. Approaches similar to this, however, have been used quite effectively in group settings for a variety of problems (Aiken & Johnston, 1973; Krumboltz & Thoresen, 1964; Napier & Gershenfeld, 1973; Varenhorst & Gelatt, 1971). In addition, the hierarchical problem-solving approach lends itself readily to the inclusion of any informational or guidance component that is relevant or necessary to the basic purposes of the group. Counselors will find that for almost any community college group a relatively strong information/guidance component is essential, regardless of the problem. This is not to advocate telling students what they should do, but it needs to be emphasized that for all the concerns listed above, some new information is going to be necessary to effect change, and this is best dealt with as part of the basic purpose of the group. Whether the information is going to be provided directly by the group leader, as might be the case with a job-hunting-skills group or a sexual-identity group, or whether the means and methods to obtain the necessary information are provided and the student must undertake the effort—as with a career-development group or a human-potential seminar, information/guidance becomes a crucial component to the entire hierarchical problem-solving process. Cramer and Herr (1971) suggest that counselors ask two questions. First, what kind of information necessary for decision making (problem solving) is best presented in a group situation? Second, what are the best ways to insure that the information will be internalized by the group members? Obviously, these will need to be addressed in terms of the purpose of

the group, but generally, facilitating discussion of the information
and its potential and/or probable utility is always a good method,
as is helping the students, wherever possible, to develop or find
the information personally.

In applying this model to group counseling procedures, there
are several components of the process to be taken into account.

Building a Facilitative Relationship

The facilitative relationship is more complex for the group
because the counselor is dealing with not one client but many.
Building this relationship begins with the intake interview and continues through the sessions. Shertzer and Stone (1980) point to the
following counselor efforts that contribute to a facilitative group
relationship: getting the group organized; explaining how it should
function for maximum results; conveying that members have a responsibility for understanding and helping each other, as well as
for striving to solve their own problems; and encouraging members
to share feelings and try out new ideas.

When the group members can see that the leader cares about
them, is working to understand them, and is expert in helping
people help themselves, the facilitative relationship is enhanced.
When these elements are present the leader will readily notice that
the group is no longer a collection of separate individuals intent on
solving only their own problems; they are a counseling group—a
unique entity, possessing cohesion. Cohesion is that dynamic force
that holds a group together and allows it to be a productive and
functioning group. The mutual trust and respect among group members is greatly influenced by the behavior and direction of the leader
(Krumboltz & Potter, 1973; Liberman, 1970). The presence or
absence of this facilitative group relationship will have considerable impact on the ensuing components of the process.

Developing Self-awareness and Understanding

The second component in this group process is basically
similar to that for individual counseling. Members must begin to
see by means of interactions with other group members and the
leader, as well as through appropriate information where relevant,
the importance of problem solving in their own lives. How problem solving is related to their own problems and life situations,
together with its long-range implications, must be conveyed.

Through verbal interactions with group members—all with their own similar concerns—the group leader can begin to help develop an awareness of the problem or situation that will aid in coming to a specific identification of the problem or problems that face each group member.

Identifying the Problem

Many times a major step toward achieving this element is begun at the initial screening interview. Accurate problem identification, however, requires sufficient self-understanding to allow precise and meaningful individual goals to be set. The group interaction and feedback will help insure that each member benefits from the help of the others. As will be recalled, helping each other is one of the member responsibilities that the leader conveys to members early in the group experience.

Setting Individual Goals

While all the members of a group at the community college level may have the same general goal in mind—for example, increased study skills, job-hunting strategies, and so on—each one will have a personal, idiosyncratic, specific goal to work toward. This applies equally whether the group is designed for individuals with the same specific problem or with a variety of problems. The process will help the members refine and specify what it is they hope to accomplish from the experience. The group interaction, in addition, will help insure that each member's goals are realistic and meaningful. This is quite important, since research has rather convincingly shown that identifying specific goals can facilitate the positive group outcomes (for example, Bush, 1971; Hilkey, 1975; Krumboltz, 1966; Ohlsen, 1977). The specific issues discussed in Chapter 5 on identifying individual goals should aid in helping group members assist each other in the formulation of meaningful personal goals.

Generating Alternatives

The real value of the hierarchical approach for groups lies in its rich potential to help group members generate alternatives both for themselves and for others. Here too, they may decide that additional information or guidance is required. The leader's task at this point is to guide the discussion and dialogue to generate meaningful alternatives. The leader can help members explore all possible and probable outcomes.

The group relationship and cohesion will help insure that members feel free to make suggestions, and perhaps, as suggested by Napier and Gershenfeld (1973), treat this component as a "brainstorming" session.

Evaluating Alternatives

Under the leader's direction, group members need to evaluate each of the alternatives developed earlier. Thus, a variety of viewpoints concerning possibilities—probabilities, reactions, and consequences—will be presented. Varenhorst and Gelatt (1971) indicate that this is a real asset for the group approach, since it conveys the various priorities of each of the members, which is, in itself, a positive side effect of evaluating alternatives in a group setting. Overall, it can help the group leader demonstrate that there are many possible, useful, and realistic answers to a given problem. This fact will apply even if all the members of the group have essentially the same problem or concern to resolve.

Selecting Appropriate Courses of Action

Selecting appropriate courses of action is similar to selecting strategies to resolve the problem. It may be the case that the strategies to resolve the problem are built into the group experience (for example, role playing to develop assertive skills), or it may be that members work together in helping each other take meaningful action to bring about individual change. Many of the specific individual strategies presented in Chapter 5 have been successfully applied to the group experience. Additional group strategies used in the community college will be presented later in this chapter.

Once again, the group will greatly facilitate each member's selection of the best possible courses of action and will also add greatly to the individual's motivation and commitment to follow through. This phenomenon works like contracting. Once a member makes a decision to do something and receives the support and encouragement of the other group members, the individual will be much more likely to be motivated to carry it through. There are several interested individuals who are helping, encouraging, and placing confidence in the member's ability to be successful. It is this cohesive force or group pressure and encouragement that should help sustain the member's motivation and commitment to change. Hansen et al. (1980, p. 522) summarize it best: "A group of peers has more sources of data, a wider range of reactions and more possibilities for identification than can be afforded by the counselor." Thus, individual commitment is enhanced by membership in the group itself (Bradford, Gibb, & Benne, 1964).

Evaluating Client Efforts

Evaluation of efforts in group as in individual counseling is an ongoing, continuous process. It is greatly enhanced by the group process because members can provide continued support and encouragement for member efforts. They can also, with the leaders' assistance, help evaluate the success of member efforts and suggest possible ways to reassess goals, strategies, and efforts, as well as ways to improve upon the members' efforts where need be.

In addition, it is always an excellent therapeutic and educational asset for group members to discuss how other efforts are succeeding or failing, since the learning that will take place from discussions of this sort will greatly benefit all the group members, either directly or indirectly. It will also be quite a meaningful learning device for the leader to convey the important issues and aspects that are related to the basic purposes of the group. For example, the leader of a career-development group may wish to convey the concept that even though individuals review career information thoroughly and interview knowledgeable people, they may still not be able to reach decisions concerning their own careers. This fact may be best conveyed by the group discussion concerning the specific incident.

Terminating the Group and Follow-up

Although the group's purpose and activities are usually structured for each meeting, termination of the group is known in advance and consequently is no surprise to the members. If the group has been especially cohesive, however, many members may not want to stop meeting. Oftentimes member relationships will have developed and participants may want to continue meeting either as a group or in some other capacity. There may also be some participants who want to continue in other counseling groups or who want to make arrangements to see the leader in individual counseling.

If the group has been a positive experience, there should be some degree of sadness at the termination stage. These feelings should be dealt with and discussed in advance of the last meeting. Here the counselor can emphasize the feelings that some members may possibly hold, as well as the progress that the participants have made toward their overall individual goals. Groups that are not time-limited in nature will have more difficulty at termination since the biggest decision to be made is when to terminate. This situation, of course, will require more leader effort to prepare for termination.

Group leaders should be aware of those individuals who want to continue in some other form of counseling or who might benefit from additional counseling. Discussing this with the member at some point individually—not during the group—is the best approach. Whether or not to see group participants individually either during the group experience or after is an issue that varies from counselor to counselor. Some counselors prefer not to see clients they have in their groups, but do not object after the group has terminated. Others may feel that it would be best for individuals who want to continue in individual counseling to see a different counselor. The best course of action depends on the situation and the individual counselor's preferences. It is not uncommon, however, for members to want to continue seeing a counselor with whom they already have a positive relationship. Regardless of the situation that may exist, these issues should be discussed with the participants in question.

Follow-up counselor efforts for group counseling can be accomplished in much the way as those discussed under individual approaches in Chapter 5. Here the counselor's continued interest in the former group member will be a positive influence, as well as convey the message that the counselor is always available, should any need arise in the future.

Some Concluding Remarks

A general hierarchical, group problem-solving model has been presented, which is felt to be a viable and useful approach to working with the types of student problems and concerns faced by the community college counselor. It will be noted that specific group techniques and approaches have been deemphasized, reserving them for later in this chapter. The contention here is that this general model can serve as a basic framework within which to conduct the group process, even when the counselor is conducting a structured or task-centered group. The model is adaptable to the specific purposes a group leader may have and should enhance attaining the group's basic purposes. As with individual counseling, each component builds into subsequent components. Finally, the model should be equally useful whether the group is focusing on guidance/information or counseling or both.

GROUP APPROACHES

Selected group appraoches that have been used in community college counseling are presented in the sections that follow. They span a variety of problems and concerns that are commonly faced by counselors. They are described in order to provide a view of the broad range of group activities that occur in the community college. Interested readers who wish to learn more about group counseling procedures should refer to the supplementary resource books on group counseling listed at the end of this chapter.

Career Counseling

The Vocational Exploration Group (VEG)

The Vocational Exploration Group is a two-part group counseling approach that uses structured group exercises that combine group counseling and decision-making skills. It focuses on job functions, job demands, and job satisfactions. The groups are kept small, and extensive participation in the group interaction is expected. Results from the use of this approach appear to be positive with adolescents and young adults, as well as with special population groups—for example, those with educational, emotional, and physical handicaps (Neely & Kosier, 1975). The approach would appear to have interest for those counselors wishing to apply a decision-making or problem-solving approach to the three basic vocational issues of VEG.

The Life Career Development System

The Life Career Development System (Waltz & Benjamin, 1974) is a group, career-development, structured procedure that has been used for high school through adult participants. The major purpose of the approach is to focus on members' outcomes and learning that are directly related to real-life situations, with experiential elements revolving around career-development tasks. The structured program is divided into modules of six to nine sessions, combining both individual and group experiences, which can easily be tailored to fit the academic semester or year.

Modules cover the following career-development areas:

Exploring self—seven sessions are related to helping participants obtain a greater understanding of their own interests and strengths, as well as an understanding of how the self is related to career satisfaction.

Determining values—six sessions are focused on determining the participant's values and their relationship to career development.

Setting goals—six sessions are provided to assist the participant in formulating meaningful goals.

Expanding options—six sessions are provided to facilitate the exploration and expansion of options as they relate to the world of work.

Overcoming barriers—six sessions assist participants in identifying and coping with the obstacles and roadblocks commonly found in one's career development.

Using information—five sessions are provided on the effective use of career information.

Working effectively—six sessions are provided to increase effective study and work performance.

Thinking for the future—six sessions are provided to facilitate looking forward in the career-development process.

Selecting mates—six sessions are concerned with dating and marriage issues.

As can be seen, the Life Career Development System is a comprehensive group approach that focuses heavily, as does the VEG discussed earlier, on decision making and problem solving. Various modules or sessions within modules can be selected for focus, or the entire package can be utilized to assist in the overall career development of the community college student.

Decisions and Outcomes

Decisions and Outcomes is another decision-making/problem-solving approach that was developed by the College Entrance Examination Board (Carey, Gelatt, Miller, & Varenhorst, 1973). It focuses on values, use of appropriate information, and effective strategies. It was developed for use as a separate program or to complement the regular college curriculum. It is especially useful as part of the community college orientation program.

Work-Exposure Approaches

Lamb (1980) described work exposure as a group approach designed to facilitate the interchange among students, business, and industry. At Tidewater Community College in Virginia Beach, Virginia, groups of faculty, students, and counselors board chartered buses and visit local business and industry sites. The observations and discussion of these experiences provides the group with real-life work exposure, and acquaints employers with prospective graduates.

Similar work-exposure programs involving group approaches have been conducted with nontraditional students and disadvantaged youth (Forrer, Cooper, Epperley, & Inge, 1977; Roessler, Cook, & Lilland, 1977, Thompson & Majunder, 1972). These programs are especially useful at the community college where special vocational attention to the disadvantaged is a major concern for the counseling staff.

The Alumni Panel

At Essex Community College in Newark, New Jersey, graduates are invited back to speak to students about the world of work (Cherichello & Gillian, 1980). Panels for discussion are organized on a variety of topics to maximize the effectiveness of this group guidance approach. The developers of this approach emphasize the fact that community college alumni are rarely organized. It is usually the four-year college that claims these alumni as their own, thus exempting the community college from utilizing its most obvious resource. Cherichello and Gillian further suggest the establishment of an alumni bank to enable interested individuals to talk to recent graduates about the world of work. Secondary schools have used this approach quite effectively in the past (Hoppock, 1976) and it can be quite a meaningful experience if sufficient attention is given to the discussion and interaction among the participants.

Exercise

Conduct a community resource survey for vocational interests. This will involve determining the business and industry resources in the community, identifying potential resource persons—alumni, faculty, and others. These are individuals who would be of assistance in discussions, field trips, and interviews to acquaint students with the world of work. It will be necessary to determine the career-development needs that are present, identify the business and industry that may be involved, identify those individuals who could serve as resource discussion participants, and plan the process the group approach should follow. A word of caution: if the community is relatively large, this could be a massive undertaking. The focus should be on a small segment of the community, if this is the case; perhaps a small geographic area of town would suffice. The basic idea is to start planning for the effective use of resource persons including graduates, faculty, and the community.

Exercise

Plan a career development group. Use the hiararchical problem-solving model as a framework to assist in identifying the problems involved, the alternatives, and the solutions to the problems. This will help develop a first-hand experience with the problem-solving approach. Go through each step in the model in planning.

Academic Concerns

Test Anxiety

Many counseling centers develop group programs for test anxiety. Generally, the research on test-anxiety effectiveness has been quite positive (for example, Crighton & Jehu, 1969; Mitchell & Ng, 1972; Gilbreath, 1968).

Osterhouse (1976) has developed a model for group desensitization of test anxiety with college students that involves training in deep muscle relaxation, constructing anxiety hierarchies, and working through the hierarchies. The approach is presented in sufficient detail to be an excellent reference for those planning groups on test anxiety. Osterhouse (1972) has also developed similar approaches that use study-skills training as well.

When underachievement is a prominent concern, central focus on study-skills training by means of behavioral self-control methods (Richards, 1975) is appropriate and is quite adaptable to the group approach in the community college. Additional studies of underachievement among college students (Jackson & Van Zoost, 1974; Spielburger & Wirtz, 1964) have found group approaches to improve study skills and college adjustment.

Considerable attention to study-skills training has been given by the behaviorally oriented writers (for example, Goldiamond, 1965; Watson & Tharp, 1972). Their approach generally involves applying principles of learning theory and self-management skills, and is quite suitable for the community college. For example,

Hudesman and Wiesner (1979) have used test-anxiety desensitization workshops at New York City Community College. These small group workshops focus on muscle relaxation and group desensitization sessions, and have been used with positive results.

Transfer Students

Group approaches to deal with the special concerns of transfer and potential transfer students are quite important among the academic concerns of the community college counselor. Rich (1979) discusses some of the myths and realities of the academic transfer student. These issues can serve as excellent discussion content for group experiences to minimize the transfer shock of new students entering the community college and as preparation for graduates who go on to a four-year college. Among the realities Rich presents are that transfer students have preconceived ideas about their new college; that most transfer students will encounter a different cultural situation; that a change in schools will not resolve academic problems; and most importantly, that adjustment involves the student, the counselor, and the total college environment.

Personal/Social Problems

Assertiveness

Assertive training groups have enjoyed widespread success in recent years, and many applications of this group approach are quite appropriate for the community college student. The best single source of assertive training approaches can be found in the work of Rimm and Masters (1979). Their comprehensive review of the theory, research, and technique of assertive training is must reading for counselors planning assertive groups.

Washington (1980) describes a ten-step approach to assertive training used at Northern Virginia Community College in Alexandria, Virginia. The ten steps reflect a decision-making group approach to student assertive behavior.

Identification of the problem
Time and person—when and with whom the feelings and behaviors
     occur
Settings—where the feelings and behaviors occur
Reaction—examination of the student's reaction to the nonassertive
     situation
Blocks—Exploring what prevents the assertive responding

Benefits—examining what the student gains by being nonassertive
Losses—examining what the student loses when displaying inappro-
    priate assertive behavior
New behaviors—how the student would change the behaviors
Failure—exploring the worst thing that could happen if the student
    did change
Success—examining what would be the best possible outcome if the
    student did change

Washington's decision-making model is basically similar in content
to other behavioral, action-oriented approaches to assertive behavior.

Bower (1976) has described an assertiveness program for
reentry women. The reentry woman is typically a returning housewife who is trying to move out into the world of work from her
previous work as a housewife and mother. This particular subpopulation of special students has become more prevalent at community colleges during the past several years. Bower's program
is a four-step approach that utilizes DESC: describing, expressing,
specifying, and consequences. Her action-oriented DESC approach
is ideally suited to the community college and has also been effectively used with men as well.

Stress-Management/Relaxation Training

Anxiety or stress-management training (Richardson, 1976) is
designed to teach people to cope with or reduce anxiety across a
variety of situations. As in test-anxiety approaches, students can
be taught in groups to control their stressful reactions that are
counterproductive. Most individuals can benefit from learning more
effective ways to control and manage stress and anxiety.

The relaxation approaches—a variety of them exist, from deep
muscle relaxation (Jacobson, 1938; Lazarus, 1971) to autogenic
training (Schultz & Luthe, 1959)—can be quite useful when used as
group training. Paradise has successfully used these approaches
with college students with encouraging results over durations less
than an academic semester.

Increasing Personal Happiness

Personal happiness, defined by various researchers (Fellows,
1966; Fordyce, 1977) as an overall emotional sense of well-being,
can serve as a relatively important determiner of satisfaction with
one's life. Fordyce (1972, 1977) reports encouraging results with

an innovative program to increase everyday happiness and satisfaction with life for normal community college students. The program is based on the notion that community college students could become happier individuals if they could modify their behaviors and attitudes to approximate more closely the characteristics of happier individuals.

Basically, Fordyce's program consists of receiving information about happiness to include nine specific activities that can be engaged in to increase happiness: spend more time socializing, develop an outgoing personality, become more active, lower expectations, develop positive thinking, get better organized, stop worrying, become more oriented to the present, and value happiness. The program, which includes goals, techniques, and procedures, can be accomplished in a relatively short period of time.

Evaluation of the program with over 200 community college students ranging in age from 17 to 50 years suggests that a psychological variable as globally defined as happiness is amenable to training and development. Fordyce (1977, p. 521) concludes that "there appears to be much about the achievement of personal happiness that anyone can develop, despite situational constraints or fundamental changes in the economic status or social condition." It is innovative and creative intervention programs such as this that can enhance the ability of community college counselors to provide valuable contributions to the students they serve.

Developmental Needs

Brimline and Klimek (1977) describe a comprehensive program to meet the developmental needs of students at Montgomery County Community College in Rockville, Maryland. Their development framework centers around the students' intellectual, social, and personal developmental tasks. The format for this group approach is a series of one-credit courses that address the following developmental tasks of the community college students (p. 405):

□ Developing personal autonomy and responsibility
□ Developing interdependence and trust
□ Developing appropriate educational plans
□ Developing realistic career plans
□ Developing mature life-style plans
□ Developing tolerance and understanding of others
□ Developing mature relationships with peers

Courses offered to achieve these objectives include career development, the human potential seminar—a course of structured group exercises to help students realize their potential—and a college survival course designed to look at the factors surrounding the college experience. Courses such as these underscore the mission of the college counseling service and provide an outreach function. The academic credit does facilitate the motivation of the student toward addressing the basic developmental issues of young adulthood. Courses that have a strong educational/guidance component can facilitate the role and function of the counseling efforts at a school. They also lend themselves quite easily to effective and meaningful orientation courses, which all too often become wasted experience for the student. Additional discussion of the utilization of freshman orientation can be found in Guber (1970) and Kopecek (1971).

Bibliotherapy in Groups

An innovative approach to the developmental problems of students is bibliotherapy—facilitation of attitudes, feelings, and behaviors through reading. West (1977) describes a group bibliotherapy approach designed to increase the self-understanding of college students. A reading discussion group of Rollo May's Man's Search for Himself (1967) was conducted with eight college students. The basic purpose of the group was to help members relate what they learned from each chapter to their own life experiences.

The idea of using reading/discussion groups to facilitate personal understanding and development has been around for at least 40 years (Bryan, 1939); it is seldom used, however, as a group counseling/guidance approach to the major development problems facing students. It should be noted that care should be taken in formulating the reading list for bibliotherapy groups, so that the overall purposes will be best served by the reading material selected.

RET Groups

Approaches using Rational-Emotive therapy (RET), which were discussed in Chapter 5 on individual counseling, have also been used in groups. Jacobs and Croake (1976) report on the use of RET for short-term discussion groups on marriage and family with college students. Their research suggests that RET group members increase their rational thinking, decrease their anxiety, and self-report problems. While their results are encouraging, the use of RET groups has not been widespread.

A Final Note

Group procedures greatly facilitate the work of the counselor as well as help achieve the goals of a community college counseling center. They do, however, require systematic staff planning and coordination if they are to be successful. They also require, as might be guessed, experienced group leaders. The best way to get needed experience for group work is to conduct groups as a co-leader with someone who does have the expertise.

SUPPLEMENTARY RESOURCE BOOKS
ON GROUP COUNSELING

Bates, M. M., & Johnson, C. D. Group leadership. Denver: Love Publishing, 1972. This manual discusses the group process from an existential, theoretical framework. It presents structured group exercises that have been used to facilitate the purposes of various groups.

Ohlsen, M. M. Group counseling (2nd ed.). New York: Holt, Rinehart & Winston, 1977. This is one of the better-known basic texts on group counseling. In addition to the basics on group procedures, it presents material on special issues and client types commonly faced by counselors.

Hansen, J. C., Warner, R. W., & Smith, E. J. Group counseling: Theory and process (2nd ed.). Chicago: Rand McNally, 1980. This revised edition presents comprehensive coverage of the theories and procedures of group counseling. It is an excellent resource text and is quite complete in its coverage of the topic.

Mahler, C. A. Group counseling in the school. Boston: Houghton-Mifflin, 1969. The text deals with the basic issues of group counseling in a practical and applied manner. The emphasis throughout the book is the issue of group counseling in various school settings. Mahler's many years of practical experience in school settings provides excellent insight into groups in the school.

Harris, G. G. The group treatment of human problems. New York: Grune and Stratton, 1977. This text presents a thorough treatment of group approaches as they apply to a wide range of human problems. Numerous author insights provide for interesting and useful information.

Berg, R. C., & Landreth, G. L. Group counseling: Fundamental concepts procedures. Muncie, Ind.: Accelerated Development Press, 1979. This relatively new text discusses the basic issues, procedures, and concepts of group counseling. It offers some new and exciting ideas in addition to discussing some of the basic elements of the group counseling process.

Napier, R. W., & Gershenfeld, M. K. Groups: Theory and experience. Boston: Houghton-Mifflin, 1973. This text deals with the group experience in detail. Readers will find the specific attention devoted to leadership and group problem solving to be especially helpful.

Williamson, E. G., & Biggs, D. A. Student personnel work. New York: Wiley, 1975. This text, though written with the student personnel worker in mind, contains some interesting and useful information on group work in student personnel.

Hanfmann, E. Effective therapy for college students. San Francisco: Jossey-Bass, 1978. While this book deals primarily with therapeutic intervention for the college student, readers will find some useful information relevant to group counseling.

Vriend, J., & Dyer, W. Counseling effectively in groups. Englewood Cliffs, N.J.: Educational Technology Publications, 1973. Vriend and Dyer discuss the effective use of counseling in groups and present many innovative ideas and procedures. Their practical experience should benefit the reader.

REFERENCES

Aiken, J., & Johnston, J. Promoting career information-seeking behaviors in college students. Journal of Vocational Behavior, 1973, 3, 81-87.

Bates, M., & Johnson, C. D. Group leadership. Denver: Love Publishing, 1972.

Bower, S. A. Assertive training for women. In J. D. Krumboltz & C. Thoresen (Eds.), Counseling methods. New York: Holt, Rinehart & Winston, 1976.

Bradford, L. P., Gibb, J. R., & Benne, K. E. (Eds.). T-group theory and laboratory method: Innovation in re-education. New York: Wiley, 1964.

Brimline, C., & Klimek, R. Developmental education. Journal of College Student Personnel, 1977, 18(5), 403-406.

Bryan, A. Can there be a science of bibliotherapy? Library Journal, 1939, 64, 773-776.

Bush, J. The effects of fixed and random actor interaction in individual goal attainment in group counseling. Unpublished doctoral dissertation, Indiana State University, 1971. (Abstract)

Carey, R., Gelatt, H. B., Miller, G., & Varenhorst, B. Decisions and outcomes. New York: College Entrance Examination Board, 1973.

Cherichello, F. J., & Gillian, C. An alumni panel: A component for National Career Guidance Week at Essex Community College. Journal of College Student Personnel, 1980, 21(2), 170.

Cohn, B. (Ed.). Guidelines for future research on group counseling in the public school setting. Cooperative Research Project, Board of Cooperative Educational Services, Bedford Hills, New York, 1964.

Cohn, B., Combs, C., Gibian, E., & Sniffer, A. Group counseling: An orientation. Personnel and Guidance Journal, 1963, 42, 355-358.

Collins, J. A comparative guidance study. Unpublished doctoral dissertation, University of Southern California, 1964.

Conyne, R. K., Lamb, D. H., & Strand, K. H. Group experience in counseling centers: A national survey. Journal of College Student Personnel, 1975, 16, 196-200.

Corey, G., & Corey, M. S. Groups: Process and practice. Monterey, Calif.: Brooks/Cole, 1977.

Cramer, S. H., & Herr, E. L. Effecting an approachment between group guidance and group counseling in the schools. In J. C. Hansen, & S. H. Cramer (Eds.), Group guidance and counseling in the schools. New York: Appleton-Century-Crofts, 1971.

Crighton, J., & Jehu, D. Treatment of examination anxiety by systematic desensitization or psychotherapy in group. Behavior Research and Therapy, 1969, 7, 245-248.

Diedrich, R. C., & Dye, H. A. (Eds.). Group procedures: Purposes, processes, and outcomes. Boston: Houghton-Mifflin, 1972.

Dinkmeyer, D. C., & Muro, J. J. Group counseling and practice. Itasca, Ill.: Peacock, 1971.

Eddy, W., & Lubin, B. Laboratory training and encounter groups. Personnel and Guidance Journal, 1971, 49(8), 625-634.

Fellows, E. W. Happiness: A survey of research. Journal of Humanistic Psychology, 1966, 6, 17-30.

Fordyce, M. W. Happiness: Its daily variation and relation to values. Dissertation Abstracts International, 1972, 33, 1266B.

Fordyce, M. W. Development of a program to increase personal happiness. Journal of Counseling Psychology, 1977, 24(6), 511-521.

Forrer, S., Cooper, J. F., Epperley, J., & Inge, J. Career skills attainment: A programmed approach. Journal of College Student Personnel, 1977, 8(3), 242-243.

Garfield, S. L., & Bergin, A. E. Handbook of psychotherapy and behavior change (2nd ed.). New York: Wiley, 1978.

Gazda, G. M., Duncan, J., & Meadows, M. Group counseling and group procedures. Counselor education and group procedures. Counselor Education and Supervision, 1967, 6, 305-310.

Gilbreath, S. H. Appropriate and inappropriate group counseling with academic underachievement. Journal of Counseling Psychology, 1968, 15, 506-511.

Goldiamond, I. Self-control procedures in personal behavior problems. Psychological Reports, 1965, 17, 851-868.

Guber, S. K. Four approaches to freshman orientation. Improving College and University Teaching, 1970, 18, 57-60.

Hansen, J. C., Warner, R. W., & Smith, E. J. Group counseling (2nd ed.). Chicago: Rand McNally, 1980.

Hare, A. Handbook of small group research. New York: Free Press, 1962.

Hilkey, J. H. The effects of videotape pretraining and guided performance on the process and outcomes of group counseling.

Unpublished doctoral dissertation, Indiana State University, 1975. (Abstract)

Hinko, P. M. A national survey of counseling services. Junior College Journal, 1971, 42, 20-24.

Hoppock, R. Occupational information (4th ed.). New York: McGraw-Hill, 1976.

Hudesman, J., & Wiesner, E. The effect of counselor anxiety on the systematic desensitization of test anxious college students. Journal of College Student Personnel, 1979, 20(5), 415-417.

Jackson, B., & Van Zoost, B. Self-regulated teaching of others as a means of improving study habits. Journal of Counseling Psychology, 1974, 21(6), 489-493.

Jacobs, E., & Croake, J. Rational-emotive theory applied to groups. Journal of College Student Personnel, 1976, 17(2), 127-129.

Jacobson, E. Progressive relaxation. Chicago: University of Chicago Press, 1938.

Johnson, J. A. Group therapy: A practical approach. New York: McGraw-Hill, 1963.

Kopecek, R. J. Freshman orientation programs: A comparison. Journal of College Student Personnel, 1971, 12, 54-57.

Krumboltz, J. D. Behavioral goals for group counseling. Journal of Counseling Psychology, 1966, 13, 153-159.

Krumboltz, J. D., & Thoresen, C. E. The effect of behavioral counseling in group and individual settings on information-seeking behavior. Journal of Counseling Psychology, 1964, 11, 324-333.

Krumboltz, J. D., & Potter, B. Behavioral techniques for developing trust, cohesiveness, and goal accomplishment. Educational Technology, 1973, 13, 26-30.

Lamb, S. H. Student interchange with business and industry. Journal of College Student Personnel, 1980, 21(2), 176-177.

Lazarus, A. Behavioral therapy and beyond. New York: McGraw-Hill, 1971.

Liberman, R. A behavioral approach to group dynamics. Behavior Therapy, 1970, 1, 141-175.

Lieberman, M. A., Yalom, I., & Miles, M. Encounter groups: First facts. New York: Basic Books, 1973.

Litwak, L. Counseling services in community colleges. Journal of College Student Personnel, 1978, 19(4), 359-361.

Mahler, C. A. Group counseling in the schools. Boston: Houghton-Mifflin, 1969.

May, R. Man's search for himself. New York: New American Library, 1967.

Miller, T. M. A study of counseling services in two-year colleges. Journal of College Student Personnel, 1979, 20(1), 9-14.

Mitchell, K. R., & Ng, K. Effects of group counseling and behavioral therapy on the academic achievement of test anxious subjects. Journal of Counseling Psychology, 1972, 19, 491-497.

Morrill, W., Ivey, A., & Oetting, E. The college counseling center: A center for student development. In J. C. Heston, & W. B. Frick (Eds.), Counseling for the liberal arts campus. Yellow Springs, Ohio: Antioch Press, 1968.

Napier, R., & Gershenfeld, M. Groups: Theory and experience. Boston: Houghton-Mifflin, 1973.

Neely, M. A., & Kosier, M. Physically impaired students and the Vocational Exploration Group. Vocational Guidance Quarterly, 1977, 26(1), 37-44.

Ohlsen, M. H. Group counseling (2nd ed.). New York: Holt, Rinehart & Winston, 1977.

Osterhouse, R. A. Desensitization and study skills training as treatment for two types of test-anxious students. Journal of Counseling Psychology, 1972, 19, 301-307.

Osterhouse, R. A. Group systematic desensitization of test anxiety. In J. D. Krumboltz, & C. Thoresen (Eds.), Counseling Methods. New York: Holt, Rinehart & Winston, 1976.

Rich, I. A. Counseling the transfer student: Myths and realities. Journal of College Student Personnel, 1979, 20(2), 175-176.

Richard, C. S. Behavior modification of studying through study skills advice and self-control procedures. Journal of Counseling Psychology, 1975, 22, 431-436.

Richardson, F. C. Amxiety management training: A multimodel approach. In A. Lazarus (Ed.), Multimodal behavior therapy. New York: Springer, 1976.

Rimm, D. C., & Masters, J. C. Behavior theory (2nd ed.). New York: Academic Press, 1979.

Roessler, R., Cook, D., & Lillard, D. Effects of systematic group counseling on work adjustment clients. Journal of Counseling Psychology, 1977, 24(4), 313-317.

Shertzer, B., & Stone, S. C. Fundamentals of counseling (3rd ed.). Boston: Houghton-Mifflin, 1980.

Shostrum, E. L. Group therapy: Let the buyer beware. Readings in Psychology Today. Del Mar, California: CRM Books, 1970.

Schultz, J. H., & Luthe, W. Autogenic training. New York: Grune and Stratton, 1959.

Spielburger, C. D., & Weitz, H. Improving the academic per- formance of anxious college freshmen. Psychological Mono- graphs, 1964, 78, 1, (Whole No. 590).

Thompson, D., & Majunder, R. Work exposure: A new concept in vocational guidance for disadvantaged youth. Research Re- ports. Annual Convention of American Personnel and Guidance Association, 1972.

Varenhorst, B., & Gelatt, H. D. Group guidance decision-making. In J. C. Hansen, & S. H. Cramer (Eds.), Group guidance and counseling in the schools. New York: Appleton-Century- Crofts, 1971.

Vocational Exploration Group Approach. Tempe, Arizona: Studies for Urban Man, undated.

Waltz, G. R., & Benjamin, L. (Eds.). A comprehensive view of career development. Washington, D.C.: American Personnel and Guidance Association, 1974.

Washington, C. Ten steps to assertive action. Journal of College Student Personnel, 1980, 21(2), 175-176.

Watson, D. L., & Tharp, R. G. Self-directed behavior. Monterey, Calif.: Brooks/Cole, 1972.

West, J. H. Group bibliotherapy: A student development program activity. Journal of College Student Personnel, 1977, 18(3), 239-240.

Yalom, I. D. The theory and practice of group psychotherapy (2nd ed.). New York: Basic Books, 1975.

7

USING TESTS IN
COMMUNITY COLLEGE COUNSELING

> Any test is an invasion of privacy
> for the subject who does not wish
> to reveal himself.
> > Cronbach, 1970

The use of psychological tests has been widespread in the educational system, touching almost all students and at times greatly affecting their futures. The whole field of testing has, likewise, received considerable criticism over the use and abuse of tests. For a wide variety of reasons, tests have become a critical issue facing counselors over the past two decades.

While tests and their use have generated considerable controversy both philosophically and practically, counselors are, by and large, ill prepared in their training on the use of test and psychometric procedures. Counselors in the community college have to contend with extensive tests and appraised data. A thorough knowledge of tests, including their development, administration, and most importantly their interpretation, is essential to competent practice. This chapter will review the abuses of tests and discuss their responsible use. In addition, tests commonly used by the community college counselor will be described and some helpful suggestions on effective interpretation will be provided. The intention here is to help the counselor use tests in effective ways as a meaningful adjunct to the counseling process and not, as has been charged by those who are critical, as a substitute for effective counseling.

THE USES AND ABUSES OF TESTS

A test is nothing more than a systematic observation of some sampling of behavior, whether it be achievement in an academic course, occupational preferences, attitudes toward some issue, behaviors that seem to characterize the person, scholastic aptitude, mechanical ability, and so on. It should be remembered that any test, regardless of how well developed and validated it may be, is just measuring limited and superficial aspects of behavior. Counselors often forget this fact and treat test results as showing the true state of affairs. In doing so, they do a considerable injustice to their clients. One need only review the various test manuals and Buros's Mental Measurements Yearbook (1978) to determine the basic weaknesses in validity and reliability in all tests, and to verify the need for caution in test use. To maximize the somewhat limited validity that all tests possess, they should be used exactly for the purpose for which they were designed and only for those individuals for whom they were validated. This will help insure that the upper limits of the validity and reliability data are maximized.

Tests and testing procedures can serve five basic purposes in the counseling process: selection, classification, prediction, evaluation, and corroboration.

Selection

Tests are used by many institutions, training programs, and schools in the admissions process. The decisions on whom to accept and whom not to accept usually rest on resulting test scores. This was one of the earliest influences on the rapid development of testing in America; obviously great efficiency and economy could result if important decisions of selection could be made by the results of a single test score. While this pragmatic view has great significance to those making the decisions, it has a considerable negative influence on those subjected to the testing. Important life-changing decisions, reduced to a test performance score, create considerable anxiety in the test taker. All too often the test is seen as something that is the determiner of the future.

This is not, of course, the most valid use of tests. They should be just one part, not the only part, of the selection process. Kirkland (1971), in reviewing test-anxiety research, concluded that less capable students have greater test anxiety than more capable students; that the more familiar a person is with the type of test to be administered, the less test anxiety is present; and that highly anxious individuals do better than the less anxious on tests that require rote memory, and perform less well on tests requiring flexibility of thought.

Attempting to use tests to make selection decisions is a difficult task for all those concerned. The increased likelihood of high levels of anxiety, combined with the state of the art of test validity, will certainly increase the probability of errors of selection. Tests used for selection in the community college—for example, aptitude tests for various training programs—should be only one part of the selection process and students should be well informed as to the nature and purpose of the testing. Legislation requiring full disclosure on this use of tests is under consideration in Congress. Called the Truth-in-Testing Act, it would require the full disclosure of exactly how a test is used and selection decisions are made. If this legislation becomes law, it will have considerable impact on the testing process.

The community college counselor should not forget that decisions of selection have great and lasting impact on the client and should not be made hastily or capriciously. Decisions of this magnitude should involve tests as only one part of the selection process and, perhaps, not even the most important part.

Classification

Tests used for classification purposes attempt to decide to which group or assignment a person should belong—for example, a particular diagnostic category or a special curriculum. In a sense, this use of testing is an attempt to match a square peg with a square hold. At the community college level, the assignment of various individuals to specialized training programs or courses of study could involve tests used for classification purposes.

Prediction

Tests used for prediction have occupied a major role in the debate over test use. The basic idea behind the predictive power of a test is simple. If a test can be dhown to correlate well to some criterion or outcome—for example, success in college—then it can be used to predict the criterion for individuals. The greater the correlation between the two measures, the stronger the predictive power. Such is the basis for aptitude tests. The Scholastic Aptitude Test is designed to predict success in college; mechanical aptitude tests are designed to predict success in some mechanical endeavor. Tests used for predictive purposes must demonstrate good predictive validity—that is, they must correlate well to the criterion.

One final point needs to be made: prediction is based upon the ability of the test to predict for large groups, and for groups, on the average, many tests may have excellent predictive power. Counseling, however, usually deals with one individual, so averages on probability of accurate prediction are somewhat irrelevant. This is why only one or only a few measures to make a prediction will never be as good as several different measures. The chance of making an error of prediction when dealing with individual clients is much greater.

Evaluation

Certain tests are used to evaluate the effectiveness of certain programs, approaches, treatments, and so on. Often these tests are attempting to discern whether objectives for a program were met or whether the treatment given was successful. Tests of this nature may take the form of surveys, opinionnaires, or rating inventories. Tests used to evaluate should provide sufficient diagnostic information to help identify where additional work is needed; the evaluation should give information about what has improved and what has not. This type of information will aid in additional counseling efforts. For example, a reading test that has an evaluative purpose should tell how well the individual can read, perhaps as a function of participation in a given remedial reading program. It should also tell where additional work is needed. This is one of the more important functions of evaluative tests for counselors. All too often evaluative and diagnostic tests are used simply to select or classify individuals and little attention is given to the information that evaluates or describes the current state of the individual. It is this information that by itself is most helpful and useful to the counselor in future treatment planning.

Corroboration

Tests used for corroboration serve the purpose of additional validation for a client who wishes more information upon which to base a decision. This may seem an ineffective use for tests, but, in fact, it is probably the most important use of testing for counselors.

Tests should be used by counselors as an adjunct to counseling—a supplement to the counseling process. They may be quite useful in corroborating client concerns, ideas, interests, and the like, but should never be used as the sole determiner of these. For example, the client may self-report various vocational interests, and testing may be used to corroborate these and perhaps help identify some new areas for discussion. It is this corroborative, adjunctive use that should be the most prominent purpose of tests for community college counselors. It is this use that can help make it easier for the nonverbal client to begin talking about issues of importance.

CRITICISMS OF TESTS

Several relevant and debatable issues concerning tests have been argued by the proponents and critics of testing procedures over the past several decades. They include the following basic concerns.

Invasion of Privacy

Tests of personality, values, attitudes, and interests are certainly an intrusion of privacy, if not an invasion. If the client understands the nature of the test, voluntarily agrees to take it, and the counselor has a definite need to have the information, then no invasion of privacy has taken place. As Cronbach (1970) has stated, it is not invading privacy if the information is freely admitted and the client has a genuine need for the information obtained (p. 510). To insure that the client's rights of confidentiality and privacy are maintained, the code of ethics of the American Psychological Association states that the psychologist should make certain that the individual is fully aware of the purposes of the test and the ways in which the information may be used. Counselors need to be aware of the clients' rights to confidentiality and privacy whenever tests are being used.

Interpretation

Often test results are not provided to the test takers for fear that they may be misinterpreted or misunderstood. Shertzer and Linden (1979) have amply pointed out that test results circulate freely among counselors, teachers, and administrators, but all too often the examinees never learn what they reveal. Nothing can be more frustrating and counterproductive than to ask or require individuals to take tests, then not provide them with in-depth feedback about the results. The fear that feedback sessions will go poorly or be counterproductive is unfounded. If the client is appropriately prepared for the testing, then the interpretation will be productive. Not interpreting test results for the test taker is a valid criticism and simply not good counseling practice.

Creation of Anxiety and Interference
with the Counseling Process

As discussed earlier, test anxiety is a main concern of community college counselors. Tests do create anxiety and counseling
centers have developed useful treatment programs to deal with test
anxiety (see Chapters 5 and 6). Counselors who use tests in the
counseling process must be aware that the tests themselves may interfere with the counseling procedure—arouse anxiety and thus not
facilitate the helping process. Many counselors of various theoretical orientations feel that tests are of little or no value and that they
can only interfere with effective counseling. Some counselors feel
that whenever one starts to rely on tests and testing, one minimizes
the counseling.

Tests do have a tendency to assume too powerful a role in the
client's eyes, so that the counseling becomes an adjunct to the testing. It is the tests that really have the answer. This attitude, unfortunately, is difficult to change, because it is fostered by some
counselors who believe that the answers—or the "truth" about the
client—will be in the test data and not in what the client has said
during counseling. Also, it may not always be the best practice to
have important client constructs, such as attitudes, values, interests, traits, and the like, reduced to a quantity. These issues, for
most clients, need to be talked out and dealt with in the counselor-
client communication, not transmitted in a sheet full of numbers.
When any of these attitudes concerning tests is present, the counseling process will face interference.

Categorization and Labeling

This criticism, on its face, seems valid, since one purpose
of tests is to categorize and label. The problem, of course, is that
the labels, whether accurate or not, tend to stick with people. These
labels do bias individuals who have contact with the labeled students
(Rosenthal, 1973; Rosenthal & Jacobson, 1968). Critics charge that
these labels create expectations and that these expectations become
self-fulfilling prophecies, usually negative. Murphy (1973) has indicated that this is true because people believe that tests are the
truth, the whole truth, and the final permanent truth. Labels can be
helpful if they have, as most do, diagnostic value. The criticism,
of course, is that the labels have a degree of permanence that can
be more potentially damaging than not using the test in the first place.

Counselors can be too quick at times to use the label "someone with a problem," rather than defining the person as someone

with a given, specific problem. Certainly this is true for academic and scholastic test data and can be just as damaging for psychological test data.

Bias and Discrimination

Tests should be used only on subjects for whom they were developed and normed. As mentioned earlier in this chapter, no test has extremely high validity and this, coupled with the typical cultural bias that is generally found in standardized tests, means that caution should be used (Mercer, 1971).

It is always prudent to use a test only if it has been normed or developed for that group to which it is being given. Results of tests with little or no validity and norming data should be treated as suspect. There is evidence from research to indicate that much of the bias problem is not with the tests per se, but with their use and interpretation (Cleary, Humphreys, Kendricks, & Wesman, 1975; Fishman, et al., 1964). The whole bias issue, however, is still unresolved. No doubt many tests exist that are biased and do discriminate unfairly against certain minority groups and client subpopulations. The best way for the counselor to insure against this possible bias is to use tests in the exact manner for which they were developed.

The above criticisms have been discussed and debated for many years and, no doubt, the criticisms will continue. Counselors should be aware of these criticisms and insure that tests are utilized in a professional and competent manner.

EVALUATING TESTS FOR USE

Before any test is used by a counselor, it should be thoroughly evaluated to determine its appropriateness. Wise counselors will not only review the test information but will take the tests themselves, so that first-hand information concerning the test can be conveyed to the client. This will help rectify any unrealistic expectations or negative initial perceptions on the part of the client. Counselors should keep in mind that, just because a test is commercially published and has some statistical data to support it, does not insure its validity. No test should be used by a counselor unless it has been subjected to the individual counselor's review and unless the counselor has had first-hand experience taking it. That will provide the most useful evaluation data possible on which to base a decision as to whether a test is appropriate for use.

In reviewing a test, the counselor should pay close attention to several factors:

Cost. Cost includes the price of test material such as booklets, answer sheets, scoring services, and so forth.

Time. Time to administer the test is important. As a rule, clients will take longer to complete almost any test than the test publisher suggests. Also, enough time is needed to score the test. Can it be hand-scored? Must it be computer scored and if so how long will scoring take?

Population. What are the populations for which the test was designed? This should include the appropriate age ranges, types of subpopulations, and so on. Remember that the test should be used only for clients similar to those for whom it was developed.

Psychometric data. This includes the normative information. How are the scores reported—as standard scores, percentiles? On what types of samples were they normed against? There should be norms that represent the clients for whom the test will be used If a test has no normative data for a young adult or college level population, results with community college students may be suspect. If the clients are older returning students, then young adult norms would be somewhat meaningless and subject to misinterpretation. The reliability measures—that is, test consistency—should be provided, and there should be several reliability estimates. Normally, the type of reliability coefficient and the samples upon which it was calculated are the minimum requirement. By far the most important psychometric information concerns the validity of the test (Sax, 1980). Does the test do what it claims? Since a test can not be reliable if it is not valid, validity becomes the key issue. Examining the data that are present helps to determine the utility and accuracy of the test. Sufficient validity data should be presented— for example, what types, how validity was determined, and the nature of the samples employed in the validation studies.

Qualitative features. Anastasi (1976) suggests that certain qualitative features of test materials be evaluated for their practical significance. These include such things as the design of the test materials, ease of using, reading level of test materials, clarity of directions, face validity, instructions for scoring and interpretation. These considerations may become quite significant.

Independent reviews. In addition to reviewing potential tests using the criteria above, it is also prudent to obtain independent reviews of tests whenever possible. Several excellent references provide valuable resource information concerning tests. Many of these reference materials should be a permanent part of the counseling service library. As mentioned previously, the single most important resource book on test reviews is the series <u>Mental Measurement Yearbooks</u>, edited by Buros. The yearbook, revised at several-year intervals, is in its eighth edition (1978), and reviews practically all commercially available psychological and educational tests. The reviews for each test are thorough, objective, and quite informative. Counselors using tests of any type should be familiar with this resource. Two additional resource books edited by Buros are also helpful to the community college counselor. These are <u>Tests in Print II</u> (1974) and <u>Personality Tests and Reviews II</u> (1975). <u>Tests in Print</u> is a comprehensive bibliography of all published tests available and serves as a classification index to the editions of the <u>Mental Measurements Yearbook</u>. <u>Personality Tests and Reviews</u> provides reviews of this type of test. Both references contain information regarding tests that are not included in the <u>Yearbook</u>. Additional test reviews can be found in the research periodicals for psychology and counseling. Tests that are unpublished or are research instruments can be found in <u>A Sourcebook for Mental Health Measures</u> (Comrey, Backer, & Glaser, 1973). This book contains over 1,000 abstracts on tests, questionnaires, rating scales, and other testing and assessment instruments. Similarly, <u>Measures for Psychological Assessment</u> (Chun, Cobb, & French, 1975) contains almost 3,000 assessment measures with an annotated bibliography of the research in which each measure was used.

These resource books can be a great asset in providing information on the appropriateness of a given test or assessment instrument. The counselor who wishes to use testing procedures wisely needs to consider the six steps in test evaluation before using any materials with clients.

TESTS FOR VOCATIONAL COUNSELING

Several tests are widely used by community college counselors for vocational counseling. If testing is to be used for vocational or career counseling it should include a variety of assessment measures, including a vocational interest survey, such as the Strong-Campbell Interest Inventory or the Kuder Occupational Interest Survey; a values inventory such as the Work Values Inventory; and a personality test such as the Edwards Personal Preference Inventory or the Sixteen Personality Factor Questionnaire. Considerable research has shown (for example, Hansen & Johansson, 1974; Scott & Day, 1972) that substantial interrelationships exist between personality and attitudinal measures and vocational interests. These psychological relationships can provide useful discussion material to assist individuals in developing self-awareness and career direction.

Strong-Campbell Interest Inventory (SC II)

The SC II developed in 1974 is, perhaps, the most widely used and researched vocational interest inventory. The inventory consists of 325 items in which the respondent is asked to indicate preferences for various occupations, school subjects, activities, recreation, types of people, and items dealing with things versus dealing with people. Finally, several self-descriptive statements are provided for evaluation. Because of the elaborate scoring patterns, the SC II must be computer-scored, which does require some additional expense and time. The greatest advantage of the SC II is that the scales are based upon the theoretical framework of John Holland (1973) on the classification of interests. The interpretation information on the SC II is well presented to the client and quite useful to the career-development process.

Minnesota Vocational Preference Inventory

The Minnesota Vocational Preference Inventory is somewhat similar to the SC II, except that, unlike the SC II, it emphasizes various skilled and semiskilled occupations. This can be quite useful to community colleges where a strong technical curriculum exists. The inventory provides 21 occupational scales and 9 general area scales such as mechanics, electronics, and so on. Many counselors will find this scale more advantageous than the SC II for clients more interested in trades and technical careers than traditional college-oriented careers.

Kuder Occupational Interest Survey

The Kuder Occupational Interest Survey (KOIS) is another widely used survey of vocational interests. The KOIS contains 77 occupational and 29 college-major scales. The occupations cover a wide range from semiskilled to highly professional levels. Clients' scores on each of the scales are expressed as a correlation between their interest patterns and those in the given group. Because of the elaborate scoring patterns, the KOIS must also be computer-scored.

The use of interest inventories in the vocational counseling process can assist clients in exploration of areas of which they may not be aware. Furthermore, it can stimulate and corroborate many of the career ideas a client may possess. Also useful in this career process is the examination and discussion of work values.

The Work Values Inventory

The Work Values Inventory, developed by Donald Super, is designed for vocational counseling of high school and college-age students. Respondents are asked to rate 45 work values on a five-point scale for their importance as a source of satisfaction from the work environment. Fifteen scores—for example, creativity, security, prestige, and so forth—are generated from the scale. These work values can play a prominent role in the development and exploration of career direction for the community college student. Discussing the work values scores together with vocational interest scores can provide a more realistic picture of the client. Even more useful to expanding the clarity of the picture is the use of a personality measure in the test battery. Several tests, such as the Sixteen Personality Factor Questionnaire or the Edwards Personal Preference Survey are quite useful in the vocational counseling process.

The Sixteen Personality Factor Questionnaire

The Sixteen Personality Factor Questionnaire (16PF), developed by Cattell and his associates (Cattell, Eber, & Tatsuoka, 1970), is a self-report inventory that yields 16 scores for such traits as outgoing versus reserved, venturesome versus shy, suspicious versus trusting, and the like. Basically the 16PF, according to Cattell, represents the identification of primary personality traits. These personality traits can be interpreted in conjunction with the interest and values test data to help identify a more complete picture of the individual.

The Edwards Personal Preference Inventory

The Edwards Personal Preference Inventory (EPPS) is a self-report personality test that assesses 15 needs drawn from the theoretical work on human needs of Henry Murray. Scores for needs include, for example, achievement, deference, order, exhibition, autonomy, and affiliation. The EPPS is an ipsative scale—that is, scores for each need are expressed in relation to the strength of other needs, rather than in an absolute sense. This is similar to an individual rank-ordering of scores so that they have direct meaning to the client, but a comparison between two clients' sets of scores would lack any real meaning.

The use of a needs test can be quite relevant to the vocational counseling practice, since many theories of vocational choice (for example, Anne Roe, Robert Hoppock, Donald Super) place a considerable emphasis on the individual's needs.

Tests for Personal/Social Counseling

A wide variety of tests used in personal/social counseling are available. They include personality tests such as those discussed above, as well as self-concept inventories, projective tests, and rating scales for a variety of personal/social problems. A discussion of the variety of tests available in this area of counseling is beyond the scope of this chapter. Several excellent texts are available, however, that provide such detailed discussions. Two are described below.

Anastasi, A. Psychological testing (4th ed.). New York: Macmillan, 1976. This text is probably the most widely used, thorough, authoritative source on the subject of psychological testing. In addition to several excellent chapters on the actual tests available, there are several very good chapters on test psychometrics. This book in its fourth edition is considered the classic in the field of testing.

Goldman, L. Using tests in counseling (2nd ed.). Pacific Palisades, Calif.: Goodyear Publishing, 1971. This textbook deals directly with tests and testing as they apply to the counseling process. Goldman's book is written on a very understandable level and deals with many texts and procedures that are relevant to the counselor. Excellent statistical and psychometric explanations are presented in an easy-to-understand approach.

SUGGESTIONS FOR TEST INTERPRETATION

The following are some suggestions for test interpretation that should be considered whenever tests or test data are to be used in the counseling process.

Know the Test Thoroughly

Anytime counselors are considering the use of a test, they should have a thorough knowledge of its uses and limitations. Review the test, as discussed earlier, to insure that the test is, indeed, valid and appropriate for use. The counselor should be able to answer most client questions concerning the test, such as those listed below:

- Where do the scores come from?
- How are scores calculated?
- What do scores mean?
- Is this score high or above average?
- How long will the test take?
- What will the results be like?
- What kind of questions will be asked?
- What kind of information will the test provide?

Being unsure of the answers to any of these questions will weaken the counselor's credibility, which could have counterproductive effects on the entire counseling process. If the counselor is not sure about the basics of the test, then it should not be used. The test manual and the test reviews should help familiarize the counselor with the test, but it should be kept in mind, and it will become obvious as various test manuals are reviewed, that the manual and the independent test reviews are often at variance. Remember, the manuals are written by the test developers and they have a tendency to view the test in a more favorable light than more objective reviewers. Review all the evidence, then make your decisions as to whether to use the test or not.

Take the Test

The single best way to become familiar with a test is to take it. This will greatly facilitate an awareness of the practical considerations for a given test that may develop. Then, when initially discussing or suggesting a given test for a client, the counselor will be in a much better position to explain the test and answer any questions the client may have. This should help assuage any erroneous preconceived expectation or anxiety a client may have. It is recommended that counselors themselves take all tests they are likely to be using in their counseling of students.

Do Not Go Beyond the Test Data

When interpreting the results of tests, do not go beyond the results with inferences about the meaning of the scores. Let the scores stand for themselves. The client should be encouraged to extract the test's meaning. If inferences about the test scores are to be made, they should be made by the client. Actually, the client should be encouraged to see the relevance and meaning of the test scores in the context of his or her counseling problems. Remember, it is usually neither good counseling practice nor a valid use of test data to infuse too much meaning into any single test. This is especially important when the test data are incongruent or conflict with what the client's perception is concerning the trait or variable being assessed.

Prepare Clients to Take Tests

The best results with test interpretation are usually obtained when the client has received good preparation on the test. This is not coaching, but information on what to expect, what the test is like, the limitations and weaknesses of the test, and so on. This type of preparation will guard against unrealistic expectations, mystical answers to client decisions, and any negative perceptions that may exist.

If a client does have considerable negative perceptions about a given test, or tests in general, that cannot be resolved during discussions, then testing ought not to be used, as the results will probably be biased. Furthermore, even if the results are accurate, the client's bias may prevent the acceptance of the test results in a useful way.

If testing is suggested by the client, the reasons for wanting tests should be discussed to correct any misconceptions that may exist and to keep the role of testing in its proper perspective—that is, as an adjunct to the counseling process. Many clients, for example, will come to the counseling center to request a vocational test or an intelligence test because they have a friend who has just taken one or because they are trying to decide on an academic major. When this is the case, the counselor should discuss the role of counseling in solving the problem and how testing might help this process. Clients will receive the maximum benefit from test information if they have been adequately prepared on what to expect and what is expected of them.

Use Test Results to Stimulate Discussion

The test results should be presented to the client in such a way as to stimulate discussion of the problem. They should not be merely summarized in a manner that overwhelms the client with numbers. They should be given to the client in small chunks or pieces with comments or reactions solicited by the counselor. For example:

Counselor: Well, this shows you to be most interested in occupations that have some level of social interaction. Do you enjoy dealing with people?

Client: Yes, I think I prefer to work with people. You know, to be of some type of help.

Counselor: Well, judging from how you compare with other individuals in social-oriented occupations, which do you feel would be of interest to pursue more information?

or

Counselor: You seem to be in agreement with the test concerning the areas you do not like, but I couldn't help notice your reaction to the first information we discussed. You seem surprised. . . .

Client: Yeah, well, it isn't what I expected. Actually, I have never liked scientific kinds of things.

Counselor: Well what do you suppose is accounting for this?

In both these cases, the counselor is asking the client to react to the test data, so that the test interpretation will not be a situation in which the counselor is actively giving out scores and the client is passively receiving them. The scores should stimulate and facilitate the discussion of the main issue of concern. If the counselor can enlist the support of the client in working together to see where and how the test information fits into the overall counseling process, the information will serve its maximum purpose. Actually, this is the primary use of test scores in the counseling process.

When doing the test interpretation, make sure that clients have adequate time to consider the meaning of the results. Do not rush through the test results; schedule adequate time to discuss the implications fully. If the test results are at variance with the client's own perceptions, discuss this. Do not accept the fact that the test is correct and it is the client who is wrong. Also, counselors should not put themselves in the position of having to justify or defend the tests to the client. The tests are what they are, and sometimes they are not very accurate. If the client is well prepared on the limitations of a given test, this issue can be dealt with as a counseling issue. Counselors who overly defend tests and testing weaken their credibility with their clients.

In addition to these suggestions, Goldman (1971) and Lister and McKenzie (1966) have commented on other useful test interpretation guidelines, including the following:

Relate the results to information clients have previously discussed, questions they have asked, or choices that have been made. This will help facilitate meaning for the results.

Help clients discuss evidence of strengths and limitations in their backgrounds and abilities. This is particularly important when ability or intelligence are part of the test discussion and the results are in conflict with how clients see themselves. Overachieving, highly motivated clients can be quite shocked to discover that their aptitude level is not as high as their achievement would indicate. Counselors need to be quite sensitive to the impact this type of awareness may have on the self-concept of the client. Any information that is in conflict with the client's perceptions may have considerable impact on the self-concept.

Discuss the test results in language the client can understand. Do not get bogged down in unintelligible statistical concepts and highly technical psychological jargon. Explain what the results mean and how they were derived. This will help demystify the testing process and greatly facilitate client understanding.

Be sure to give reasonable emphasis to any physical or environmental factors that may have influenced the test scores. How individuals feel when they take tests, as well as the situational factors present, will exert influence on the test scores. This is true not only with ability and achievement tests but also with personality and attitude tests. If the client feels that such factors were important, then perhaps the results should not be considered valid.

Finally, be sure to reemphasize that test scores are only one part of the overall evaluation or assessment process and only one small part of the overall counseling process.

CONCLUSION

This chapter has presented some of the important issues and considerations of tests and testing procedures. Tests can provide useful adjunctive service to the counseling process and counselors using tests and test data as part of their counseling need to be quite familiar and skilled in the test use. Much of the controversy over the use of testing has developed because the individuals who administer and interpret tests have misused, misapplied, or misinterpreted them. Counselors administering tests should do so only when they have acquired the necessary skills and competencies for test use and interpretation.

REFERENCES

American Psychological Association. Standards for education and psychological tests. Washington, D.C.: American Psychological Association, 1974.

Anastasi, A. Psychological testing (4th ed.). New York: Macmillan, 1976.

Buros, O. K. (Ed.). Tests in print II. Highland Park, N.J.: Gryphon Press, 1974.

Buros, O. K. (Ed.). Personality tests and reviews II. Highland Park, N.J.: Gryphon Press, 1975.

Buros, O. K. (Ed.). The eighth mental measurements yearbook. Highland Park, N.J.: Gryphon Press, 1978.

Cattell, R. B., Eber, H. W., & Tatsuoka, M. Handbook for the 16 PF. Champaign, Ill.: Institute for Personality and Ability Testing, 1970.

Chun, K., Cobb, S., & French, J. Measures for psychological assessment. Ann Arbor, Mich.: Institute for Social Research, 1975.

Cleary, T. A., Humphreys, L. G., Kendrick, S. A., & Wesman, A. Educational uses of tests with disadvantaged students. American Psychologist, 1975, 30, 15-41.

Comrey, A. L., Backer, T., & Glaser, E. M. A source book for mental health measures. Los Angeles: Human Interaction Research Institute, 1973.

Cronbach, L. J. Essentials of psychological testing (3rd ed.). New York: Harper and Row, 1970.

Fishman, J., Deutsch, M., Rogan, L., North, R., & Whiteman, M. Guidelines for testing minority students. Journal of Social Issues, 1964, 20(2), 137.

Goldman, L. Using tests in counseling (2nd ed.). Pacific Palisades, Calif.: Goodyear Publishing, 1971.

Hansen, J., & Johansson, C. Strong vocational interest blank and dogmatism. Journal of Counseling Psychology, 1974, 21, 196-201.

Holland, J. L. Making vocational choices: A theory of careers. Englewood Cliffs, N.J.: Prentice-Hall, 1973.

Kirkland, M. C. The effects of tests on students and schools. Review of Educational Research, 1971, 41(4), 303-350.

Lister, J. L., & McKenzie, D. A framework for the improvement of test interpretation in counseling. Personnel and Guidance Journal, 1966, 45, 61-66.

Mercer, J. Institutionalized Anglocentricism. In P. Orleans & W. Russell (Eds.), Race, change and urban schools. Urban Affairs Annual Review, Vol. 5. Los Angeles: Sage Publications, 1971.

Murphy, L. B. The stranglehold of norms on the individual child. Childhood Education, 1973, 49, 343-347.

Rosenthal, R. The pygmalion effect lives. Psychology Today, 1973, 7(4), 56-59.

Rosenthal, R., & Jacobsen, L. Pygmalion in the classroom. New York: Holt, Rinehart and Winston, 1968.

Sax, G. Principles of educational and psychological measurement (2nd ed.). Belmont, Calif.: Wadsworth, 1980.

Scott, W. E., & Day, G. Personality dimensions and vocational interests among graduate business students. Journal of Counseling Psychology, 1972, 19, 30-36.

Shertzer, B., & Linden, J. D. Fundamentals of individual appraisal. Boston: Houghton-Mifflin, 1979.

8

OUTREACH PROGRAMS

> The college counseling center is a paradoxical posi-
> tion—the greater its investment in the counseling of
> individuals, the less general impact it has on the
> solution of student problems.
>
> Warnath, 1972

As discussed in Chapter 2, the philosophical model a counseling center adopts will guide the services it provides. Too often the
choice has been a remedial or medical model, reflecting an attitude
of waiting patiently and enthusiastically for students to bring their
problems to the counselor for resolution. As long as there was a
steady flow of students seeking help, these models gave the appearance of being viable. The overwhelming portion of the counselor's time was thus spent in crisis intervention, and although
such a service is of vital importance, it effectively prevented the
counseling staff from engaging in proactive, preventive, and developmental activities. Gradually, more and more counselors began to see the shortcomings in this practice and sought to find
effective means for minimizing the almost inevitable crises common
to a large majority of the student population. It became apparent
that it is more economical to teach a group of students coping
skills than it is to help each one individually in overcoming a crisis
situation.

As a result of searching for a better way, prevention seemed
to be the obvious route to follow. Counselors soon found that to
help students prevent or cope with crises required a good deal of
personal and psychological education. It was evident that many of
the problems encountered by students were common to most students in that particular age group or life situation, and were problems only because the students lacked the necessary coping skills.

Researchers have long been interested in patterns of growth and development of children and adolescents, but the focus on the young adult has been a recent trend, reflecting the changing emphasis of student personnel work. The writings of several authors have contributed greatly to knowledge of the developmental needs (Chickering, 1969), the educational preparation (Cross, 1971), and the personality dimensions (Koos, 1970) of college students. An awareness of the needs, values, and aspirations that community college students hold will help counselors anticipate how they are likely to react to the environmental presses that confront them. As a result, it will be possible to develop programs and strategies to intervene before the crises have a chance to take effect. Because students are unlikely to be aware of developmental crises and develop effective coping mechanisms, counselors have a moral obligation to identify such crises beforehand and to take the steps necessary to help students prevent the avoidable and cope with the inevitable. This makes sense not only from an ethical standpoint but from an economical one, as well.

This chapter will discuss the meaning of outreach, some target areas, and suggestions for implementing a number of programs. The reader is encouraged to expand and modify the ideas presented here to fit individual needs in this area. In addition, it is hoped that counselors' creative potential in designing and developing even more programs in this needed area will be stimulated. The ideas set out in this chapter are the result of creating, adapting, or borrowing from what is known of the state of the art. The reader is invited to use these ideas directly or as a source of brainstorming. Do not be convinced that something will not work until there is proof. Some of the authors' zaniest ideas have given the best results. Take a risk and let the results be the judge.

DEFINING OUTREACH

Outreach can mean many different things to many people, so before proceeding it is important to discuss what outreach activities are. In its simplest sense, outreach is defined as those activities initiated by the counselor that are aimed at providing preventive and developmental services traditionally provided by counselors to students on a request basis—usually through individual contacts. According to Drum and Figler (1976) outreach consists of all those efforts on the part of the counselor to diversify the counseling mission by offering multiple modes of intervention as well as one-to-one direct service, thus providing widespread benefits to the majority of students.

Greater emphasis is presently being placed on the efficiency with which time, energy, and money are being spent in relation to student benefit. Obviously, the direct-service model cannot meet the efficiency levels demanded by tightening budget restrictions, with the present, and most likely continuing, student/counselor ratios under which counselors function.

An additional rationale for initiating outreach programs, aside from budget concerns, is that a far larger number of students can be served with no additional effort, save planning. Students can be provided with the type of information and coping skills required to take charge of their lives, set goals, and take action, thereby becoming more independent and self-directed. The ultimate goal is that students will be better prepared to anticipate, prevent, or minimize sources of conflict in their lives.

Such a developmental and preventive approach is clearly in the best interests of the students, counselors, faculty, and administrators. A well-planned and effective outreach program will have the added benefit of making the counseling function visible and viable. This is not to be taken lightly, since student personnel services are usually the first to feel the budget crunch.

In essence, outreach programs can be seen as restructuring the major role of the counselor from that of problem solver to that of resource person. No longer can the counseling service afford as its primary function the luxury of reactive intervention for a limited number of students. Counselors are at a point where they must take the initiative for student contact. Some proven methods for doing so will be discussed later in this chapter. Before engaging in a variety of outreach programs, however, it is necessary to have a functional counseling model to guide counseling activities, lest they be caught in what is faddish or gimmicky. A model that has been found to meet this need follows.

AN OUTREACH MODEL

While it is the rare community college counseling service that follows the clinical/medical model, many can be classified as favoring the direct-service model. This model has worked because there have always been students at the counselor's door with one crisis or another. As long as counselors were busy and could document their activities, the illusions of viability and accountability were present. This is not to say that those students have not been helped, but rather that in doing so the great majority of the student population has been overlooked. Those who sought out the counselor have been those who hurt too much or those who had no where else to turn, and there is no doubt that many times more students have sought help outside the counselor's office than inside it. Counselors can no longer assume that they are doing their jobs on the basis of providing crisis intervention services for 5 to 10 percent of the student body.

The recent trend in the philosophical orientation of counseling centers, away from the direct-service model to one of human development, growth, and prevention, has come about through the influence of several factors, not the least of which are economic considerations. The cost/benefit ratio of counseling services has come under close scrutiny by those in control of the budget. Many people within the profession, as well as outside it, have come to realize that remediation is not a cost effective approach, either economically, or more importantly, from a student benefit standpoint.

American college students are, perhaps, the single most widely studied group in the world. Enough is known about their interests, needs, motivations, abilities, personality, and so on to anticipate and prevent a vast majority of the developmental crises, and this information can be utilized to enhance preventive efforts. Several factors influence developmental crises. First is the passage of time between recognition of an unfulfilled need and the resolution of that need. Second is the presence or absence of useful and effective information on which to base meaningful life decisions (Drum & Figler, 1976). It is the task of the developmental outreach program to help students anticipate areas of personal concern and initiate appropriate intervention strategies before the fact. This is not to say that crisis intervention will be rendered obsolete; on the contrary, effective reactive programs must be maintained as an adjunct for those students who are not able gracefully to master their psychological, vocational, or academic growing pains.

Before embarking on a program of developmental outreach, counselors must have a model to guide their efforts. As Morrill and Hurst (1971) have put it, the fact that programs are new and exciting is not a sufficient criterion to justify their use. The counselor must ensure that it is the students' needs, not those of the counselor, that are being met through these programs. Among other things, a well-thought-out model is required to structure the counselor's action. Perhaps the most comprehensive model to date has been developed by Drum and Figler (1976). Their model has been designed in general terms, so that it is applicable to and adaptable by any educational institution. In this model there are ten components categorized into four major sections, briefly outlined below:

Providing additional sources of help
   Identifying people with helping potential
   Providing counselor training for helpers
   Utilizing community resources
Identifying sources of students' problems
   Determining problem areas
   Dealing with environmental factors
Providing self-help programs
   Encouraging self-direction
   Providing programs for self-direction
Providing for evaluation
   Using developmental testing
   Examining the counselor as a unit of research
   Assessing counseling programs

     The remainder of this chapter will provide the reader with descriptions of successful programs in operation at various community colleges, and some ideas for innovation and implementation of new programs. The topics in this chapter are not designed to be exhaustive, but rather to be representative of what is and what can be for the progressive student development program. The topics to be covered herein include orientation, environmental management, consulting services, going where the students are, information dissemination, testing for nonstudents, community service programs, and ideas for minicourses on student development topics.

ORIENTATION

     The design of programs to familiarize new students with their college environment is not a new concept in higher education; however, the way in which it is conducted at the community college is, by necessity, different from that of the residential, four-year colleges and universities. It is different from several standpoints, the most obvious of which is that the community college student is a commuter and has a limited amount of time to spend on campus prior to enrolling. Even though a majority of these students live in close proximity to the community college, it is surprising to learn how many are unaware of even the most basic features of the college and its offerings.

     Many of these students, unlike their counterparts at the four-year colleges, are the first members of their families to enroll in any form of higher education. The challenge is clear; these students need much more basic information and must get it in a shorter period of time. This matter is further complicated by the fact that the open-door admissions policy allows for the acceptance of walk-ons—that is, those students who make application for admission on the first day of classes, and are accepted, registered, and enrolled on the spot. This number of students can be quite substantial, as any veteran community college counselor can attest. When administrators and counselors do not know who is coming and when they will arrive, a real strain is put on the counseling staff and other student personnel workers who are responsible for acquainting the new students with community college life.

From a developmental point of view the orientation program, as one of the first contacts between counselors and new students, provides the counseling staff with an opportunity to educate students to the known pitfalls of academic failure, to make initial assessments of their education-related needs, to inform them of the various help providers on campus, and to relieve initial anxieties that may be present.

One of the authors explains to his orientation groups that one of the main purposes of such an experience is to prevent students from asking the rhetorical question, "Well, why didn't someone tell me sooner?" It would be naive, however, to assume that all students will assimilate everything they are told during their orientation program. Therefore, it is essential that counselors make a favorable impression upon the new student to such an extent that each student perceives the counselor as the person to seek out for information. For this reason the counselor must appear competent, concerned, and accessible, if the outreach efforts of the orientation presentation are going to be effective.

Orientation programs generally take one of two forms in the community college: the day-long, preenrollment session, or the once-weekly, hour-long, credit course lasting the duration of the term. Both have their relative merits for the groups they are designed to serve and both have their shortcomings. With the large part-time enrollment found in most community colleges, a full day away from work or family is not really feasible for many. For those who do participate in a day-long program, overexposure and the law of diminishing returns may effect retention of information.

Regardless of how the program is presented, several important ingredients must be present:

Key members of the administration and staff should be introduced with emphasis on who the counselors are.
A guided tour of the campus should be provided, indicating the academic as well as the support services of the college.

Basic rules and regulations, rights, and responsibilities must be
reviewed.

Registration and schedule-change procedures must be explained to
ensure that students enroll in all and only the classes they need.
Community college students are notorious for changing class
schedules, and unless the proper procedures are followed, a
failing grade may be issued for a class never attended.

Any other information peculiar to the institution, pertaining to
academic survival, must be provided.

It is always advantageous to supplement the orientation presentation with written material for students to peruse later.
Typically, students are given copies of the college catalog and the
student handbook. These two documents usually contain most, if
not all, the information students need. It might be wise to pick
key pieces of information from the various resources and summarize them on one or two sheets of paper, to serve as an easy
guide for solving the problems of the new freshman. Such essentials as a campus map and a list of whom to see when certain
questions arise should be included.

The once-weekly class version of orientation allows the
counselor and student to become familiar with one another, to solve
problems as they arise, or to forestall those identified early. The
student being oriented in this way needs as much survival information, as early as possible, as those receiving the day-long, preenrollment session, but has less of the counselor's time to receive
it. Therefore, the need for clear and concise written material
becomes foremost. Homework assignments, as such, must supplement any in-class activity, if the program is to be effective.

In cases where course credit is given for the orientation
class, grades must be assigned. This may be a source of contention for many counselors and is often resolved on the basis of
attendance. An alternative method that relieves the counselor from
the grading dilemma and serves the developmental needs of students
involves the idea of contract grading. This assigns the responsibility to the students for determining their grades and selecting
those projects that meet real student need.

Projects may include assessing personal and vocational
preferences, occupational evaluations through the career center,
job interviews, evaluation of and/or visits to transfer colleges,
surveying study habits and improving them, outside readings, or
observing and reacting to various multimedia programs on personal growth (often found in the learning lab). Students may design projects of their own in cooperation with the counselor, when
those available do not meet their needs. The counselor is encour-

aged to brainstorm, design, revise, and update projects on a regular basis to insure that student needs are being met.

A third alternative to the traditional orientation format is that of independent study. Initially, such a concept might appear inappropriate; however, it has been quite effective on a limited basis in a number of community colleges in Virginia. Many students often cannot schedule the orientation class due to work/school/family commitments, but nevertheless can and do benefit from receiving such information. Other students take courses off campus and never see the community college whose rules and regulations govern their academic experience.

A well-conceived, self-instructional manual will serve the purpose of getting needed information to the new student. To make such a program work, the orientation student must meet with the counselor during the first week of school to review the requirements and to schedule subsequent meetings. The contract method of grading described above can be very useful here as well. The table of contents from one manual is shown in Figure 8.1.

Perhaps one of the most important aspects of any orientation program is that the counselor is the initial contact between the community college and the new student. While first impressions are not always valid, they are usually lasting and, therefore, it cannot be overemphasized that the counseling staff should demonstrate that they are ready, able, and willing to assist students with their concerns in a professional, confidential, and nonjudgmental fashion. The extent to which this is accomplished will determine the nature and extent of future contact initiated by students.

GOING WHERE THE STUDENTS ARE

The number of students who voluntarily seek the counselor when needs arise generally ranges between 5 and 15 percent of the student enrollment, with these figures being considerably lower for part-time and night students. The reasons for this small involvement with the counseling staff vary from a lack of awareness that such people as counselors exist to a matter of inconvenience or outright avoidance.

Community college students seem prone to ask help from whoever is available at the time of the concern. Often this is a fellow student or the classroom instructor, who may or may not have the time, expertise, energy, and inclination to help. Given such a situation, it is difficult to justify the counselor's role when fewer than 20 percent of the student population have contact with the counseling staff.

FIGURE 8.1

Table of Contents

The authors believe that outreach activities can increase and improve the delivery of direct service as well as a host of preventive and developmental programs. In an attempt to reach the reluctant or unaware student, the counselor should, in the words of Pappas and Smith (1976) "pick it up and move it out." Counselors are urged to go where students congregate—the student lounge, the learning lab, patio areas, the gym and sports fields, club meetings, student activities. Wherever students are likely to gather is where the counselor should be on a regular basis. Let it be known that the counselor will be available on an informal basis to talk with whomever about whatever.

Since the student lounge is where a majority of students spend time between classes, this would be a prime area of the counselor's concern. Members of the staff could take turns manning a counselor's table or just roving and rapping, as suits the individual style of the counselor and the response of students. This will put counselors in the mainstream of student life, making them visible, accessible, and concerned.

For the counselor concerned with moving in closer to the academic aspects of the students' lives, serving as liaison to a particular academic division is suggested. By this is meant maintaining full ties with the counseling service, while spending time in division faculty meetings, keeping office hours within the division, consulting with the faculty, and being available to students in their academic setting.

As a note of caution, O'Banion (1971) warns of the dangers of having counselors assigned and reporting to division chairmen, but fully endorses the liaison function. Under ideal circumstances, counselors should be assigned to divisions on the basis of having either an academic or work background consistent with the type of division. This is likely to facilitate acceptance of the counselor by the faculty. In such cases the counselor is also able to give first-hand educational and/or vocational advice to students in this division. If such a match-up is possible, fine, but it is not a prerequisite to building and maintaining a viable relationship between counseling and the various divisions.

CONSULTING WITH FACULTY

The consulting function as a form of outreach can be one of the most important roles the counselor can perform in an attempt to reach a majority of the students. The faculty has more student contact than any other group on campus, a fact that should make most counselors take note of the potential impact the classroom instructor has. By seeking and obtaining the cooperation of the faculty, the counselor has the opportunity of influencing a far greater number of students than through any other procedure. The counselor may initiate contact with the faculty by explaining the functions of the counseling staff and encouraging them to refer students who appear likely to benefit from these services. Once a relationship is built and faculty members see the counseling staff as a group with something to offer classroom instructors, then cooperative efforts to enhance the total educational experience of students may begin.

Faculty members in the community college are trained as academicians, specialists in their particular areas, who may not have an understanding and appreciation of the community college student. More and more graduate schools are including special programs for community college instructors, but a great majority of those currently teaching in the community college have not received any coursework or instruction on the unique students they teach. Counselors, more so than anyone else on the staff, have the training and direct experience with the needs of these students to help the faculty and the administration to become more sensitive to those needs. An awareness of needs, learning styles, motivation, and so on can have an important impact on classroom instruction and eventual student satisfaction.

Because all segments of higher education face budget and economic concerns, the consulting function can provide a very strong basis of support for the continued existence of the counseling program. Kopplin and Rice (1975) maintain that the long-term advocacy of the faculty will have more impact than the testimonials of students helped through individual counseling sessions.

Counselors have long been involved in various sorts of outreach activities, but according to Pyron (1974) the focus has been primarily on extracurricular activities with a clear lack of involvement in academic affairs. In order to correct this situation he recommends that counselors aid the administrative decision-making process by collecting student data on a number of variables. Policies that affect students must consider their needs, and it is the counselor who is in an ideal situation to convey knowledge of those needs to policy makers. Pyron also suggests that student development factors can influence curriculum development, instructional practices, scheduling, and so on. He warns, however, that the faculty may become suspicious of counselors interfering in their domain. Therefore, he recommends that counselors be knowledgeable about teaching methods, learning theory, and curriculum development before venturing into this aspect of consulting.

Pyron's advice is well taken, for more harm than good can be done if the faculty views counseling as overstepping its bounds. A great deal is to be accomplished, however, by a well-planned, cooperative effort. DeOrdio (1974) summarizes some of the benefits, suggesting that effective consultation will result in a reduction of the resistance to innovation, an increase of acceptance of feedback or suggestions for improving instruction, an increase in morale, the greater facilitation of teacher/student interaction, and a reduction in the anxiety about students. Even if only one of these outcomes suggested by DeOrdio were to result, then the consulting process would have to be considered a success.

Once the confidence of the faculty has been gained, many pssibilities open up for the innovative counselor. For example, counselors may make themselves available to fill in when the instructor is absent from class by reason of illness, committee meetings, conventions, or whatever, as well as on an invited basis to present a program or to share responsibilities with the instructor. Prior to making oneself available, the counselor must plan and prepare a presentation that will be both interesting and informative.

Pappas (1976) has designed what are called "traveling road shows" to meet this purpose. His staff has at least 17 different programs ready to go at the request of the faculty or at their own suggestion. Included in his growing list are such programs as how to study, test-taking strategies, time management for the college student, job-hunting skills, group vocational and personality testing, the placement file—how to set it up and how to use it to the best advantage—and constructing a resume. The list need be limited only by counselors' creative talents and abilities. When executed properly, all concerned will reap benefits. Effective execution, however, requires considerable planning, and this fact cannot be stressed enough.

Perhaps one-half or more of all effective outreach programming involves planning and preparation. And as is true for any method of intervention, follow-up feedback and evaluation of the programs are essential for continued success. This may be casual or sophisticated, but must be done to assess where the programs stand.

Successful consulting practices will have long-term benefits for the counseling program as it moves from the periphery into the mainstream of the educational process. It would behoove counseling programs not already doing so to make a major effort to design and provide outreach activities consistent with the needs of their students. The dividends paid by such efforts will be many, and will benefit all those involved.

ENVIRONMENTAL MANAGEMENT

For quite some time a belief has existed among educators that when students fail it is either a result of poor teaching or poor student motivation. A closer look at the situation suggests that there are a host of other explanations, exclusive of teacher or student, that may be responsible. These can be called, collectively, environmental variables, which can have positive, negative, or neutral effects on the teaching/learning/developmental aspects of education. Noisy, inadequate, inaccessible study areas will take their toll on even the most motivated student who receives the best of instruction. In many instances it is the environment that must be dealt with directly, and not the student's impression of it. The counselor can be instrumental in identifying environmental barriers and assume an active stance in helping to remove them.

Several authors (Lamb & Rapin, 1977; Rapin, Lamb, Matthews, & Rademacher, 1977) have presented categories of environmental variables affecting educational institutions. The following is an attempt to integrate these variables into four categories. The first consists of all physical aspects of the environment, including all natural and man-made barriers. The most obvious of these are those that affect the mobility of handicapped students, but also included are such situations as overcrowded classrooms, inadequate study facilities, inaccessible laboratory time and/or equipment, limited parking, lack of recreational and relaxation areas, poor acoustincs, and lack of student storage facilities. The support materials in the form of personnel, facilities, and equipment play a major role in shaping the physical environment.

The next category is defined as the behavioral environment found within the college, which represents the characteristics of all those people involved in the day-to-day operation of the college, including everyone from students to the academic and support staffs. As a matter of fact, different campuses of the same community college have been described as having separate personalities, and thus drawing different types of students (Klimek & Hodinko, 1977). Such a report should cause others to investigate the existence and impact of such a phenomenon on their own campuses. The implications for admission and retention could be staggering. This topic is worthy of investigation on several accounts, not the least of which is the relationships students have or could have with significant others within the college environment.

Closely aligned with the behavioral category is the psychological one. This may be seen as the overall impression of the college and is influenced by, among other things, the general classroom atmosphere and the quality of teaching. This may be the most nebulous to identify and alter, but should not be avoided on that basis. Any accounting of this variable will be purely subjective, but valid to the extent that students perceive it to be so.

A final category may be termed the institutional environment, composed of the official college policies, rules, and regulations that affect the student. Institutional policies are second only to the physical environment in their effect on the student's life, and may be the most difficult to alter.

In order to have a clear understanding of the specific effects of the various environmental variables on the educational process, some form of evaluation must be undertaken. In line with this, Astin (1968) has developed the Inventory of College Activities (ICA). While not designed specifically for any one education level, it is readily adaptable to community college use. The ICA is comprised of three main categories with various subcategories. The first category taps the college environment by addressing such issues as peer environment, classroom environment, administrative environment, and physical environment. Next, the college image is assessed by subjective opinions, ratings of environmental traits, and evaluations of satisfaction of the college experience. The final category determines personal characteristics of students along the following lines: educational and vocational plans, self-ratings of various personal and intellectual characteristics, and ratings of roommates (peers) on the same traits as in the self-ratings. This type of assessment, or one similar to it, can be of much help to the counselor and other members of the student personnel staff in their efforts to determine student perspectives of their college environment. Once such an assessment has been made, plans for correcting or enhancing the environment can be arranged and carried out.

Counselors must be concerned with both the academic and the social climates if they hope to have a major influence on student development, according to Morrill and Hurst (1971), who describe three primary functions of environmental managers. First, they should contribute to, support, and enhance the learning environment through such activities as reducing noise levels in study areas, reducing or alleviating student/administration tensions, and helping faculty and students make better use of educational media. Second, they should strive to facilitate maximum utilization of the learning environment by the students. This might include teaching study skills, use of the library, socialization skill building, and teaching students how to manage the environment themselves. And finally, the authors suggest that counselors study the students, the college environment, and the interaction effects of the two to form a data base for implementing the first two roles. Continued reassessment and evaluation is required for the college and the counseling program to remain viable.

More recently, Coyne (1977) has suggested six specific roles for the counselor who is interested in environmental management. He has even given such a person a new title, the Campus Change Advocate (CCA). Briefly, these six roles are as follows:

The initiator of linkages, who establishes conduits or linkages between students and hard-to-reach administrative decision makers

The catalyst, who changes existing policies when they are inconsistent with student development values

The politico, who learns how the system works and acts within it to change the status quo

The applied researcher, who must determine if issues are real and verifiable and then supply the data to the decision makers

The social architect, who does more than merely bring awareness to problems, working cooperatively with others to redesign ineffectual or noxious aspects of the environment

The persistent facilitator, who must know how to communicate his or her point of view effectively through relentless perseverance, since change is often slow.

Several more roles for the CCA to assume, which may be critical to the success of this function, can be added.

The investigator, who does not wait patiently for student complaints, but makes determinations for change based on knowledge of student development needs

The public relations specialist, who effectively communicates to students the interest and availability of the CCA.

For this new role of the counselor to be truly effective, the CCA must work to make this role obsolete. To do so, Coyne recommends that the ideal role of the Campus Change Advocate will be that of trainer of students to be their own change agents, but until that time comes, the counselor or CCA must assume the tasks outlined above. With the frequent turnover of students in the community college, this may be a role the counselor will play on a continuing basis.

GETTING THE WORD OUT

It stands to reason that students will take advantage of counseling service programs only to the extent that they are aware of them. From this perspective, then, the counselor must engage in a continuous public relations/information campaign to all prospective users and referrers of the various and sundry offerings. Unless counselors are willing and able to provide such information dissemination, many of their best designed programs will never be implemented.

Prior to launching an "ad campaign," it is wise to determine consumer needs. This can be accomplished through familiarity with the literature on the community college student, and through ongoing institutional research. A second important facet of this process is to determine who the audience will be. Does the counselor hope to reach just those students currently enrolled, or also the faculty, the administration, high school counselors of feeder schools, the employment commission? Usually, a slightly different approach is necessary, depending on who is to be informed or convinced. The administration will want to see data, the faculty will want to know how it will help instruction, students will want to know the personal gains involved, high school counselors and the employment commission will want to know who is eligible and associated administrative details, and other members of the student development staff may want to know how they can help.

Once these preliminar details have been worked out, the counselor is ready to bring the product to the marketplace. There are an infinite number of ways of going about this, several of which are described briefly below.

The Faculty

One group that can contribute much to successful outreach programming is the faculty. A cooperative, working relationship is essential if the counselor is going to have access to the classroom or expect referrals from instructors. If the faculty are going to invite counselors into their classrooms or send students to them, they must know what can be done to help them and their students. This task is simplified if the counselor acts in a liaison capacity with an academic division, where there is close, daily contact with the individual faculty member, and attends division staff meetings. Often having coffee or lunch with the various faculty members can be as productive as the best-prepared formal presentation. These informal chats, however, should not be substituted for memos, news letters, program announcements, and other forms of written communication. Presentations of new programs at divisional meetings are also encouraged, and may be necessary for those counseling services that do not use the divisional liaison format. The faculty must be kept well informed on a regular basis by whatever means are most productive.

The High School Counselor

High school counselors from the various feeder schools should also be kept informed of programs available to their students. Members of the counseling staff can be assigned as contact persons to a number of high schools. Periodic visits will serve to maintain a good working relationship between the college and the high school. In cases where the community college requires an admissions and/or placement test, it is always a good policy to administer these tests at the high school as a matter of convenience to these students.

Few if any four-year colleges are able to offer such personal attention to high school students and counselors. It does not take much effort to deliver this type of service and the mutual benefits possible can be tremendous.

Using the Media

When programs are offered to the public, the local newspapers and radio stations can be used to advantage in publicizing special courses, open-house days, and special events such as National Vocational Guidance Week.

Informing potential sources of referral, such as the high school guidance personnel and the general public, is important, to be sure, but the most important task faced is that of getting the word to enrolled students. After all, this is the group for whom the programs have been designed. Several possibilities exist to meet this end. The student newspaper might be a good place to start. Articles by the counselors on new programs, interviews with a counselor, a regular column on careers or personal adjustments are all newsworthy topics. Talk to the editor; most are cooperative and eager for timely contributions.

Bulletin Boards

Student bulletin boards are usually so cluttered they defy communication. Students tend not to pay much attention to them as a result. To catch the student's eye requires something out of the ordinary. One way to use a bulletin board to good advantage is to place it on wheels and move it to a prominent spot in the lounge or other major area of student congregation. To ensure novelty, the message and the board itself should be moved frequently. Bulletin boards located in the various academic divisions can also be used to keep students informed of counseling activities and other news items pertinent to their goals.

Slide/Sound Presentations

In an attempt to reach students and other audiences through a livelier medium, the counseling staff at Central Virginia Community College has produced a 15-minute sound/slide program. The program includes a brief description of the college's goal and the curricula offered. The counseling staff is introduced and the services available are discussed. An art instructor was responsible for the photography and an announcer from the local radio station edited and narrated the audio, which includes subdued background music. The entire project required much time but very little money. In fact, the only expense was the cost of the film. This program is used in all orientation classes, has been shown to various civic clubs, displayed at the local and state Personnel and Guidance Association meetings, and presented at the first general faculty meeting of the year.

Public Dissemination

A final suggestion is for contacting potential students in areas where they are required to wait for one thing or another. In such a situation you have a captive audience. Sound/slide programs such as described above could be placed in banks, bus, train and airport lounges, and so on. If this is too intrusive or obtrusive to the management, then perhaps placing a copy of the college catalog with the other reading material may be a better solution. This latter method is preferred for small businesses such as barbershops and doctors' and dentists' offices. When people are forced to wait, they will generally browse through reading material if it is available. Why not make your college literature available?

Getting the word out is an extremely crucial aspect of the outreach effort, regardless of the type of service being offered. The best-designed, most germane student-development program will be canceled for lack of enrollment unless significant efforts are made to inform the target population of its existence. Counselors must pay particular attention to the effectiveness of their advertising efforts and constantly seek ways to enhance these efforts.

MINICOURSES

Outreach programs can range from the intensive to the extensive and cover topics from skill-building techniques to personal development. Described below are a number of ideas for minicourses to be conducted by the counseling staff, designed to aid students in coping with problem situations typically encountered by community college students. This list could easily be expanded according to the needs of the students and the resources of the counseling staff.

Career Awareness

Many students come to the community college with no clear idea of the career they hope to pursue and therefore are undecided about a curriculum choice. This may include as many as 50 percent of the entering freshmen. Others who have stated a choice may have done so to please their parents, to reduce cognitive dissonance, or on the basis of job/sex stereotyping. Of course, many students will have a firm idea of their goals and how to attain them, but many will not. Choices are limited, in part, by the amount of information students have about jobs and about themselves. Courses designed to teach students how to use the Dictionary of Occupational Titles, the Occupational Outlook Handbook, the career resources center, vocational interest inventories, and so on can be of tremendous value to this group of students. Such minicourses can be individually designed or follow the structure of commercially produced programs such as the Life Career Development System (LCDS) available from the Human Development Services, Inc. of Ann Arbor, Michigan. All students, including those who have made realistic and firm choices, can benefit from this type of course, since it conveys the skills necessary to make a systematic career choice. It is important for all, since it is becoming the trend to change careers several times before choosing the job from which a person retires. Furthermore, with the rapid growth of knowledge and technology, many jobs that will exist in the future do not exist today. Members of the faculty and administration may also be interested in learning more on this topic.

Study Skills

Since the community college attracts many nontraditional students and those who have been away from academics for some time, building adequate study habits and skills is of prime importance. A number of published assessment devices are available to students who are not sure that their study skills are up to snuff. For some students such assessments are not necessary—they know their skills are deficient. The greatest demand for classes on this topic generally occurs prior to the fall term for those who know they need help, and again after midterms for those who had to do some reality testing to find out.

The delivery of the study skills program may take various forms—an intensive week-long (five-hour) session, a term-long class usually offered through the English department in conjunction with reading improvement, or on a self-instructional basis such as the Points About Study Skills (PASS) program available from Sound Guidance Consultants, Inc. Any or all three of these should be available to community college students in an attempt to keep the open door from becoming a revolving door of easy access and easy attrition.

Employment Skills

The ultimate purpose a large majority of community college students is to train for a career, and as graduation draws near many will begin the job search. To facilitate this process a short course in job-hunting skills should be offered. Topics to be covered should include writing resumes, where to find sources of job listings, writing letters of interest, interviewing skills, follow-up correspondence, and an orientation to human relations on the job. There are many excellent books on writing resumes and related correspondence. Several recent ones are by Bostwick (1976) and Reed (1976). For job-hunting skills, Richard Bolles's (1977) book What Color Is Your Parachute? is an excellent resource. A very good resource to use for the human relations aspect is Your Attitude is Showing by Elwood N. Chapman (1977). For this course, it would be a good idea to enlist the aid of the director of the Career Planning and Placement Office who could be an excellent resource person, if not the actual leader.

All components of higher education are facing tests of accountability to the sources of funding, which monitor the academic programs according to the number of graduates placed in jobs related to their curriculum. The importance of helping students in this regard cannot be understated. In the final analysis, job placement will determine the fate of the academic programs.

Test Anxiety

While test anxiety is not peculiar to community college students, it nevertheless presents a real problem to be resolved. Key features of anxiety to bear in mind when designing a program to counteract it are its worry and emotionality components. Emotionality is the autonomic arousal aspect of anxiety, while worry is described as the cognitive concern over performance (Meichenbaum, 1972). It is the latter component, worry, that affects test performance, since worry takes the student's attention away from the task (Morris & Liebert, 1970) and on to self-evaluative ruminations (Wine, 1971). Systematic desensitization, the usual treatment of choice, addresses the emotionality component but does not challenge the internal, cognitive cues that result in task-irrelevant behavior (Meichenbaum, 1972). For the intervention in a test-anxious situation to be instructive rather than palliative, cognitive restructuring should be a vital part of the counselor's concern.

The literature is rich in research on this topic, indicating the pervasiveness of test anxiety. From a developmental point of view, a program designed to teach study skills should also include a unit on dealing with the distractive aspects of test anxiety. The counselor should be prepared to help students deal with their test anxiety as it arises, especially during midterms and finals.

Assertion Training

Failure to assert oneself may be attributed to one of two situations: where individuals have never had the opportunity to assert themselves and therefore lack the experience and know-how; or where individuals have asserted themselves in the past and met with some aversive consequence, and therefore have discontinued that behavior lest the same consequences occur. This position suggests that assertive behavior is learned and is maintained or eliminated on the basis of its effects. Alberti and Emmons (1975) believe that behavior can be classified as nonassertive, aggressive, or assertive. These behaviors may be situationally specific or any one of them may characterize a person's life style.

Many excellent resources are available to the interested counselor, including Your Perfect Right by Alberti and Emmons (1975) and Responsible Assertive Behavior by Lange and Jakubowski (1976). Both books contain an explanation of the theoretical and philosophical foundations for assertive training, as well as guidelines and ideas for leaders. Perhaps the largest problem facing the counselor is to convince otherwise shy people, first, to admit it to themselves and second, to voluntarily step forward and ask to join the group. Several rating scales are available for identifying or screening members for an assertive training group. Among them are the Rathus Assertiveness Schedule (Rathus, 1972) and the College Self-Expression Scale (Galassi & Galassi, 1973).

Students who lack assertive skills may be handicapped in their academic, social, marital, or job-related effectiveness. Thus, the idea of conducting assertion training as skill building for personal development is consistent with the objectives of developmental counseling.

Transfer Shock

Many students who attend community colleges do so with the intention of transferring to a four-year college or university. The now famous Knoell and Medsker (1965) national study of the transfer student indicates that community college transfer students are generally successful in attaining the baccalaureate degree, although they require more time than four-year students. Even though these students are competitive academically and perform as well as they did at the community college, there has been found an initial drop in grade-point average for the first semester after transfer. This phenomenon has been termed transfer shock (Hills, 1965). Nolan and Hall (1978) found transfer shock discussed in a large number of studies in the literature. The likelihood that transfer students will have difficulty in adjusting to the new environment is sufficient to warrant a program designed to provide them with an awareness of the situation and to teach coping skills to handle it.

Students should be prepared for such situations as living with a roommate, budgeting time and resources, increased academic competition and degree of difficulty, a less personal relationship with the faculty, a feeling of anonymity, and getting around in a new city—to name but a few of the many adjustments to be made. Programs designed to address these issues will have their greatest impact when conducted as close to the actual transfer date as possible. Because many students transfer after summer break, this means that sometime late in the spring term will be the most appropriate time for this program.

In this case, a familiarity with the various transfer colleges rather than with the literature is the best preparation for leading one of these sessions. The counselor should be familiar with the colleges to which most students transfer, both through visiting them and through reading materials published by those institutions.

Students who have transferred from these colleges to the community college and faculty members who have attended these colleges can be a great source of first-hand knowledge.

Orientation for transfer students is usually available at the four-year college or university; however, the counseling staff at the community college can effectively supplement this effort by anticipating potential pitfalls and teaching coping skills to deal with them.

These are but a few of the many possible topics that can serve as the basis for the minicourse approach to outreach. Pappas (1976) has listed many more ideas, which he calls, collectively, his traveling road show. Other topics such as human sexuality, new directions for women, reentry counseling for the older student, human potential seminars, and dating skills are all real possibilities, depending on the needs and interests of the students. Again, the need to conduct institutional questionnaire research, in order to determine the needs and interests of the students, is emphasized.

Minicourses, such as those described above, provide an opportunity for the counselor to reach a large number of students with similar concerns and to help that group deal with the issues in a proactive rather than a reactive fashion. From a delivery standpoint, this appears to be the most efficient method for accomplishing the goal. And from the recipient's point of view, this seems to be in the best interests of developing potential and conserving human resources. Everyone concerned, therefore, benefits from these efforts and will continue to benefit, provided real needs are being met.

SUMMARY

This chapter has offered a definition of outreach from a developmental counseling perspective and provided a description. The balance of the chapter has been devoted to identifying means by which to deliver the outreach function. The following topics were offered as suggestions for possible inclusion in an outreach program: the need and alternatives for orienting new students; ways of having the counselor move into areas where students congregate; a rationale and means for consulting with the faculty; dealing with environmental barriers to education; conducting a public relations campaign to get the word out on what the staff is doing or can do; and finally, minicourses as a proactive means of meeting student needs.

Throughout, this chapter has emphasized the importance of careful planning and suggested that planning should involve more time than the delivery. In addition, the need for research of student needs before the fact, and for program evaluation after it, has been stressed. The benefits to students are obvious, but the benefits to the counseling staff should also be noted.

Today, few if any community colleges do not engage in some fashion of outreach; the percent of time devoted to this area must increase, however, if community college counseling centers are to remain accountable and viable.

REFERENCES

Alberti, R., & Emmons, M. Your perfect right. San Luis Obispo, Calif.: Impact Press, 1975.

Astin, A. The college environment. Washington, D.C.: American Council on Education, 1968.

Bolles, R. What color is your parachute? Berkeley, Calif.: Ten Speed Press, 1977.

Bostwick, B. Resume writing: A comprehensive how-to-do-it guide. New York: Wiley, 1976.

Brawer, F. New perspectives on personality development in college students. San Francisco: Jossey-Bass, 1973.

Chapman, E. Your attitude is showing: A primer on human relations. Chicago: Science Research Associates, 1977.

Chickering, A. Education and identity. San Francisco: Jossey-Bass, 1969.

Coyne, R. The campus change advocate. Journal of College Student Personnel, 1977, 18, 312-316.

Cross, K. Beyond the open door: New students to higher education. San Francisco: Jossey-Bass, 1971.

DeOrdio, J. Rising to the challenge: Counseling center outreach. Improving College and University Teaching, 1974, 22, 65-66.

Drum, D., & Figler, H. Outreach in counseling. Cranston, R.I.: Carroll Press, 1976.

Galassi, J., & Galassi, M. Validity of a measure of assertiveness. Journal of Counseling Psychology, 1973, 2, 193-197.

Hills, J. Transfer shock: The academic performance of the junior college transfer. Journal of Experimental Education, 1965, 33, 201-216.

Klimek, R., & Hodinko, B. Psychological climate of the multicampus community college: A campus amalgam? Journal of College Student Personnel, 1977, 18, 482-485.

Knoell, D., & Medsker, L. From junior college to senior college— A national study of the transfer student. Washington, D.C.: American Council on Education, 1965 (ERIC Document ER 013 632).

Koos, L. The community college student. Gainesville: University of Florida Press, 1970.

Kopplin, D., & Rice, L. Consulting with faculty: Necessary and possible. Personnel and Guidance Journal, 1975, 3, 367-372.

Lamb, D., & Rapin, L. An ecological model for categorizing and evaluating student development services. Journal of Counseling Psychology, 1977, 24, 349-353.

Lange, A., & Jakubowski, P. Responsible assertive behavior. Champaign, Ill.: Research Press, 1976.

Meichenbaum, D. Cognitive modification of test anxious college students. Journal of Consulting and Clinical Psychology, 1972, 30, 370-380.

Morrill, W., & Hurst, J. A preventive and developmental role for the college counselor. The Counseling Psychologist, 1971, 2, 90-95.

Morris, L., & Leibert, R. Relationship of cognitive and emotional components of test anxiety to physiological arousal and academic performance. Journal of Consulting and Clinical Psychology, 1970, 35, 332-337.

Nolan, E., & Hall, D. Academic performance of the community college transfer student: A five-year follow-up study. Journal of College Student Personnel, 1978, 19, 543-548.

O'Banion, T. New directions in community college student personnel programs. Washington, D.C.: American College Personnel Association, Student Personnel Series No. 15, 1971.

Pappas, A. Traveling road shows: An outreach strategy in counseling. Journal of College Student Personnel, 1978, 19, 73.

Pappas, A. Traveling road shows. Mimeographed. University of South Carolina at Spartanburg, 1976.

Pappas, A., & Smith, C. Pick it up and move it out: Strategies for outreach in counseling. Paper read at Southeast Conference for Counseling Center Personnel, Boone, N.C., 1976.

Pyron, T. The consultant role as an organizational activity of student personnel workers. Journal of College Student Personnel, 1974, 15, 265-270.

Rapin, L., Lamb, D., Matthews, C., & Rademacher, B. Environmental assessment and design in a university counseling center. Journal of College Student Personnel, 1977, 18, 321-322.

Rapin, L., Lamb, D., Matthews, C., & Rademacher, B. Environmental design in a university counseling center. Journal of College Student Personnel, 1977, 18, 321-22.

Rathus, S. An experimental investigation of assertive training in a group setting. Behavior Therapy and Experimental Psychiatry, 1972, 3, 81-86.

Reed, J. (Ed.). Resumes that get jobs: How to write your best resume. New York: Arco Publishing Co., 1976.

Warnath, C. New myths and old realities. San Francisco: Jossey-Bass, 1971.

Wine, J. Test anxiety and direction of attention. Psychological Bulletin, 1971, 76, 92-104.

9

THE FUTURE OF COMMUNITY COLLEGE COUNSELING

> A nation of educated people is a peak to which human
> beings have never ascended, a planet which they have
> never explored. Given human curiosity and adven-
> turousness, universal higher education is a goal for
> which people must strive.
>
> Howard R. Bowen, 1979

Since 1965, enrollments in two-year colleges have increased
to approximately 3.5 times that year's figure, and if the reported
number of people participating in community education programs is
included, two-year institutions are serving 6 times the number of
students they served then. There are also today about 1.6 times
the number of two-year colleges there were in 1965. If quantitative
effectiveness is the key to success, two-year institutions have been
very successful. The impact of this growth, however, has largely
been to extend a traditional system of higher education to increasing
numbers of students for whom the traditional system was never intended.

The future of community and junior colleges now depends on
qualitative growth, precise program response to specific population
needs, and a clear definition of the place of two-year institutions in
the educational structure of the United States. Competition for the
traditional student market is sure to increase as this population
shrinks and as four-year colleges enter the associate degree market
and attempt to sponsor career and technical training in addition to
their traditional curricular offerings. It is now the challenge of
community and junior colleges to change as rapidly as the nature of
the new clientele and the needs of society demand without, however,
attempting to be all things to all people. It is within the context of
the great challenges facing two-year institutions that counseling in
these institutions must change.

Of all sectors of U.S. higher education, two-year colleges are the most dynamic. As a result, their future course is most exciting, least settled in function, and most unpredictable. Two-year colleges have also developed certain strengths which, if capitalized upon, will keep them far ahead of any competitors. These strengths will likely determine, in some measure, future areas of development for two-year colleges and consequently determine areas of counseling needs.

Two-year colleges have more collective experience with high-risk students than other educational systems in this country. Along with military training programs, two-year institutions also evidence greater commitment to disadvantaged students than other types of educational institutions. Community and junior colleges, vocational-technical training programs, and the military have a near corner on the experience of developing career education programs responsive to current local and national needs. Two-year colleges also have great experience in developing programs responsive to the needs of youth and maturing adults.

The expertise and commitment of two-year college staffs to community-directed education has a solid foundation in experience. This experience is growing, as staffs of these colleges stabilize, and as in greater numbers professionals find their career goals associated with the excitement of being team members of these dynamic institutions. The growing cohort of people who find their employment futures linked with community and junior college education and the increasing numbers of people who experience this education provide a solid support base for future growth and development. Alumni of two-year colleges constitute a great, growing population of higher education. One out of every six students was enrolled in a two-year college in 1960; one out of every three in 1980.

Community colleges, which have generally been less well financed than state colleges and universities, have also learned how to perform the task of education at lower cost. This experience of making do with less should prove an advantage to community colleges as all educational institutions find themselves contending with increased expenses and less income.

AREAS OF EXCITEMENT AND CHANGE

An Educated People

There is an overarching question for all of higher education in the United States. Do people want to become a nation of educated people? This was a goal first stated for the country after the Second

World War. It is not a goal that has been achieved. It is a goal that is currently being questioned. If the country decides to become truly a nation of educated people, the future of higher education and counseling in higher education will be lit up as never before. Even the events of the post–World War II period, during which college enrollments increased eightfold, will pale by comparison.

A renewed commitment to become an educated nation must mean massive improvement in current investment in learning. At current rates of improvement, it will take 50 to 60 years before even one-fourth of the population achieves the status of college graduate. Such a commitment to become an educated people will catapult the efforts of two-year colleges into the future. In order to speed up the current timetable, the percentages of youths attending all institutions of higher education must be radically increased, and the educational opportunities for adults beyond the usual college age must be increased. It has been the history of community and junior colleges to be the recruiters of new learners. It is probably the future of these colleges to continue in this role. Moreover, it appears to be the mission of two-year colleges to open the doors of education to people for the sheer purpose of developing themselves.

Given the current economic nervousness, there is an excessive focus on education as a path to a better job. The goal of an educated nation, however, is a goal based on the desirability of developing human potential as an intrinsic value. As Howard Bowen (1979, p. 8) has aptly stated, education helps people

> . . . develop themselves through expanding their knowledge, enhancing their ability to learn, identifying their talents and interests, liberating their minds from prejudice and superstition, augmenting their aesthetic sensibilities, and developing their interpersonal skills. It also helps by strengthening their practical competence for citizenship, work, family life, health and leisure pursuits.

Accepting the goal of extending education to provide for full human development would not only eliminate the worry college administrators now feel regarding enrollments in the foreseeable future, but would also place student personnel workers, especially counselors, firmly on a course of student development.

The authors believe that the American people desire a higher quality of living. Within the constraints of less readily accessible energy, the quality of one's life will be advanced through greater involvement in intellectual and cultural pursuits, better management of time and available opportunities, and improved, self-managed care of health. Each of these areas will be developed through education.

Growth in each of these areas is not limited to a select age group. In fact there are currently eight times as many people living in this nation who want to improve their quality of life as there are people in the traditional 18- to 21-year-old age group. As a general result of sheer numbers of people looking for a better life, education across all institutions of higher learning must become more involved in adult learning. And two-year colleges should continue to be the leaders in this area.

The future direction of counselors, pushed by growing concern for a higher quality of life and a more generally educated people, should be to become developers of human potential. This means knowing how to respond to the requests of youth and especially adults in their desire to develop all of their potential. The counselor must learn how to help people orchestrate programs that weave together intellectual and cultural pursuits. The counselor must become a master of helping people manage their time and life pursuits effectively. The counselor and other student affairs professionals must be prepared to help people take charge of their own health care, leisure time, and preparation for and participation in an extended old age.

Focus on a fully educated population will also demand greater concern for and participation in the creative and performing arts; increase use of the formal storehouses of knowledge—libraries, resource centers, and museums—and the expansion of the perspective of the American people to global dimensions. A global perspective is virtually made mandatory by communication and technological revolutions. The counselor must keep pace through continued learning in order to be of maximum service to students. Expanded, planned, continuous professional development of student affairs workers is seen as necessary despite curtailed budgets.

Furthermore, counselors must prepare for and help their institutions prepare for a student population comprised for the most part of students who ten years ago would never have been enrolled in college. Life-span learning demands acceptance of the concept of interrupting one's schooling as a normal part of life. The processes for entering and leaving institutions must be streamlined. Better and more widespread processes for incorporating credit for life experiences must be developed. Instruction must be individualized with an emphasis on people. Arrangements for delivering instruction must not be limited to traditional times or carried out in traditional spaces. Evaluation systems must be developed that are experienced by students as encouraging rather than punitive. The pace of instruction must be set to assure individual success.

Counselors need to gain more knowledge and experience with adult learners. Adult learners need assistance in determining what they should learn and how to learn it. Counseling services need to keep pace with the development of instructional services in order to avoid making unwarranted assumptions about the self-directed nature of adult learners. Adult learners will need guidance about mid-career changes and assistance in assessing past and present experiences and planning for future ones.

It is to be hoped that a nation of educated people will produce a creative society in which the resources of the society are put to work on problems within and identified by the society. In such a society people will feel that they are growing, realizing their abilities and mastering skills. It is entirely likely that the basic unit of such a society will be the school district. It is further likely that the central organization in which the majority of the people of a community will find a forum to pursue interests and develop skills, to communicate easily with one another and spur each other on, will be the community, junior, or local college.

Counselors should see, as part of their future growth, a change to involve the uninvolved in the community and through involvement help people grow, find companionship and the dignity that goes with accomplishment.

The Student Population

In the 50 years from A.D. 1950 to 2000, the college student population will have changed more than during the previous 500 years of education. This change is brought on by the influx of older learners, women's rush to education and into the labor force, and the education of minority, poor, handicapped, and less talented students in record numbers.

Older adults are the fastest growing minority in the United States (Webbers, 1978). By A.D. 2000 half the population will be 50 years of age (Shalka, 1978). Counselors must be prepared to work with this segment of the population and its concerns. For many counselors, preparation will mean learning the developmental tasks that must be encountered after age 30 and how to cope with them.

Although large numbers of women have been entering educational institutions, the tide has not yet abated. Even though 50 percent of women of working age are now employed outside the home, it is not likely that the numbers of women entering the labor force will level off until two out of every three are so employed. The path to fuller employment for most women will be through continued education. Student personnel workers, in addition to encouraging the institution to be more flexible in its delivery of services, must pay more attention to back-up support for the learning process, including involving families in the educational process and providing inexpensive child care.

The racial and ethnic composition of the population will also change significantly. The minority population in the United States will increase from 14 percent in 1977 to 20 percent by 2000. Since minority populations tend to be younger on the average and to have higher fertility rates, the minority share of the younger age groups should be even higher. Including people of Hispanic background, the minority population should account for about one-third of the total population under 24 years of age by the year 2000.

Two-year college counselors will be challenged as never before to provide services for persons who are culturally and linguistically different. More than this, the younger and possibly full-time college student will tend to be increasingly racially, culturally, and linguistically different and come from more diverse economic levels, including that lowest third of the economic ladder that has been traditionally underserved by all types of higher educational institutions.

The Labor Force

The labor force in the United States will be influenced by two precipitating factors: the changing composition of the population and the shifting rates of participation. The labor force will also ultimately be influenced by two responses to these factors: an increasing substitution of capital for labor and a gigantic boom in new technology. As the number of young workers declines in succeeding years, even increased participation rates will not fully offset the impact of the decline, unless immigration shores up the loss. For an economy that has come to depend on cheap and plentiful labor, such a change will probably mean the development of a high rate of labor-saving technology, especially in areas where young, unskilled workers have been plentiful in the past. The expansion of high technology will have the effect of upgrading many occupational areas, making higher skill demands in formerly routine jobs, and creating entirely new skilled positions.

These developments are likely to cause as dramatic an impact in types of workers sought as that experienced between 1900 and 1980, a time during which the percentage of the labor force engaged in professional, technical, and executive work rose from 10 percent to nearly 25 percent. The expected change will also be influenced as much by the kinds of work people want to do as by the work employers want them to do. And as technology shifts and develops, job demands—even job classifications—will turn over more rapidly.

Careers, as a consequence, will become even more serial, with workers changing careers several times during the course of their work lives. Counselors must be prepared to help people cope with rapid career change, even anticipate change and plan for it, just as colleges must prepare people for such changes by developing in students problem-solving skills, a future orientation, and the necessary training for new work orientations.

Counselors must also be the master articulation links between secondary and vocational-technical schools and two-year colleges. Two-year colleges are likely to increase their role as the vital link between secondary and vocational-technical education and professional advancement. Further, the two-year college is likely to see much expanded cooperation between business and education. The counselor will be increasingly expected to foster this cooperation, to search out areas of business-college cooperation, to make the business contacts, and to consult on possible types of cooperation. Ability to develop this cooperative arrangement with business, and even with the military, will be increasingly important as the young adult population shrinks. The armed services are likely to improve pay and training benefits to attract more of the 18- to 28-year-old group. A tightening labor market will mean increased competition by industry for young adult labor. Many young people may opt to skip postsecondary schooling in favor of employment and on-the-job or employer-sponsored training. Unless cooperative arrangements between two-year colleges and business and military interests can be developed at reasonable prices, an array of in-house training programs is likely to be spawned, which will compete rather than cooperate with community college programs.

Edmund Gleazer (1973, p. 120) has said that he believes that there is a need for

> . . . a social institution which could bring together the now separate streams of work and education and which would provide an organized way to relate those educational institutions that offer a variety of services and environments to the potential student so that information and counseling could be readily available.

The community college appears to be the most acceptable and available social institution to offer this service.

The Carnegie Council (1979) suggested an even broader role for community colleges, going beyond job counseling and the offering of job-preparation classes to providing job-placement services, advising on legal and medical services, offering assistance in developing and maintaining apprenticeship programs, developing a referral service that would identify opportunities for volunteering one's services, increasing cooperative education programs, and sponsoring new service projects in the community. These additional suggested responsibilities are also being placed at the counselor's doorstep.

Community and junior college counseling services should jump at the chance to become the career and vocational development center of the community. In no other type of institution do the opportunities for education, training, personal development, job-related community development, and counseling come together so well. Community and junior college counseling services that fulfill this broad function as the career and vocational development center of the community will find themselves more than paying for any expansion such a service would demand. Even if the mechanisms for the individual purchase by consumers of services provided were not established, it is hard to imagine community industry and individual taxpayers not making such services worthwhile in terms of increased contributions to the college in general.

Knowledge and Values

It is daily being seared into our collective consciousness that today's information is tomorrow's misinformation. Of the information learned by the typical engineer of today, for example, one-half will be obsolete within ten years. The perishability of knowledge and the multiplicity of choices that assault people each day set the stage for the increased importance of counseling to help sort through the conditions of overchoice confronting students.

Every institution of higher education must accept as an obligation teaching students how to learn. For many students learning to learn will demand remediation. In general, skills for learning, including specific study skills, will be taught by counseling personnel. Counseling personnel are also being called upon to take the lead in introducing students to the impact of various technological and social developments of the present and future in order to help students think in terms of probability and values in decision making, and, in general, developing interest in and ways of coping with the future.

Increased and changing knowledge, which of itself increases choices, will force everyone to become selective in tasks undertaken. Because attitudes are formed and behavior is guided by the values held, counselors will increasingly be called upon to assist in values exploration, assessment, and ranking. In a world characterized by intense change, individuals must learn to become quickly and directly aware of their values, because values direct change while providing a stabilizing force. Counselors are key change agents in helping students to develop and strengthen personal values, to learn to anticipate the future, and to learn to live comfortably with change. A prime objective of tomorrow's two-year college will be to increase the individual's coping ability. The counselor will be required to help people adapt to continual change with speed and economy through private consultations, but also through group instruction during which students are offered an opportunity to examine, refine, and reinforce their individual frameworks of values. It is also likely that counselors will be called on by the institution to assist administrators in assessing and ranking the values that will guide institutional policy.

Administration

Rapid changes in communication technology and increased instantaneous access to data, added to a greatly heightened interest among workers in becoming involved in the decision-making processes of institutions, will all contribute to radical shifts in administrative configurations and activity in community and junior colleges in the future. The technology is already available to provide individuals with private television channels. The Dick Tracy TV wrist receiver-transmitter is no longer a comic-strip fantasy. But the novelty of such communication advances is not as important as the impact of massive amounts of instantly available data with which people are already daily bombarded. Information forces respond at a pace that would have boggled the minds of our grandparents. Rapid reply, then, demands rapid access to additional information in order to formulate the next response. The volume of change decreases the time available to make decisions.

It is entirely likely that colleges will soon be organized to use special administrators whose job it is to monitor the institution to determine whether or not it is being responsive to changing social needs. It is not improbable that in some organizations a unit like Student Affairs will need a futurist as an administrative assistant, simply to project the next development the unit should take. Nor is the time too far away when every major administrator will have a desk-top computer to provide immediate access to information on the basis of which decisions will be made.

There is clear evidence that student affairs personnel are now concerned about their ability to participate in the decision-making processes of their unit and the whole college. During the 1960s and early 1970s, when enrollments were rapidly increasing, student affairs workers struggled simply to keep abreast of the student tide. There was little effort to carry out critical analyses of the services rendered or to evaluate their effectiveness as a basis for further planning. Now, during a time of tight budgets and in the absence of an effective evaluation system for determining the impact of student personnel services, student services personnel are coming to realize that their very survival can be threatened unless they have some say in determining or adjusting the priorities of the institution, as well as those of their particular unit.

Student services personnel will increasingly become aware that they must design systems of accountability that can be used in decision-making processes for their own benefit. Further, they must learn that their accountability system must be predicated on identifying a series of needs that are integrally related to the overall goals and objectives of the whole institution, including an understanding of the target populations to be served.

Student services personnel must become involved with assessing the environment within which their services are to be exercised, including the community's attitudes toward the college, the financial picture of the college, the political forces operating within and outside the college, and the needs and demands coming from the environment. From this assessment, student personnel services workers must define their own goals and objectives and those of specific areas under their sway. Then they must relate these objectives to the objectives of other areas of the college and to the college as a whole.

Student personnel workers can no longer remain aloof from the priority-setting process of the college. While ultimately the governing board will have to assume responsibility for the decisions by which a college sets its course, such decisions are not made in a vacuum. Student personnel workers must work to influence the decisions made about their unit and the college in general at every juncture. In order to do this, they must keep abreast of every bit of information available about a changing society and translate this information into budgetary decisions flowing out of the real priorities of the institutions. A rapid rise in the process of program budgeting is projected for the near future, in which resources are allocated according to articulated and justified program needs. It is further projected that student services personnel will increasingly rise to the challenge of involvement with the whole spectrum of administrative development throughout two-year colleges.

PROGRAMS FOR THE FUTURE

For the near future, programs already in existence in some institutions must continue to be developed. The presence of large numbers of women in community colleges places a demand on counselors to develop support programs for women. Such programs include those for dealing with spouses and families unsympathetic with the woman's desire for self-improvement and vocational advancement; programs for dealing with financial realities, especially for women who are single heads of households; day-care programs sponsored by the college; programs dealing with family development, personal sexuality, and self-defense; and programs for personal and family recreation.

The great development, enormous change, and continuing complexity in the world of work means that counselors will need better and more sophisticated computer assistance for vocational and career guidance. More than this, counselors will need to know the real relationship between career decisions and computerized counseling, and between career maturity and computer-assisted career guidance activities.

The role of the paraprofessional counselor will have to be better defined and the effectiveness of these helpers in carrying out their roles assessed. Better peer-helper training programs must be developed, so that peers with usable skills can act as adjuncts to counseling staffs.

Evening and weekend counseling services models must be developed and extended to better serve the part-time or evening-only student. These models should also include ways to extend services to all the community. The counselor must be in the forefront of integrating the college and its services with the community. Counselors must revamp their attitudes and behaviors in order to take the lead in destroying the barriers that have traditionally separated institutions of higher education from the societies they serve.

The counselor must become infinitely more involved in programs for the culturally and racially diverse, the handicapped, and the high-risk student. In each of these areas it is not enough to develop programs that increase access to the college for these populations; counselors must focus their attention on making occupations, indeed the entire community, accessible to the handicapped and racially and culturally diverse.

Technical skills programs and life-skills programs that are not employment-related are expected to increase in the future. There are currently five times more people engaged in various kinds of postsecondary education than are enrolled in any kind of school or college. Counselors will expand their role as teachers in the foreseeable future. Increasingly, counselors will be asked to be master teachers with special skills for moving people ahead in their thinking.

Counselors will increasingly be required to cope with government. This will include both knowing how to obtain access to the services offered by various branches of the government on local, state, and national levels and knowing how to provide governmental units the services and information they demand. Despite the nation's current shift to the political right, it does not appear that bureaucracy will decline.

Traditional counseling services, one-to-one counseling, and work with transfer students are the areas in which declines, as a percentage of total demand, are projected. It might happen that before the end of this century the title of counselor will disappear from community colleges, to be replaced with titles such as career development specialist, learning skills developer, and community liaison developer. On the other hand, counselors may find themselves involved with a variety of community clinics sponsored by two-year colleges: family planning clinics, family life transitions clinics, career development clinics, economic resource development clinics, personal development clinics, and health clinics.

OUTLOOK FOR THE FUTURE

Rejecting the atmosphere of gloom that surrounds many in higher education, the authors are very optimistic about education's future. It is true that many have come to question whether the nation has a manifest destiny. And the national consumer mentality has run headlong into the realities of limited energy sources. Even the two-year colleges, which have operated as enrollment-driven organizations, are forced to rethink their strategies. But none of these pose potential disasters that cannot be coped with.

With the enormous increases in lifelong learning, enrollments are not likely to diminish in those institutions adapting to new society demands. Even with a reduction in the percentage of the gross national product spent on education, huge sums of money will be available for those institutions adaptable enough to obtain them. Even as population shifts in age configuration and geographical location occur, no catastrophe is foreseen for those institutions and programs that plan adaptation for the future.

Of all institutions of higher education, two-year colleges appear to be in the most favorable position, partly because the new composition of the student body works heavily in favor of community and junior colleges. The Carnegie Council (1980) projects that two-year colleges will account for 40 percent of enrollments in higher education by the year 2000. Counselors can play a central role in developing the exciting future of two-year colleges by maintaining services for children and the employed and facilitating the entry of the young, the elderly, the unskilled, the poor, and the unemployable into an educated nation that appreciates the qualities of wisdom, social responsibility, personal integrity, human understanding, and spiritual development more than one's ability to contribute measurably to the gross national product.

REFERENCES

Bowen, H. R. A nation of educated people. Community and Junior College Journal, 1979, 49(8), 6-14.

Carnegie Council on Policy Studies in Higher Education. Giving youth a better chance: Options for education, work and service. San Francisco: Jossey-Bass, 1979.

Carnegie Council on Policy Studies in Higher Education. Three thousand futures: The next twenty years for higher education. Final Report. San Francisco: Jossey-Bass, 1980.

Gleazer, E. J. Project focus: A Forecast study of community colleges. New York: McGraw-Hill, 1973.

Shalka, P. Farewell to the youth culture. TWA Ambassador, April 1978, 43-48.

Webbers, P. J. Community colleges and older adults: Facing the issues. Interface, 1978, 3, 1-2.

INDEX

ABOUT THE AUTHORS

LOUIS V. PARADISE is Associate Professor of Education at the Catholic University of America. He maintains a private practice of psychology in Washington, D.C., and serves as a consultant to several Washington-based consulting firms.

Dr. Paradise has authored and coauthored two other books and numerous articles in the field of counseling and psychology. He holds a B.S. from Pennsylvania State University, an M.S. from Bucknell University, and a Ph.D. from the University of Virginia.

THOMAS J. LONG is currently Associate Professor of Education at the Catholic University of America, Washington, D.C., and coordinator of the Program in Counseling and Guidance. He was formerly Associate Professor of Educational Psychology at the University of Illinois, Urbana, Illinois; Director of the Office for Professional Services in Education; and Acting Chairman of the Department of Educational Psychology.

Dr. Long has coauthored two other books and numerous articles in the areas of counseling and behavior problems of children. He has served as consultant in the National School Resource Network, as a member of the Advisory Council for the public schools of the District of Columbia, and as a consultant for Parkland Community College, Champaign, Illinois.

Dr. Long holds a B.A. from Saint Meinrad College. He was awarded a National Defense Education Act fellowship and received his M.A. and Ed.D. from Arizona State University.